T0301000

# MOVING UP THE LADDER

Development Challenges for
Low and Middle-Income Asia

# MOVING UP THE LADDER

Development Challenges for
Low and Middle-Income Asia

Editors

**Shigesaburo Kabe**
Nikkei Inc., Japan

**Ryuichi Ushiyama**
Japan Center For Economic Research, Japan

**Takuji Kinkyo**
Kobe University, Japan

**Shigeyuki Hamori**
Kobe University, Japan

 **World Scientific**

EW JERSEY · LONDON · SINGAPORE · BEIJING · SHANGHAI · HONG KONG · TAIPEI · CHENNAI · TOKYO

*Published by*

World Scientific Publishing Co. Pte. Ltd.

5 Toh Tuck Link, Singapore 596224

*USA office:* 27 Warren Street, Suite 401-402, Hackensack, NJ 07601

*UK office:* 57 Shelton Street, Covent Garden, London WC2H 9HE

**Library of Congress Cataloging-in-Publication Data**
Moving up the ladder (Kabe and others)
  Moving up the ladder : development challenges for low & middle income Asia / [edited by]
Shigesaburo Kabe (Nikkei Inc., Japan) [and three others].
    pages cm
  Includes bibliographical references.
  ISBN 978-9814723565 (alk. paper)
    1. Income--Asia.  2. Middle class--Asia.  3. Economic development--Asia.  4. Asia--Economic
conditions--21st century.  5. Asia--Economic policy--21st century.  I. Kabe, Shigesaburo, editor.
II. Ushiyama, Ryuichi. Current situation and challenges of Asia's middle-income economies.
Container of (work):  III. Title.
  HC415.I5M68 2016
  338.95--dc23
                                                              2015032181

**British Library Cataloguing-in-Publication Data**
A catalogue record for this book is available from the British Library.

In-house Editors: Harini/Lum Pui Yee

Typeset by Stallion Press
Email: enquiries@stallionpress.com

Printed in Singapore

# Contents

# Chapter 10. The Role of Judiciary in India's Economic Development 215
*Sukanya Natarajan*

# About the Editors

Shigesaburo KABE:

Mr. Shigesaburo Kabe is a Senior editor of editorial bureau, Nikkei Inc. He had worked for Japan Center for Economic Research (JCER) as a Principal Economist until March 2015. He is a Ph.D. Candidate (Keio University) and received Master of International Economics from Aoyama-gakuin University, Tokyo. His research interests include population study focusing on low fertility and ageing in Asia, human resource development (HRD), and transnational movement of people. He has published papers in refereed journals, such as Asian Economic Policy Review.

Ryuichi USHIYAMA:

Mr. Ryuichi Ushiyama is a Principal Economist of Japan Center for Economic Research (JCER). He previously worked as Singapore correspondent, Singapore Bureau Chief, and Hanoi Bureau Chief of Nihon Keizai Shimbun (NIKKEI), covering politics and economy of ASEAN countries. He received Master of International Economics from Aoyama-gakuin University, Tokyo. His research interests include foreign direct investment, international trade, and economic integration in Asia. His has published many papers on Asian economy, including analysis of emerging economies such as Cambodia and Myanmar, and middle-income trap issues among ASEAN countries. These papers have been published by JCER in both English and Japanese.

Takuji KINKYO:

Dr. Takuji Kinkyo is a Professor of Economics at Kobe University in Japan. He received his Ph.D. from University of London. He previously worked as Director at International Department in Ministry of Finance. His research interests include exchange rate economics, finance and development, and Asian economic integration. His work has been published in leading academic journals. He is also the co-editor of Global Linkages and Economic Rebalancing in East Asia (World Scientific, 2013) and Financial Globalization and Regionalism in East Asia (Routledge, 2014).

Shigeyuki HAMORI:

Dr. Shigeyuki Hamori is a Professor of Economics at Kobe University in Japan. He received his Ph.D. from Duke University and has published many papers in refereed journals. He is the author or co-author of An Empirical Investigation of Stock markets: the CCF Approach (Kluwer Academic Publishers, 2003), Hidden Markov Models: Applications to Financial Economics (Springer, 2004), Empirical Techniques in Finance (Springer, 2005), Introduction of the Euro and the Monetary Policy of the European Central Bank (World Scientific, 2009), Rural Labor Migration, Discrimination, and the New Dual Labor Market in China (Springer, 2014), Indian Economy: Empirical analysis on Monetary and Financial Issues in India (World Scientific, 2015), and The European Sovereign Debt Crisis and Its Impacts on Financial Markets (Routledge, 2015). He is also the co-editor of Global Linkages and Economic Rebalancing in East Asia (World Scientific, 2013) and Financial Globalization and Regionalism in East Asia (Routledge, 2014).

# Introduction

Shigesaburo Kabe

*Nikkei Inc.*
*1-3-7, Otemachi, Chiyoda-ku, Tokyo 1008066, Japan*
*skabe0727@yahoo.co.jp*

Ryuichi Ushiyama

*Japan Center for Economic Research*
*1-3-7, Otemachi, Chiyoda-ku, Tokyo 1008066, Japan*
*ushiyama@jcer.or.jp*

Takuji Kinkyo\* and Shigeyuki Hamori[†]

*Faculty of Economics, Kobe University*
*2-1, Rokkodai, Nada-Ku, Kobe 657-8501, Japan*
*\* kinkyo@econ.kobe-u.ac.jp*
*[†] hamori@econ.kobe-u.ac.jp*

## 1. Perceived problem and objectives

Recent global financial crises triggered an economic downturn in many developed countries, such as the United States and several European countries, while the dynamic growth of Asian countries stood out. This brought about a new image of Asia as a potential growth center on a global scale, rather than an economic region lagging behind advanced economies. The Asia Development Bank (ADB) forecasts that the region will maintain a higher growth rate than that of advanced economies throughout 2015 — an average of 6% compared to 1–3% of advanced economies.

Not only export expansion, but also a growing middle class in Asia has contributed to the area's economic expansion, providing Asian countries with a window of opportunity to leap from low- and middle-income levels to high-income levels, as measured by per capita

GDP or GNI. It may sound easy for these countries to run up the ladder of economic growth, but the potential risks of quickly shifting from low- and middle-income to high-income levels are often over-looked. In other words, a country should be careful not to fall into stagnation by focusing only on its growth path. Careful studies in history reveal that the experience of moving up the ladder of economic growth has varied among countries: very few countries experienced constant growth, while most countries were forced to run a spiral course.

Therefore, it is not realistic for Asian countries to assume that they can continuously grow without difficulty. That is, unless adequate policies are adopted, it is possible, if not likely, that Asian countries will fall into a stage of stagnation — specifically, the so-called middle-income trap of middle-income countries, defined as having a GNI per capita (2012) of 1,036–12,615 USD (World Bank classification). The middle-income trap has been a hot topic of discussion among international institutions such as the International Monetary Fund and ADB, as well as in academia, throughout the last few years.

The probability of falling into the trap highlights an important issue, which can be illustrated by the impacts of quantitative easing (QE) tapering, a policy implemented by the Federal Reserve Bank (FRB). The start of QE tapering by the FRB is expected to cause a huge financial flow out of emerging countries, including Asian countries, into the United States and other advanced economies. Hence, it is likely that this will expose structural weaknesses by the subsequent capital shortfall in Asian countries, at least in some specific countries, and will have a negative influence on their economies.

Coping with the negative impacts of QE tapering will require an improvement of economic fundamentals — namely, structural reform — which is also the case with the middle-income trap. If Asian countries want to avoid such a trap, structural reform must address the structural problems they face by, for example, promotion of investment, human resource development, strengthening of infrastructure, and expansion of the social system, including social security. The QE tapering policy raises problems in the short run, while the middle-income trap relates to primal challenges in the long run.

Thus, Asian countries exhibit vulnerability of structural problems in addition to potential growth dynamism. This does not mean that potential growth dynamism in Asia might be cancelled out by vulnerability, because, from a developmental viewpoint, potential growth dynamism and vulnerability under changing external circumstances are two sides of a coin. Transformation into a leading engine of the world economy requires Asian countries to develop potential ability and mitigate vulnerability.

Based on the views expressed above, this book explores (1) the current state of Asian economies and (2) the conditions or policy counter-measures that lead to higher income levels under changing external circumstances, illustrated by case studies on five Asian economies and their structural problems. It also aims to paint a comprehensive picture of necessary policies, which will encourage Asian countries to move up the ladder of growth.

## 2. Structure

### 2.1. Current status and development challenges of Asia

Chapter 1, by Ryuichi Ushiyama, is titled "Current Situation and Challenges of Asia's Middle-income Economies." The emerging Asian economies have achieved high growth; however, after the global financial crisis that erupted in the late 2000s, China's and India's growth has slowed down. Similarly, the growth of ASEAN countries has also decelerated after the Asian financial crisis. For these reasons, there are concerns over the future of emerging Asian economies. These countries are all middle-income economies; therefore, the discussion on the middle-income trap has become more spirited. Against this background, this chapter specifically focuses on the economic challenges surrounding middle-income countries in Asia. The phenomenon of the middle-income trap occurs when the growth model — which involves cheap labor and the introduction of technology from foreign countries — reaches a limit, while the advancement of industry and export structures fail to progress smoothly. Slowdown can be observed with the decline of the total factor productivity (TFP) growth rate. The emerging Asian economies are attempting to strengthen various policy efforts to sustain high growth. While the termination of monetary-easing policies in advanced nations is a negative factor for emerging Asian economies, there are positive factors, such as the expansion of demand within Asia. In order for emerging Asian economies to overcome the middle-income trap and be on a steady growth path, each nation has to consistently implement various reforms, promote the advancement of industry and export structures, and establish an economic foundation to take advantage of positive factors.

Chapter 2, by Hiroyasu Hasegawa and Shigeyuki Hamori, is titled "Determinants of Economic Growth in East Asia: BMA Approach." This paper attempts to identify the key determinants of economic growth in the East Asian region using a Bayesian model averaging (BMA) approach. The authors use this approach because it offers robust results in the environment of many competing theories and many possible determinants. The empirical results indicate that the important determinants of economic growth in the East Asian region are human capital, the index of upgrading industrial structure, and population growth rate. These three factors are also found to be consistently important over time.

## 2.2. Common policy issues in Asian countries

Chapter 3, by Fumihide Takeuchi, is titled "Industrial Structural Change and Productivity Growth in the Era of Global Value Chains (GVCs)." This chapter analyzes the impact that GVCs have on the real side of world economies. GVCs have expanded rapidly in the 2000s, especially in Asian countries. The basic assumption behind this chapter's analysis is that gross trade, including foreign inputs, no longer reflects the country's industrial structure in the era of GVCs. In Asian economies, the share of high-tech industries is extremely high given their levels of development. As this high share of high-tech industries is due to a great dependence on the importing of intermediate goods, the high share does not result in improvements in domestic productivity. In certain Asian countries, labor-intensive multinational enterprises (MNEs) address processing and assembling activities while simultaneously exporting and importing large amounts of half-finished goods. As a result, the amount of added value attributed to these economies is relatively small, and similarly, the productivity level is inevitably low.

The upgrading of industrial structures is redefined by referring to the new indicator, the relative VaR of high-tech industries, and we analyzed the impact of outsourcing foreign intermediate goods on industrial structural upgrading and productivity improvement. The results reveal that the size of the impact differs between high-income and low- and middle-income economies and that the Asian countries are less affected by outsourcing from abroad than are other countries.

Chapter 4, by Wang Chen and Takuji Kinkyo, is titled "Financial Development, Openness, and Growth Performance." This chapter empirically investigates the possible heterogeneity in finance–growth relationships across countries. To this end, a dynamic panel regression model is estimated using the first-differenced GMM estimators. The sample includes 108 countries over the period 1970–2010. The conventional regression model is extended to include the interaction term between financial deepening/openness and income levels to capture the heterogeneity in the finance–growth relationship across countries. The major findings can be summarized as follows. First, deeper banking sectors have a positive effect on growth across almost all income levels. Moreover, the benefit of deeper banking sectors becomes greater in countries with higher income levels. Second, greater financial openness has a stabilizing effect on growth volatility only when the income level reaches approximately 2,800 constant US dollars. Moreover, the stabilizing effect of financial openness becomes greater in countries with higher incomes. Third, there is considerable diversity in the development stages of financial systems across Asian countries. Reflecting this diversity, the effect of financial openness on growth differs significantly across countries. However, the effect of financial openness changes over time, and greater openness can be stabilizing once a country reaches the threshold level of income.

A group of middle-income countries including Malaysia, Thailand, and China crossed the threshold level at various points during the sample period.

Chapter 5, by Shigesaburo Kabe, is titled "Human Resource Development in Asia: Expected Role of Higher Education." The accumulation and development of human capital contributes to economic growth in the long term. This indicates that education has been a key determinant for economic growth, especially for Asian middle-income countries trying to shift from middle-income to high-income, socio-economically. In the current globalized world, higher education is considered pivotal for such development, rather than primary and secondary education. The rise in population and economic power of countries such as China and India, low fertility, and aging populations also enhance the significance of higher education in the 21st century.

Currently, most middle-income countries in Asia maintain lower completion levels for tertiary and secondary education, while completion levels of primary education is high. It is important to increase the overall level of education in these countries, which will improve productivity to maintain sustainable economic growth. Enhancing productivity requires highly educated people able to utilize technology, and thus, higher education is expected to play a key role for economic growth, especially in the initial development process of human capital. It is worth mentioning that developing human capital takes time, due to a spiralling process in which new technology is researched, learnt, applied, and absorbed. The characteristics of this long-term process assume various opportunities are available for the educational development of human resources. To expand higher education, it is important to diffuse secondary or primary education and diminish the gender gap that exists for the attainment of secondary education.

## 2.3. Case studies: Current status and challenges of five Asian countries

Chapter 6, by Hwok-Aun Lee, is titled "Affirmative Action and Transformation in Malaysia." Malaysia's transformation agendas —

to attain high-income status, while pursuing inclusive and sustainable development — demand policy responses toward affirmative action, the nation's massive program for promoting Bumiputera upward mobility through preferential selection. These policies stand in tension against broader aspirations of becoming a high productivity, high income economy, and particularly need to be reconciled with the principle of inclusiveness. However, public and academic discourses largely omit critical and systematic analyses, and tend to dwell on generalities and simplistic positions, such as need-based policies which offer only partial, even misguided, solutions. This chapter presents an overview of Malaysia's affirmative action regime and its interactions with broad development visions, with particular focus on transformation agendas and reform rhetoric in recent years. Affirmative action programs have made quantitative gains over time but have fallen short qualitatively, and in crucial aspects have become less effective, particularly in higher education where the capacities for productive and sustained change are also the greatest. Charting a reform path away from the current affirmative action regime, and its quota-based and highly centralized mode, will require these interventions to be made more effective again, toward generating sufficient Bumiputera capability, confidence, and self-reliance, in order that ethnic preferential treatment might be scaled back and modified, in line with national aspirations of being a fully developed nation, and mature, inclusive society.

Chapter 7, by Nguyen Cao Duc, is titled "Vietnam: New Doi Moi: Strategy and Priorities of Development Policies for Lower Middle Income Country." Vietnam's Doi Moi policy since 1986 has been successful with its high economic growth and fast significant poverty reduction as well as higher human development index improvement. On the one hand, the Doi Moi policy helped Vietnam to successfully transform from the centrally-planned economy to the multi-sector commodity economy under market mechanism with the State management in line with socialist orientation. On the other hand, the Doi Moi policy helped Vietnam to take advantage of its width-based growth model with low-skilled and cheap labor advantage as well as the resources-intensive inputs in the "factor-driven stage of development." Although the Doi Moi policy has helped Vietnam to successfully transform from a low-income economy to a lower middle-income economy since 2009, the dynamics of the renovation policy have been limited significantly. Thus, to transform Vietnam's economy from the lower to upper middle-income economy and to successfully avoid the middle-income trap risk, it is necessary to carry out the "new renovation policy" in the deeper and more widespread globalization context with the aim of creating Vietnam's new sustainable growth model towards its higher efficiency, productivity, competitiveness in transition to the "efficiency-driven stage of development."

Chapter 8, by Worawan Chandoevwit, Tirnud Paichayontvijit, and Yos Vajragupta, is titled "Thailand: How to Consolidate Social Security Systems: Universal Healthcare/Pension Systems." The public health insurance and pension policies development in Thailand has developed in the shorter period compared to the other developing countries. The country's economic, employment environment and the bureaucracy have shaped Thailand's public health insurance and pension for elderly to the fragmented inefficient and unfair systems. Three public healthcare schemes provide unequal basic benefits package, receive unequal subsidy per head from the government, and pay to service providers using different mechanisms. People were treated according to the type of health insurance they are entitled to which could lead to unfair health treatments and outcomes.

The pension systems cover only one-third of working age population. The delay of an implementation of the new National Saving Fund and lack of portability of pension systems could make elderly end up with very low amount of pension. In this chapter, the authors recommend the harmonization of public health insurance and an implementation of saving for retirement policy. These policies will benefit Thailand during the anticipated demographic transition and improve its capital accumulation in the long-run.

Chapter 9 by Yongzhong Wang, Guoxue Li, and Bijun Wang, is titled "China: Economic Structure Change and Outward Direct Investment (ODI)." Based on a comprehensive investigation on the current circumstances, challenges and prospect of Chinese economy, Chapter 9 discusses over the necessities and approaches of China's upgrade in GVCs and the industrial structure through outward direct investment. Due to the rising costs of production factors, rapid aged tendency of population, lack of advanced technology and gloomy global economy, China's current growth mode featuring with overdependence on export and investment can't be sustainable. As a large nation with huge oversea assets and an important player in the global international investment scene, China can make use of ODI activities to effectively upgrade its industrial structure and improve the status in the international specifications and GVCs, through acquiring advanced technology, well-known brands, marketing networks and resources, and transferring domestic overcapacity industries. The initiative of "One Belt One Road" will provide large potential for Chinese enterprises to go globally. However, as a late comer in international investment field, Chinese enterprises have faced more obstacles and risks than those of their western counterparts, such as investment barriers and resistance, national security fears, investment risks, insufficient international business experience, and political intention suspicions. To enhance China's capacity to create and capture value-added in the GVCs, and build a multinational diamond model with China as the core by ODI, China should transfer its low-end marginal industries to other developing countries, and attempt to link the high-end advantageous industries in developed countries.

Chapter 10, by Sukanya Natarajan, is titled "Role of Judiciary in India's Economic Development." The chapter aims to examine the relationship between legal institutions and economic growth. The intention is to examine the underlying mechanisms through which the law, the judiciary, and the legal profession influence the economy. In the context of India, the chapter traces the current state of the Indian Economy, the Investment Climate, Make in India policy, the role of legal institutions and manner in which law matters for economic growth, the challenges that judicial reforms pose and how they are all interlinked. India is one of the few developing countries where the legal machinery in action, adjudicated by judges and enforced by the Indian state plays a crucial role despite well-known shortcomings which can be altered by implementing judicial reforms.

## Acknowledgement

The editors are grateful to Ms. Pui Yee Lum and Ms. Harini Lakshmi Narasimhan and their excellent editorial work. We are also grateful to Mr. Shuairu TIAN for his research assistance.

Part I

# Current Status and Development Challenges for Asia

CHAPTER 1

# Current Situation and Challenges of Asia's Middle-Income Economies

Ryuichi Ushiyama

*Japan Center for Economic Research*
*1-3-7, Otemachi, Chiyoda-ku, Tokyo 1008066, Japan*
*ushiyama@jcer.or.jp*

## 1. Introduction

Discussions on the future of emerging Asian economies have become increasingly vigorous. After the global financial crisis that erupted in the late 2000s, China — which was experiencing high growth — has lost its momentum. India also does not have as much momentum as it did before the crisis. The other pillar that supports the economies of emerging Asian countries is the Association of Southeast Asian Nations (ASEAN). The economies of the ASEAN member states have also been declining since the Asian financial crisis of the late 1990s. For these reasons, there are concerns over the future of emerging Asian economies, but since these countries are all categorized as "middle-income countries," stagnant economic growth is often associated with the issue of the "middle-income trap." This book aims to discuss how emerging Asia can move up the ladder of economic development. For this purpose, this chapter specifically focuses on the economic challenges surrounding middle-income countries in Asia. Section 2 of this chapter examines the current situation of the economies of China, India, and the ASEAN member states after reviewing the presence of emerging Asian countries in the global economy. Sections 3 and 4 outline the background and details on how the discussion of the "middle-income trap" has grown. Section 5 reviews the major challenges in the context of the subject and discusses how they could possibly be overcome. Section 6 outlines the changes in internal and external environments surrounding emerging Asia in general, and Section 7 examines the issues that emerging Asian countries are facing respectively.

## 2. The current situation of the Asian economy

The path by which emerging Asia has made its presence known in the global economy is examined from an economic perspective. The emerging Asian economy's[1] share of the world's nominal gross domestic product (GDP) distinctly increased in the 2000s, and in 2014, it reached approximately 20% (Figure 1). The region's share of GDP based on purchasing power parity (PPP) was even higher at approximately 30% (Figure 2). In 2014, the share of GDP of emerging Asia to the nominal GDP of advanced economies[2] was approximately 30%.

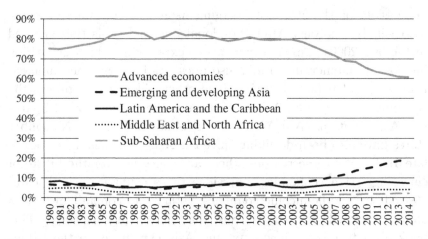

Figure 1. GDP, current prices, share of the world.
*Source*: IMF, World Economic Outlook Database.

---

[1]This refers to the 29 countries that belong to emerging and developing Asia according to the definition of IMF.
[2]This refers to 36 countries that belong to the advanced economies according to the definition of IMF.

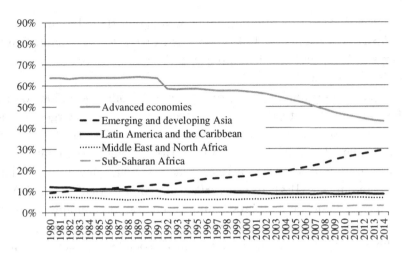

Figure 2. GDP based on PPP share of world total.
*Source*: IMF, World Economic Outlook Database.

Based on PPP, it reached approximately 70%, which is catching up with that of the advanced economies. The country that contributed the most to the rapid progress of emerging Asia is China. China's share in the world nominal GDP increased from 4% in 2000 to 13% in 2014; based on PPP, it rapidly increased from 7% to 17%. During the same period, India's nominal GDP increased from 1.4% to 2.6%, and based on PPP, it increased from 4.4% to 6.8%. The nominal GDP of the ASEAN 5[3] increased from 1.5% to 2.6%, and based on PPP, it increased from 4.3% to 5.1%.

In the nominal GDP ranking by country, China overtook Japan in 2010 and is now the world's second largest economy after the United States. In 2014, the nominal GDP of China was approximately 2.2 times higher than that of Japan (the third largest economy) and approximately 60% that of the United States. In the top 30 nominal GDP rankings, among Asian countries, India was ranked 10th and Indonesia was ranked 17th. Meanwhile, in terms of GDP based on PPP, China replaced the United States at the number 1 slot.

---

[3]ASEAN 5 comprises Indonesia, Thailand, Malaysia, the Philippines, and Vietnam.

India was third in this ranking, which was higher than Japan. Among the ASEAN 5 countries, Indonesia was ranked 9th, Thailand 22nd, Malaysia 28th, and the Philippines 29th, and these countries were also in the top 30.

Japan underwent a high-growth period from the 1950s to the 1960s, and in the late 1960s, Japan became the second largest economy in the world after the United States. In the 1970s, the four Asian tigers — namely, South Korea, Taiwan, Hong Kong, and Singapore — grew rapidly and attracted attention as the Asian newly industrializing economies (NIEs). In the 1980s, some members of the ASEAN, such as Thailand and Malaysia, underwent rapid economic growth. In the early 1990s, China underwent a period of reform and opened up the country, turning its economy into a socialist market economy. Following an economic crisis after the Gulf War in 1991, India also focused on economic liberalization policies. With these changes, both China and India's economies experienced rapid, steady growth.

New movements can be observed in the current Asian economy. Apart from the abovementioned countries and regions, the "new and emerging countries" in Asia are also growing. More specifically, ASEAN's latecomers (such as Cambodia, Laos, and Myanmar, which were behind in development) also promoted reforms and liberalization policies. Using the promotion of foreign investment and trade expansion as leverage, these countries experienced high growth, which reached approximately 7% to 8% in 2012–2014. In particular, Myanmar pushed democratization and liberalization of the economy under President Thein Sein, who was elected in 2011. Given that Myanmar is creating more ties with the international community, it is attracting attention as "Asia's final frontier."

As Asia has continued to increase its presence in the global economy, there have been more discussions on the future of emerging Asian nations, such as China and India. This situation is caused by the economic slowdown after the global financial crisis of 2008. The real economic growth rate of the emerging Asian nations[4] greatly declined after the Asian financial crisis of the late 1990s; however,

---

[4]As mentioned in footnote 1, the term refers to the 29 countries.

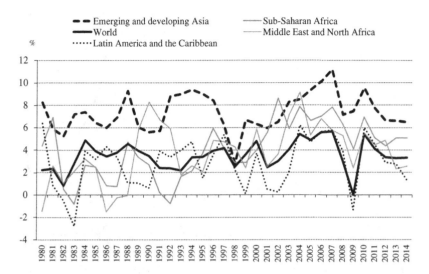

Figure 3. Real GDP growth rates.

*Source*: IMF, World Economic Outlook Database.

it showed an upward trend in the 2000s, and in 2007, it reached its peak at over 11% (Figure 3). Then emerging Asia has experienced a blow from the global financial crisis, and the real economic growth rate dropped to approximately 6% between 2012 and 2014. Even though economic growth had slowed, compared with other regions, it remains at a high level. However, the growth rate gap, which had been almost consistently expanding between emerging Asia and the advanced economies in the 2000s, peaked at 11 percentage points in 2009. Since then, the gap has shrunk rapidly (Figure 4). Therefore, it cannot be denied that emerging Asia's role as the driving force of the global economy is fading. This situation also creates growing concern that emerging Asia is having difficulties moving up the ladder of economic development.

The economic growth of emerging Asia by country shows that China's growth rate has remained around 7% since 2012. After the global financial crisis, China introduced a four trillion yuan stimulus package to boost its economy, and from 2008 to 2011, it experienced high growth of approximately 9% to 10%; however, growth stagnated after 2011. India recorded double-digit growth in 2010, but from 2012

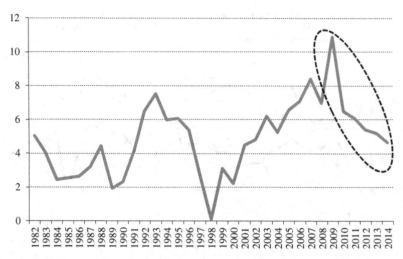

Figure 4. Difference in real growth rates between advanced economies and emerging Asia.

*Source*: IMF, World Economic Outlook Database.

to 2014, it decreased to around 5% to 7%. The growth rate of the ASEAN 5 has not decreased as much even after the global financial crisis, but compared with the period before the Asian financial crisis of the late 1990s, it has clearly slowed down.[5] The stagnation of economic growth that is evident in emerging Asia is believed to be related to structural factors in addition to cyclical economic factors.[6]

## 3. The "middle-income trap"

Let us examine the development stages of China, India, and the ASEAN 5 (the key players of emerging Asia) in terms of gross national income (GNI) per capita using the classification by the

---

[5] According to IMF's World Economic Outlook Database, the average real economic growth rate of the ASEAN 5 was 7.2% between 1988 and 1997 before the Asian financial crisis, but it decreased to 5.0% between 1999 and 2008 after the Asian financial crisis. After the global financial crisis, it was 5.5% between 2009 and 2014.

[6] See IMF (2013) and OECD (2014).

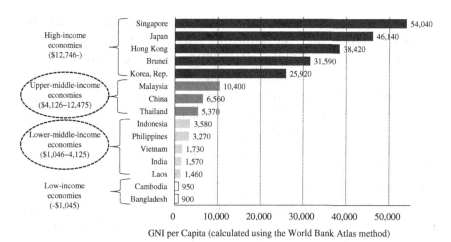

Figure 5. GNI per capita of Asian countries (2013).

*Source*: World Development Indicators.

*Note*: Categories are based on the World Bank. Brunei's figure is in 2009.

World Bank (Figure 5).[7] Middle-income economies are divided into two groups: upper middle income and lower middle income. Countries in the upper-middle-income category are Malaysia, China, and Thailand. Indonesia, the Philippines, Vietnam, and India all belong to the lower-middle-income category. Together, the entire range of GNI per capita for middle-income economies is between $1,000 and $10,000, and all the emerging Asian countries fall into this range. Therefore, the future of their economy can be translated into that of middle-income countries in Asia. As a result, the "middle-income trap" is discussed widely when the future of emerging Asian economies is brought up.

The first mention of the "middle-income trap" with regard to emerging Asia was in a report by Gill and Kharas (2007). This report was published by the World Bank at the tenth anniversary of the Asian financial crisis. It focused on five countries — China, Indonesia, Malaysia, the Philippines, and Thailand — and

---

[7]GNI per capita is converted to U.S. dollars using the World Bank Atlas method (a method that averages the exchange and interest rates).

indicated how important it was that these countries avoid the "middle-income trap." Subsequently, major international organizations, such as the ADB (2011), IMF (2013), and OECD (2013a, 2014), published reports on the subject of the "middle-income trap." Multiple researchers also analyzed this issue, including Eichengreen *et al.* (2011, 2013), Felipe (2012), and Agenor *et al.* (2012). Furthermore, the prime minister of Malaysia commented on the middle-income trap and indicated that even emerging Asia itself had begun to consider the "middle-income trap" as a grave concern that needed to be addressed through economic policy.[8]

In its 2011 report, the ADB laid out two scenarios: the "Asian century scenario" and the "middle-income trap scenario"[9] (Figure 6). The former scenario assumed that the 11 middle-income economies[10]

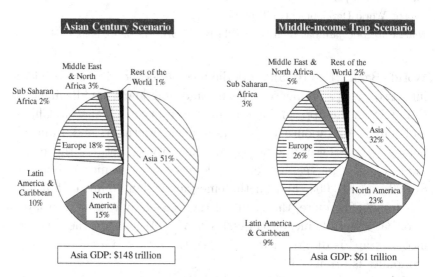

Figure 6. "Asian Century Scenario" versus "Middle Income Trap Scenario". *Source*: ADB (2011).

---

[8]In his speech at the meeting held in Kuala Lumpur in 2010, Prime Minister Najib said, "Do we have the courage and boldness to rise out of the middle-income trap?"

[9]See ADB (2011) for details on the assumptions of each scenario.

[10]Armenia, Azerbaijan, Cambodia, China, Georgia, India, Indonesia, Kazakhstan, Malaysia, Thailand, and Vietnam.

in the region with a demonstrated record of sustained economic growth over the past 30 years would continue this trend and that Asia's[11] share of global GDP (at market exchange rates) would double from 27% in 2010 to 51% by 2050. The latter scenario assumed that the growth of the current middle-income economies would stagnate. In other words, these countries would fall into the "trap," and Asia's share of global GDP would remain at only 32% in 2050. The total nominal GDP of Asia in 2050 would reach $148 trillion in the Asian century scenario but only $61 trillion in the "middle-income trap" scenario — a difference of 2.4 times. Until the industrial revolution, which occurred about 250 years ago, Asia's share of the global GDP (with China and India at the center) was over half. If the Asian century scenario does occur, then Asia would once again reclaim its dominant place in the global economy (ADB, 2011).

What is the "middle-income trap"? The term does not hold a clear or strict definition; however, it generally refers to the phenomenon of hitherto rapidly growing economies to stagnate upon reaching middle-income levels and failing to graduate into the ranks of high-income countries (IMF, 2013). Many international organizations and researchers have analyzed whether a "trap" actually exists or not; however, in any case, there are a number of countries that have stagnated after reaching the middle-income level. For example, a report published by the World Bank and China's Development Research Center of the State Council (DRC) in 2013 states that of the 101 countries that were middle-income economies in the 1960s, only 13 countries/regions[12] became high-income economies by 2008. In particular, many Latin American and Middle Eastern countries reached the middle-income status as early as the 1960s and 1970s but have remained there ever since. These cases provide compelling support for the trap hypothesis.

---

[11]Here, it refers to 49 economies, including Japan and the Asian NIEs (South Korea, Taiwan, Hong Kong, and Singapore).
[12]Equatorial Guinea, Greece, Hong Kong, Ireland, Israel, Japan, Mauritius, Portugal, Puerto Rico, South Korea, Singapore, Spain, and Taiwan.

Additionally, the IMF stated in a 2013 report that a quantitative analysis using past data shows that the probability of a middle-income economy experiencing slowdown episodes within a given five-year time span is approximately 1.5 times greater than that for low- or high-income countries and that a "middle-income trap" does exist.[13] Eichengreen *et al.* (2013) specified that there are two income levels at which many countries experience slowdowns. One is in the $10,000–11,000 range of GDP per capita (2005 PPP) and another in the $15,000–16,000 range. Eichengreen *et al.* (2013) also pointed out that this analysis — that middle-income economies would experience slowdowns at several phases in their growth — is gaining support.[14]

## 4. "Trap" and emerging Asia

Japan and the Asian NIEs (namely, South Korea, Taiwan, Hong Kong, and Singapore) are often referred to as "success cases": middle-income economies that graduated to high-income economies. Countries that are attempting to follow their example include emerging Asian nations, such as China, India, and the ASEAN member states. However, the period at which they reached middle-income status and their current income levels vary widely. Within the diverse, emerging, middle-income Asian economies, which country is starting to show signs of having fallen into the "trap"?

For example, Felipe (2012) divided the middle-income economies into upper- and lower-middle-income groups and used the number of years that countries spend in the upper- or lower-middle-income groups to determine whether these countries have fallen into the "trap."[15] Using this evaluation method, as of 2010, Malaysia has

---

[13] Middle-income economies are those with a GDP per capita of over $2,000 and less than $15,000 (2005 PPP). See IMF (2013) for more details.

[14] Eichengreen *et al.* (2011) stated that evidence suggests that rapidly growing economies slow down significantly when their per capita incomes reach approximately U.S. $17,000 a year (in 2005 PPP).

[15] This paper defines income groups of GDP per capita in 1990 PPP dollars: the lower middle income is between $2,000 and $7,250, and the upper middle income is between $7,250 and $11,750. Further, 14 and 28 years are the median number of

been an upper-middle-income country for 15 years, the Philippines has been a lower-middle-income country for 34 years, and Sri Lanka has been a lower-middle-income country for 28 years. According to Felipe, these three countries have fallen into the "trap."[16] Meanwhile, Agenor *et al.* (2012) listed the economies of Malaysia and Thailand as good examples of the growth slowdown that characterizes the "middle-income trap." Both these countries have not been able to change the pattern of labor-intensive production and exports in the past 20 years and have faced growing competition from low-cost producers, such as China and India (and more recently Vietnam and Cambodia). Consequently, their growth has slowed down significantly.

Another aspect of the "trap" discussion is how developing countries are playing catch-up with the advanced economies. The trend of relative income of Asian economies to that of advanced economies shows that Asian NIEs sustained their growth even after graduating to the middle-income group and are reaching a level that is at par with advanced economies (Figure 7). Meanwhile, while there are variations among the ASEAN nations, the general pace of convergence of the ASEAN member states to the living standard of the advanced economies has slowed down since the Asian financial crisis in the late 1990s (Figure 8). China's growth is outstanding, but it is only at the initial stage of the convergence process. Compared with China, India's pace is slow. With their income per capita currently standing at 10% to 40% of average G-7 levels, China, India, Indonesia, Malaysia, the Philippines, Thailand, and Vietnam all face the challenge of sustaining their convergence process (IMF, 2013).

---

years that countries spent in the lower-middle-income and upper-middle-income groups before graduating to the next income group. See Felipe (2012) for more details.

[16] China (two years) and Thailand (seven years) have not spent a sufficient number of years in the upper-middle-income group to be classified as having fallen into the "trap."

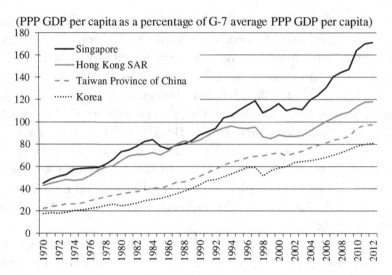

Figure 7.  GDP per capita convergence in Asian NIEs.
*Source*: IMF (2013).

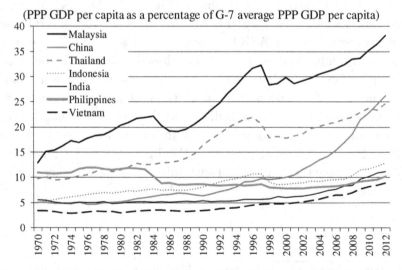

Figure 8.  GDP per capita convergence in China, India, and ASEAN 5.
*Source*: IMF (2013).

## 5. Why a country falls into the "trap" and how to overcome the "trap"

Why do countries fall into the "middle-income trap"? In other words, why do middle-income countries struggle to smoothly move to a higher-income group?

Gill and Kharas (2007) argued that middle-income countries are squeezed between the low-income countries that dominate in mature industries and the high-income countries that dominate in industries undergoing rapid technological innovation. In other words, middle-income economies cannot compete against low-income economies with low wages, but they also do not have industrial competitiveness that is at par with advanced economies because they lack technological strength. Therefore, middle-income economies struggle between the two groups.

According to the OECD (2014), many previously low-income economies have graduated to middle-income economies by exploiting a labor cost advantage and foreign-investment-led development of export industries. Trade and investment liberalization, the first typical steps of opening up to the outside world, appear to bring about quick wins in terms of growth performance. However, after harvesting the low-hanging fruit of international integration, it becomes more difficult to sustain high growth rates. In the beginning, countries are able to take advantage of their own low-wage workers and to grow a labor-intensive, export-driven manufacturing industry. However, when inexpensive labor decreases and technology that was available from abroad becomes scarce, growth slows down.

The "middle-income trap" can be explained in the process of catching-up industrialization diagrammed by Ohno (2010) (Figure 9). According to him, a country's development can be categorized into five stages, from stage 0 to stage 4, according to industry development. There is a glass ceiling between stages 2 and 3. Unless the country breaks the glass ceiling, it cannot attain a high-income status. To transition from stage 2 to stage 3, a country needs to reduce foreign dependency and build a production system for high-quality manufactured products by accumulating human capital and internalizing skill and knowledge. However, this is not an easy task.

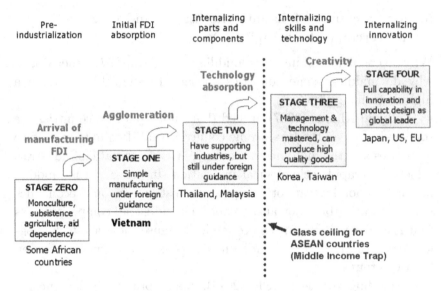

Figure 9. Stages of catching-up indutrialization.
*Source*: Ohno (2010).

According to Kanchoochat (2014), the existing literature on the "middle-income trap" that analyzes and offers solutions can be categorized into three groups.[17] The first group lists the inadequate quality of education and institutions to be the main cause for the "trap" and calls for improving education and institutions. The second and third groups list inadequate capabilities to produce and export higher-technology products as the main causes and call for countries to change their export composition. The difference between the second and third groups is the role of the state. The former group calls for the state to be "facilitating," whereas the latter calls for the state to be "proactive."[18]

---

[17]The review here is limited only to those that explicitly use the term "middle-income trap." Most of the existing literature does not deny the importance of education, institutions, and exports. The classification here is based on (a) the different emphasis each work places on the main cause of the "middle-income trap" and (b) the extent to which the state should be involved in remedying the problems.

[18]Refer to Aiyar *et al.* (2013) for the first group, Eichengreen *et al.* (2013) for the second group, and Ohno (2009, 2010) for the third group.

The issue of an inadequate capability to produce and export higher-technology products, which is featured in the second and third groups, is related to Ohno's report (2010). Meanwhile, the inadequate quality of education and institutions, which the first group indicates, is a factor that hinders the upgradation of industrial and export structures. Having no institutions to promote high-quality human resources, entrepreneurship, and technological innovations prevents the advancement of industrial and export structures. In short, the problems that are indicated in the first, second, and third groups are all related. Improvement in education and institutional quality would lead to advancement in industrial and export structures, which would then prevent and help countries escape from the "middle-income trap."[19]

From the viewpoint of growth accounting, when middle-income economies experience slowdowns, the main cause is usually a decrease in the growth rate of total factor productivity (TFP). This decrease in TFP was observed in Latin America from the 1970s to the 1980s and, although smaller in scale, in ASEAN member states after the Asian financial crisis of the late 1990s (IMF, 2013). Physical capital, human capital, and employment serve as the driving forces of growth; however, when there are slowdown episodes, the decrease in TFP growth rate has significant impacts. This shows that it is vital to pull up the TFP growth rate in order for countries to avoid and escape the "middle-income trap."

## 6. Changes in environment

It is also necessary to study the changes in internal and external environments when discussing the future of the emerging Asian economies (Table 1).[20] In terms of external factors, particularly in

---

[19] In terms of institutional quality, the five factors that would impact TFP are politics, openness, gender, entrepreneurship, and labor (Yamazawa, 2013). The institution evaluation index, calculated from these indices, shows that compared with high-income economies, such as the United States, Japan, and South Korea, emerging Asian nations all have lower scores, which indicates that there is room for improvement. See Yamazawa (2013) for more details.

[20] This argument is based on Cubeddu *et al.* (2014) and OECD (2013b).

Table 1. Change of environment for Asian emerging economies.

|  | 2000s | Now and the future |
|---|---|---|
| | [External change] | |
| | Expansion of world trade → | Slower growth of world trade |
| | Increase in commodity price → | Decline in commodity price |
| | Quantitative easing (QE) policies → | QE tapering |
| | [Internal Change] | |
| | Demographic bonus → | Demographic onus |
| | Rich labor with lower wages → | Rapid increase of wage |
| | Promoting economic growth as a top priority → | Shift to inclusive growth |
| | Less integrated economy among Asian countries → | Integrated economy among Asian countries (AEC, TPP, RCEP, etc.) |
| | Weak domestic demandx (local production for export) → | Expansion of domestic demand (local production for local consumption) |

*Source*: Cubeddu *et al.* (2014) and OECD (2013b).

the 2000s, world trade on a global and regional scale expanded, as developing technologies resulted in a reduction in transportation and telecommunications costs. Furthermore, the prices of primary commodities significantly increased, and the monetary easing policy in advanced nations resulted in excessive liquidity. These factors stimulated global investment and capital flows, which had a positive impact on the emerging Asian economies. However, the situation might change. For example, it is predicted that world trade is likely to experience a slowdown driven by structural factors (World Bank, 2015). Meanwhile, with China's economy stagnating, primary commodity markets would decline, and the United States would tighten its monetary policy. These changes could translate to the harsh environment surrounding developing economies, including emerging Asian nations.

In terms of domestic factors, there has been a decrease (or sluggish growth) of the working-age population in some emerging Asian nations, which may lead to the end of the "demographic bonus." The rapid rise in wages that is occurring in China and ASEAN member states is anticipated to continue in the future as governments aim to promote domestic demand and reduce disparities. Furthermore, in emerging Asian economies, the disparity issue is being highlighted as a political and social instability factor, and there are voices that call for inclusive growth that includes people and regions that are poor. While the development fund is limited, strategies to strengthen competition are also needed, and how the two must be managed remains a challenge.

There are positive factors as well. The first is the progress of integration between Asian economies. Within Asia, there have been movements toward reducing and eliminating barriers relating to trade, investment, and the flow of people, and these measures will continue to be implemented. Specific examples include the ASEAN Economic Community (AEC) that is planned to be created by the end of 2015, the Trans-Pacific Partnership (TPP), and the Regional Comprehensive Economic Partnership (RCEP). The second is the expansion of demand in Asia. The market for final goods, including automotive and household electronics, has rapidly grown because of the swelling middle class as a result of economic development. In the past, a tight production network was extended throughout the Asian region, but with progress on economic integration, it is possible to establish a division of the labor system that is more efficient. Furthermore, advanced economies are the final destination for Asia's production network; however, if the idea of local production for local consumption is strengthened, then new growth opportunities will arise.

## 7. Challenges and measures for each country

With regard to the "middle-income trap," there is some skepticism.[21] However, attention must be paid to the fact that the emerging Asian

---

[21]Bulman *et al.* (2014) find that "escapees" — countries that "escaped" the middle-income trap and became rich — tend to grow fast and consistently produced high income; they do not stagnate at any point as the middle-income trap theory would suggest. By contrast, "non-escapees" tend to have low growth at all levels of income.

nations themselves are focusing on the "middle-income trap" when drawing up strategies for the future. The following is a brief summary of the challenges and policy trends of the countries that will be further examined in part 3 of this book. Countries will be discussed in the same order that they are listed in Figure 5, from the highest to the lowest GNI per capita.

## 7.1. Malaysia

The Prime Minister of Malaysia himself showed recognition that Malaysia has fallen into the "middle-income trap."[22] The Malaysian government understands that many of the traditional policies and strategies of Malaysia are inadequate to pull the economy to the next level and that the approach toward economic development must undergo a dramatic transformation.[23] The GNI per capita of Malaysia has already exceeded $10,000 and is one of the top countries in emerging Asia. However, the government is disappointed that Malaysia's performance compared with the Asian NIEs (such as South Korea and Taiwan) is inferior.

The challenges of Malaysia's economy include excessive presence of government-linked companies (GLCs), brain drain, and dependency on foreign labor (Ushiyama, 2013). The excessive presence of GLCs (which have a close relationship with the government) prevents competition and new entries and has a negative influence on private investment (Menong and Ng, 2013). The phenomenon of "brain drain" and dependency on foreign labor are two sides of the same coin. For example, the departure of skilled workers from Malaysia depresses Malaysia's industries. Simultaneously, this frees Malaysia to maintain its labor-intensive industries that depend on low-wage foreign workers. In Malaysia, the percentage of exports for higher-technology products is high, but it relies on the labor-intensive assembly industry (World Bank, 2012).

In 2010, Malaysia unveiled new economic policy guidelines called the "New Economic Model," which proposed eight strategic reform

---

[22]See footnote 8.
[23]NEAC (2010, pp. 3, 4).

initiatives. Measures to escape the "middle-income trap" include reenergizing the private sector, developing a quality workforce and reducing dependency on foreign labor, and creating a competitive domestic economy. The main purpose of these measures is to move from growth primarily based on capital accumulation to growth through productivity, from dominant state participation in the economy to private-sector-led growth, and from favoring specific industries and firms to favoring technologically capable industries and firms. However, since issues such as excessive GLC presence and brain drain are related to *bumiputera* affirmative action policies, the situation is complicated (Ushiyama, 2013).

## 7.2. China

The Chinese economy has slowed down recently. China is the driving force not only for the Asian economy but also for the global economy; however, the working-age population has begun reducing,[24] and there are concerns that the Chinese economy may fail to catch up as rapidly as in the past to the leading world economies, thereby getting stuck in the "middle-income trap" (OECD, 2013a). Zhuang *et al.* (2012) posit that the challenges that the Chinese economy faces are (1) despite significant gains, continual large gaps in China's technological and productivity gaps with advanced economies; (2) declining rural surplus labor and rising wages; (3) imbalances in the sources of growth and rising income inequality; and (4) enormous pressures on resources, such as energy, water, and the environment, created by rapid growth.

In a joint report published in 2013 by the Chinese government and the World Bank,[25] China expressed concerns over the risks of the "trap" and emphasized the need to discover new growth drivers. In other words, policies focusing on increased efficiency in input use, higher human capital investments, increased innovation, and

---

[24]Since China's one-child policy was introduced in 1979, the youth population has declined, and in 2012, for the first time, the working-age population (15 to 59 years old) shrank.

[25]World Bank and DRC (2013).

a shift to high-value services were needed for China to avoid the "middle-income trap." Zhuang *et al.* (2012) also stated that measures for avoiding the "trap" include stepping up innovation and industrial upgradation; deepening structural reforms of enterprises, factor markets, and the fiscal system; expanding services; and scaling up urbanization.

Along with the expansion of China's economic scale, the influence China has over other emerging Asian nations through trade and investment is increasing, which is a matter of huge interest for the emerging Asian nations. With regard to the outlook on China's economy, there are risks regarding the "transition trap," in addition to the "middle-income trap" (Kwan, 2012). The "transition trap" refers to a situation whereby certain vested interests, such as state-owned enterprises, resist further reform, which results in distorted economic and social development. Reform measures under the Communist Party's one-party rule will be of key importance.

## 7.3. Thailand

The Thai government recognized the challenges of middle-income economies from an early stage. The "Strategy for Enhancing Thai Competitiveness in a New Global Economic Environment," announced in June 2002 by the National Economic and Social Development Board (NESDB), said that the Thai economy "is caught between the countries with low labor costs and the countries with high technological strength, and is a walnut in a nutcracker, so to speak." The Thai government was clearly worried that Thailand might lose competitiveness between low-income countries, such as China and Indonesia, and high-technology countries, such as South Korea and Taiwan (Oizumi, 2013). Therefore, the then-prime minister Thaksin Shinawatra designated five strategic industries, namely, (1) automotive, (2) food processing, (3) fashion, (4) tourism, and (5) software. In addition to these five strategic industries, he introduced policies to strengthen the invitation of foreign capital through actively concluding free-trade agreements (FTAs) and attempted to cluster these strategic industries. However, after the collapse of the Thaksin government, the successive prime ministers could not launch significant policies, as they were preoccupied dealing with political turmoil (Oizumi, 2013).

In "The Eleventh National Economic and Social Development Plan 2012–2016," the Thai government states that one of the risks the country faces is a vulnerable economic structure. In the past, Thailand primarily relied on foreign direct investment and exports based on low-wage labor, but now this is preventing an increase in competitiveness. While the Thai government is dealing with the rapid progress of the population characteristics of low birthrate and aging population and the rapid increase in domestic wages by transferring labor-intensive industries to nearby countries, such as Cambodia, it is also planning to add value to its domestic industries while improving the overall business environment and strengthening infrastructure and logistic systems.

## 7.4. Vietnam

Vietnam achieved high growth through the Doi Moi Policy implemented since the mid-1980s; in the late 2000s, it became a middle-income economy. From 2000–2007, before the global financial crisis, Vietnam's average growth exceeded 7%; however, between 2008 and 2014, after the crisis hit, it decreased to approximately 5%, and growth slowed down. Therefore, at the 2011 National Congress of the Communist Party, the need to shift to the growth model was stated as one of the country's main tasks. One major target is the transition from an economy that depends on physical capital investment to an economy based on labor productivity and technological improvement. Specific measures include increasing the TFP contribution rate to the economic growth rate to at least 35% in the next 10 years and increasing the ratio of trained workers to 55% by 2015 and to 70% by 2020 (Nguyen, 2012).

Vietnam has three main areas of structural problems: (1) delay in reform of state-owned enterprises (SOEs), (2) lack of fiscal and financial regulations, and (3) waste or inefficiency of public investment (Tran, 2013). At the 2012 National Assembly, the following reform policies were adopted, and the Vietnamese government began to reestablish their economy. SOE reforms include establishing corporate governance and phasing out preferences for SOEs, such as priority in access to financing, land, and certain economic sectors. Fiscal and financial reforms include downsizing banks, addressing non-performing loans, and strengthening banking power. Public investment reforms include increasing the transparency of the decision-making process of projects and strengthening the management system for public projects (Tran, 2013). As in China, the results of these reforms under the Communist Party's one-party rule will be intriguing.

## 7.5. India

After the global financial crisis, it became apparent that India's economy had slowed down. Similar to Vietnam, India's GNI per capita is still low at less than $2,000; therefore, it is essential to maintain high growth and improve the standard of living. Narendra Damodardas Modi, a leader of the Bharatiya Janata Party (BJP), achieved success in revitalizing the economy of Gujarat as the chief minister of Gujarat. Then he became the prime minister of India in May 2014, as India witnessed a change in administration for the first time in 10 years. Prime Minister Modi aims to establish a swift decision-making system, including significantly reducing the number of ministers. In terms of the economy, India must work on issues such as electricity shortages and a vulnerable transportation infrastructure. It must also review complicated tax system and regulations, as well as unclear trade practices. It is also important to further deregulate and invite foreign capital. India faces numerous challenges. While India requires a large sum of funds to develop infrastructure, it also needs to establish a sound fiscal system. However, whether India can manage these two issues is unclear.

## 8. Conclusion

The emerging Asian economies have achieved high growth; however, after the global financial crisis, China's and India's growth has slowed down. Similarly, the growth of ASEAN countries has also decelerated after the Asian financial crisis. These countries are all middle-income economies; therefore, the discussion on the "middle-income trap" has become more spirited. There is no strict definition for the term "middle-income trap," but experts have noted many cases in which a country is unable to transition to a high-income status after rapid growth. The emerging Asian economies are concerned regarding this issue. The phenomenon of the "middle-income trap" occurs when the growth model — which involves cheap labor and the introduction of technology from foreign countries — reaches a limit, while the advancement of industry and export structures fail to progress smoothly. Slowdown can be observed with the decline of the TFP growth rate. The emerging Asian economies are attempting to strengthen various policy efforts to sustain high growth. Specific wide-reaching measures are being adopted, from strengthening human capital and technology development capability to revising the government's role. In addition to these, resistance from vested interest groups is also anticipated, which leaves a sense of uncertainty. While the termination of monetary-easing policies in advanced nations is a negative factor for emerging Asian economies, there are positive factors, such as the expansion of demand within Asia. In order for emerging Asian economies to overcome the "middle-income trap" and be on a steady growth path, each nation has to consistently implement various reforms, promote the advancement of industry and export structures, and establish an economic foundation to take advantage of positive factors.

### References

Aiyar, S., R. Duval, D. Puy, Y. Wu, and L. Zhang (2013). Growth Slowdowns and the Middle-income Trap. IMF Working Paper No. 13/71.

Agenor, P. R. and O. Canuto (2012). Middle-income Growth Traps. World Bank Policy Research Working Paper 6210.

Asian Development Bank (ADB) (2011). *ASIA 2050, Realizing the Asian Century*.

Bulman, D., M. Eden, and H. Nguyen (2014). Transitioning from Low-Income Growth to High-Income Growth. World Bank Research Working Paper 7104.

Cubeddu, L. M., A. Culiuc, G. Fayad, Y. Gao, K. Kochhar, A. Kyobe, C. Oner, R. Perrelli, S. Sanya, E. Tsounta, and Z. Zhang (2014).

Emerging Markets in Transition: Growth Prospects and Challenges. IMF Staff Discussion Note.

Eichengreen, B., D. Park, and K. Shinn (2011). When Fast Growing Economies Slow Down: International Evidence and Implications for the People's Republic of China. ADB Economics, Working Paper Series No. 262.

Eichengreen, B., D. Park, and K. Shin (2013). Growth Slowdowns Redux: New Evidence on the Middle-income Trap. National Bureau of Economic Research, Working Paper No. 18673.

Felipe, J. (2012). Tracking the Middle-income Trap: What is it, Who is in it, and Why? Part 1. ADB Economics Working Papers 306.

Gill, I. and H. Kharas (2007). *An East Asian Renaissance.* The World Bank, Washington, DC.

IMF (2013). *Regional Economic Outlook.* International Monetary Fund, Washington, DC.

Kanchoochat, V. (2014). The Middle-income Trap Debate: Taking Stock, Looking Ahead. Kokusai Mondai (International Affairs), 633.

Kwan, C. H. (2012). China Challenges Middle-income Trap and Transitional Trap (Chusyotokukoku no wana to taiseiikou no wana no kokuhuku ni idomu chugoku). Japan Center for Economic Research (JCER).

Menon, J. and T. H. Ng (2013). Are Government-Linked Corporations Crowding out Private Investment in Malaysia? ADB Economic Working Papers 345.

National Economic Advisory Council (NEAC) (2011). *New Economic Model for Malaysia, Part 1: Strategic Policy Directions.*

Nguyen, Q. H. (2012). The Current Status and Challenges of Vietnamese Macro Economy (Vietnam no macro Keizai no genjyou to kadai). *Vietnam in Transition,* Institute of Developing Economies, Japan External Trade Organization, pp. 53–81. (In Japanese)

Oizumi, K. (2013). Thailand Upholding a 'Creative Economy' — Concerns that Political Stability Will be a Heavy Weight ('Souzoutekikeizai' wo kakageru Thai — Seiji fuan ga omoshi to naru kikenmo). Japan Center for Economic Research (JCER) Asia Research Paper, pp. 75–94. (In Japanese)

OECD (2013a). *The People's Republic of China, Avoiding the Middle-income Trap: Policies for Sustained and Inclusive Growth.* OECD, Paris.

OECD (2013b). *Economic Outlook for Southeast Asia, China, India 2014.* OECD, Paris.

OECD (2014). *Perspectives on Global Development 2014.* OECD, Paris.

Ohno, K. (2009). Avoiding the Middle-Income Trap: Renovating Industrial Policy Formulation in Vietnam. *ASEAN Economic Bulletin*, 26(1), pp. 25–43.

Ohno, K. (2010). Avoiding the Middle-Income Trap: Renovating Industrial Policy Formulation in Vietnam. Revised paper. Available at http://www.grips.ac.jp/vietnam/KOarchives/doc/EP32_ADB_HQ_MIT.pdf. (Accessed 17 October 2015).

Tran, T. V. (2013). Vietnam is Facing Economic Slowdown (Vietnam, seichou gensoku ni chokumen). JCER Asia Research Paper, pp. 143–164. (In Japanese)

Ushiyama, R. (2013). Malaysia Aims to Become a High-income Country — The Difficulty in Demolishing Long-standing Abuses So As To Maintain High Growth (Kousyotokukoku iri wo mezasu Malaysia — kouseicho jizokuhe kyuhei daha no nandai). JCER Asia Research Paper, pp. 47–74. (In Japanese)

World Bank (2012). *Malaysia Economic Monitor.*

World Bank (2015). *Global Economic Prospects.*

World Bank and the Development Research Center (DRC) (2013). *China 2030 — Building a Modern, Harmonious, and Creative Society.* Washington D.C. and Beijing.

Yamazawa, N. (2013). The Middle-income Trap Verified by Data — The Exit Key is Developing Institutions (Data de kensho suru chusyotokukoku no wana). JCER Asia Research Paper, pp. 23–45. (In Japanese)

Zhuang, J., P. Vandenberg, and Y. Huang (2012). *Growing beyond the Low-Cost Advantage: How the People's Republic of China can Avoid the Middle-income Trap?* Asian Development Bank and Peking University, Manila and Beijing.

CHAPTER 2

# Determinants of Economic Growth in East Asia: A BMA Approach

Hiroyasu Hasegawa

*Graduate School of Economics, Kobe University*
*2-1, Nada-Ku, Kobe 657-8501, Japan*
*brandon_90240@hotmail.com*

Shigeyuki Hamori

*Faculty of Economics, Kobe University*
*2-1, Rokkodai, Nada-Ku, Kobe 657-8501, Japan*
*hamori@econ.kobe-u.ac.jp*

## 1. Introduction

The East Asian region suffered significant economic damage owing to the 1997 Asian financial crisis but has made a remarkable recovery since then. However, as stressed in Chapter 1, some countries in this region attain a certain level of income, but fall into the "middle income trap" whereby rapidly growing economies stagnate at middle-income levels and fail to graduate into the ranks of high-income countries. Gill and Kharas (2007) discuss the problem of the "middle income trap" in emerging Asian countries.

Since the seminal work by Barro and Sala-i-Martin (1991) and Mankiw *et al.* (1992), many research articles have analyzed long-term economic growth. On analyzing the determinants of economic growth, however, we find many candidates for explanatory variables, such as the initial level of income, the investment rate, various measures of education, indicators of trade openness, indicators of financial development, and some policy indicators. Thus, we may encounter a problem in that the number of proposed explanatory variables may exceed the number of countries in the cross-country regression.

To formally address this specification uncertainty, we need to recognize that we do not know the "true model" and attach probabilities to various possible models. This approach is known as the BMA approach and has been used in recent empirical growth literature (see Fernandez *et al.*, 2001; Horvath, 2011; Asatryan and Feld, 2014).[1] Researchers are assumed to have a specified model in the classical methodology. Researchers, however, a priori declare that the true model is unknown in the BMA approach. In the BMA approach, the first step is to attach prior non-informative beliefs to the model parameters instead of conditioning on a specified model. The next step (averaging) is to compute the estimator as a weighted average of these conditional estimators (Asatryan and Feld, 2014).

The BMA approach has several merits (Horvath, 2011). First, this approach assesses the robustness of the model to the choice of many competing theories and many possible determinants. Second, this approach enables researchers to compute the posterior inclusion probability (PIP), which is the probability that an explanatory variable is contained in the "correct model." Third, this approach offers a rigorous way to average across models and systematically assess the robustness of results.

Some studies have analyzed the determinants of economic growth using the BMA approach. Fernandez *et al.* (2001) analyzes the determinants of economic growth using the data of 140 countries over the period from 1960 to 1992. The explained variable is the real per capita economic growth rate from 1960 to 1992, and the number of explanatory variables is 62. According to their results, the most important explanatory variables are GDP level in 1960, fraction confusion, life expectancy, and equipment investment.

Horvath (2011) focuses on the role of research and development on economic growth using the data of 72 countries over the period

---

[1]In addition, see Sala-i-Martin *et al.* (2004).

from 1960 to 1992. The explained variable is the real per capita economic growth rate from 1960 to 1992 and the number of explanatory variables is 41 including research and development. Horvath (2011) captures the investment in R&D by the number of Nobel prizes in science. According to his empirical results, R&D has a positive effect on long-term growth.

Asatryan and Feld (2014) analyze the relationship between output growth and fiscal federalism using the data of 23 OECD countries over the period from 1975 to 2000. The explained variable is PPP-adjusted per capita GDP growth rates from 1975 to 2000. Their empirical results indicate that there is no robust link between output growth and fiscal federalism.

This chapter analyzes the determinants of economic growth in the East Asian region from 1980 to 2010 using the BMA approach. The rest of this chapter is organized as follows. Section 2 briefly explains the empirical techniques. Section 3 describes the data. Section 4 reports the empirical results. Section 5 concludes.

## 2. Empirical techniques

In this section, we briefly summarize the BMA. (For the BMA approach, see, for example, Hoeting *et al.*, 1999.)

The BMA approach is effective in producing robust results in the case of model uncertainty. Note that by model uncertainty, we mean the uncertainty about the choice of regressors, that is, the model includes a lot of comparative or decidable factors (Fernandez *et al.*, 2001).

Suppose that we have a regression model as follows:

$$y_i = \beta_0 + \beta_1 x_{i1} + \beta_2 x_{i2} + \cdots + \beta_k x_{ik} + u_i \quad i = 1, 2, \ldots, n, \quad (1)$$

where $y_i$ is a dependent variable (long-term growth rate in this paper), $x_{i1}, x_{i2}, \ldots, x_{ik}$ are explanatory variables and $u_i$ is an error term. In the classical context, researchers assess the robustness of empirical results by changing the set of control variables. However, in reality, this procedure contains substantial uncertainty because researchers do not know the "true model" and thus the choice of explanatory variables $(x_{i1}, x_{i2}, \ldots, x_{ik})$ are often ad hoc in many empirical studies.

The BMA approach offers a useful alternative procedure because it considers all possible explanatory variables and averages the estimated parameters in a rigorous way. As a result, the BMA approach enables researchers to avoid the possibility of omitted variable problems. (Horvath, 2011) In principle, we consider $l = 2^k$ subsets of explanatory variables $(x_{i1}, x_{i2}, \ldots, x_{ik})$ and thus $M_1, M_2, \ldots, M_l$ models.

According to Bayes' theorem, we have the following relationship:

$$p(\theta|D) \propto f(D|\theta) \times \pi(\theta), \tag{2}$$

where $\theta$ is the vector of parameters, $D$ is the available data, $p(\theta|D)$ is the posterior distribution, $f(D|\theta)$ is the likelihood, and $\pi(\theta)$ is the prior distribution. Equation (2) indicates that the posterior distribution is proportional to the product of the likelihood and the prior distribution. This is the theorem to derive the posterior distribution form the prior distribution and data.

Thus, the posterior distribution of model $M_i$ $(i = 1, 2, \ldots, l)$, given available data, is obtained as follows:

$$p(M_i|D) \propto f(D|M_i)\pi(M_i), \tag{3}$$

where $\pi(M_i)$ is the prior distribution that $M_i$ is a correct model. Then we can calculate the PIP of a particular explanatory variable by taking the sum of posterior model probabilities across these models that include the explanatory variable.

## 3. Data

We construct a cross-sectional dataset of the following 15 countries (or regions): Japan, Korea, Taiwan, Singapore, Hong Kong, Malaysia, Philippines, Sri Lanka, China, Thailand, Cambodia, India, Indonesia, Pakistan, and Vietnam.

In order to check the robustness of the empirical results over time, we use the following two sample periods:

Case 1: from 1980 to 2010;
Case 2: from 1990 to 2010.

Table 1. Definition and sources of data.

| Variable | Definition | Source |
|---|---|---|
| Growth | Growth rate of real GDP | Penn World Table (World Economic Outlook for Taiwan) |
| Per capita Growth | Growth rate of per capita real GDP | Penn World Table (World Economic Outlook for Taiwan) |
| HC | Index of human capital per person, based on years of schooling and returns to education | Penn World Table |
| INV | Ratio of Investment to GDP | Penn World Table |
| EXP | Ratio of Exports to GDP | Penn World Table |
| FDI | Foreign direct investment, net inflows as percentage of GDP | World Development Indicators |
| OPEN | Ratio of Exports plus Imports to GDP | Penn World Table |
| POP | Population growth (annual %) | Penn World Table |
| M2 | M2 as percentage of GDP | World Development Indicators (World Bank) |
| UIS | Index of upgrading industrial structure | Provided by Professor Takeuchi |
| Initial GDP | Log of initial level of GDP for the sample period | Penn World Table (World Economic Outlook for Taiwan) |

The explained variable is per capita real economic growth rate during the sample period or real economic growth rate during the sample period.

We use the following nine factors as possible explanatory variables (Table 1):

(1) HC: Index of human capital per person;[2]
(2) INV: Ratio of investment to GDP;
(3) EXP: Ratio of exports to GDP;
(4) FDI: Foreign direct investment, net inflows (% of GDP);

---

[2]This index is based on years of schooling (Barro/Lee, 2010) and returns to education (Psacharopoulos, 1994).

(5)  OPEN: Exports plus imports as a proportion of GDP;
(6)  POP: Population growth (annual %);
(7)  M2: Money and quasi money (M2) as a percentage of GDP;
(8)  UIS: Index of upgrading industrial structure;
(9)  Initial GDP: Initial level of GDP.

The source of most of this data is Penn World Table ver. 8.0.[3] However, the foreign direct investment data is obtained from World Development Indicators (World Bank),[4] and the GDP data of Taiwan is obtained from World Economic Outlook (IMF).[5] Furthermore, Professor Fumihide Takeuchi (the author of Chapter 3) kindly supplied us with the data of the index of upgrading industrial structure.

## 4. Empirical results

Empirical results using the sample from 1980 to 2010 are reported in Tables 2 and 3. Table 2 presents the BMA estimation results with per capita real growth rates from 1980 to 2010 as the dependent variable. In each table, PIP indicates the PIP, which is the probability that an explanatory variable is contained in the "correct model." As is clear from this table, three variables, namely, POP, UIS, and HC, are found to be the most important variables in explaining per capita real economic growth. Table 3 present the BMA estimation results with real growth rates from 1980 to 2010 as the dependent variable. As is clear from this table, three variables, that is, UIS, HC, and POP are found to be the most important variables in explaining real economic growth.

Empirical results using the sample from 1990 to 2010 are reported in Tables 4 and 5. Table 4 presents the BMA estimation results with per capita real growth rates from 1990 to 2010 as the dependent variable. As is clear from this table, three variables, that is, POP, HC, and UIS are found to be the key factors in explaining per capita

---

[3]See https://pwt.sas.upenn.edu/.
[4]See http://data.worldbank.org/data-catalog/world-development-indicators.
[5]See http://www.econstats.com/weo/CTWN.htm.

Table 2. Empirical results: Growth rate of real
GDP per capita from 1980 to 2010.

| Variables | PIP |
|---|---|
| POP | 0.47812 |
| UIS | 0.38544 |
| HC | 0.35700 |
| Initial GDP | 0.34712 |
| M2 | 0.31752 |
| OPEN | 0.31042 |
| EXP | 0.30888 |
| INV | 0.30422 |
| FDI | 0.29122 |

*Note*: PIP: PIP, POP: population growth rate,
HC: human capital, INV: ratio of investment to GDP, EXP: ratio of exports to GDP,
FDI: foreign direct investment, net inflows as
percentage of GDP, OPEN: ratio of exports
plus imports to GDP, M2: M2 as percentage
of GDP, UIS: index of upgrading industrial
structure, Initial GDP: Log of initial level of
GDP for the sample period.

Table 3. Empirical results: Growth rate of real
GDP from 1980 to 2010.

| Variables | PIP |
|---|---|
| UIS | 0.46534 |
| HC | 0.38360 |
| POP | 0.36490 |
| Initial GDP | 0.33384 |
| M2 | 0.33108 |
| INV | 0.31336 |
| EXP | 0.30916 |
| FDI | 0.30872 |
| OPEN | 0.29754 |

*Note*: See the footnote to Table 2.

Table 4. Empirical results: Growth rate of real GDP per capita from 1990 to 2010.

| Variables | PIP |
|---|---|
| POP | 0.44458 |
| HC | 0.41204 |
| UIS | 0.35558 |
| Initial GDP | 0.33334 |
| INV | 0.32494 |
| M2 | 0.32066 |
| EXP | 0.31992 |
| OPEN | 0.31330 |
| FDI | 0.30086 |

*Note*: See the footnote to Table 2.

Table 5. Empirical results: Growth rate of real GDP from 1990 to 2010.

| Variables | PIP |
|---|---|
| HC | 0.44316 |
| UIS | 0.42420 |
| POP | 0.35564 |
| INV | 0.34674 |
| M2 | 0.34468 |
| Initial GDP | 0.34188 |
| OPEN | 0.32828 |
| EXP | 0.32098 |
| FDI | 0.31424 |

*Note*: See the footnote to Table 2.

real economic growth. Table 5 presents the BMA estimation results with real growth rates from 1990 to 2010 as the dependent variable. As is clear from this table, three variables, namely, HC, UIS, and POP are found to be the key factors in explaining a real economic growth.

Our empirical results thus suggest that the main determinants of economic growth in East Asia are POP, HC, and UIS. This selection of explanatory variables is robust to the choice of sample period or explained variable.

## 5. Conclusion

This paper attempts to identify the key determinants of economic growth in the East Asian region using a BMA approach. The BMA approach has several merits (Horvath, 2011). First, this approach assesses the robustness of the model to the choice of many competing theories and many possible determinants. Second, this approach enables researchers to compute the PIP, which is the probability that an explanatory variable is contained in the "correct model." Third, this approach offers a rigorous way to average across models and systematically assess the robustness of results.

Our empirical results indicate that the important determinants of economic growth in East Asian region are human capital, the index of upgrading industrial structure, and population growth rate. These three factors are also found to be consistently important over time.

The key policy implication derived from our analysis is that governments in East Asian countries should introduce policies that focus on human capital, industrial structure, and population growth in order to accelerate economic growth. The details of these points will be analyzed in Chapter 3 and Chapter 5.

## Acknowledgments

We are grateful to Prof. Takeuchi for his kindness in providing us with the index of upgrading industrial structure.

## References

Asatryan, Z. and L. P. Feld (2014). Revisiting the link between growth and federalism: A Bayesian model averaging approach. Forthcoming in *Journal of Comparative Economics*.

Barro, R. and J.-W. Lee (2010). A new data set of educational attainment in the world, 1950–2010. *Journal of Development Economics*, 104, pp. 184–198. Available at http://siteresources.worldbank.org/INTUNIKAM/Resources/BL.pdf (accessed 18 October 2015).

Barro, R. and X. Sala-i-Martin (1991). Convergence across states and regions. *Brookings Papers on Economic Activity, Economic Studies Program*, 22, pp. 107–182.

Fernandez, C., E. Ley, and M. J. Steel (2001). Model uncertainty in cross-country growth regressions. *Journal of Applied Econometrics*, 16, pp. 563–576.

Gill, I. and H. Kharas (2007). *An East Asian Renaissance*. The World Bank, Washington, DC. Available at http://siteresources.worldbank.org/ INTEASTASIAPACIFIC/Resources/226262-1158536715202/EA_Ren-aissance_full.pdf (accessed 18 October 2015).

Horvath, R. (2011). Research & development and growth: A Bayesian model averaging analysis. *Economic Modelling*, 28, pp. 2669–2673.

Hoeting, J. A., D. Madigan, A. E. Raftery, and C. T. Volinsky (1999). Bayesian model average: A tutorial. *Statistical Science*, 14, pp. 382–417.

Mankiw, N. G., D. Romer, and D. N. Weil (1992). A contribution to the empirics of economic growth. *Quarterly Journal of Economics*, 107, pp. 407–437.

Psacharopoulos, G. (1994). Returns to investment in education: A global update. *World Development*, Elsevier, 22, pp. 1325–1343.

Sala-i-Martin, X., G. Dopperlhofer, and R. I. Miller (2004). Determinants of long-term growth: A Bayesian averaging of classical estimates (BACE) approach. *American Economic Review*, 94, pp. 813–835.

Part II

# Common Policy Issues in Asian Countries

CHAPTER 3

# Industrial Structural Change and Productivity Growth in the Era of Global Value Chains (GVCs)

Fumihide Takeuchi

*Department of Economics,*
*School of Political Science and Economics, Tokai University*
*4-1-1, Kitakaname, Hiratsuka-shi, Kanagawa 259-1292, Japan*
*ftake@tokai.ac.jp*

## 1. Introduction

This chapter analyzes the impact that Global Value Chains (GVCs) have on the real side of the economies in the world. GVCs have expanded rapidly in the 2000s, especially in Asian countries. A value chain is a series of value-added processes that are involved in the production of any goods or service. GVCs or production networks are divided into discrete steps — from upstream to downstream production stages — and are located in different countries that started to actively trade intermediate (half-finished) goods in the 2000s. This type of production is known as fragmentation and the trade of intermediate goods is categorized as intra-industry and/or intra-firm trade. These new phenomena have become important topics in international economics.

When investigating the impact of outsourcing intermediate goods in GVCs, most research has investigated the implications for domestic labor markets and productivity. This chapter addresses the impact of GVCs on productivity and on industrial structural change, which is closely associated with productivity change.

Standard trade theory tells us that international outsourcing of intermediate goods is beneficial for the economy, as it enables the reallocation of resources for their best use. The economy purchases higher quality intermediates abroad and reorganizes production to concentrate the most efficient stages in the country (Görg *et al.*, 2008).

In certain Asian low- and middle-income countries, however, it may not be possible to apply this standard theory because in a portion of Asian countries, labor-intensive multinational enterprises (MNEs) deal with processing and assembling activities and export and import large amounts of half-finished goods simultaneously. As a result, the amount of added value, export minus import, that is attributed to these economies is relatively small, which means that the productivity level is inevitably low.

To verify this supposition, we must use the data of value-added exports, which are equivalent to domestic content that deducts foreign content from gross exports. Based on these recent research interests, several studies have analyzed certain countries' trades in value added to clarify the extent of the domestic content of gross exports (e.g., Dai, 2013; Timmer *et al.*, 2014; OECD *et al.*, 2013). This chapter introduces a new indicator to measure the extent of the upgrading of industrial structures (referred to as the relative value-added ratio (relative VaR) hereafter). First, we define high-tech manufacturing industries and subsequently calculate the relative size of the ratio of added value to production of high-tech industries relative to the ratio of other manufacturing industries. This new indicator, relative VaR, is almost equal to the comparative advantage index calculated using value-added trade data relative to the index calculated using gross trade data. Using the relative VaR of world economies, including Asia, this chapter analyzes the degree to which international outsourcing of intermediate goods affects industrial structural upgrading and the closely associated economic variable — total factor productivity (TFP) change. The focal point is the differences in the impacts of international outsourcing between low- and middle-income economies, including those of Asia and high-income economies.

The structure of this chapter is as follows. In the next section, we first discuss the expansion of GVCs in the 2000s and the background for this new trend. After discussing the importance of the difference between gross and value-added trade data for understanding the implications of GVCs on the world economies, we introduce the relative VaR as a direct measure of the extent of industrial structural upgrading. With respect to the relative VaR indicator, we also present the difference between this new indicator and other traditional indicators to measure industrial structural upgrading, such as the share of high-tech industries in total production and in total added value. Section 3 discusses the empirical methodology for analyzing the link between international outsourcing on one side and industrial structural upgrading and TFP on the other and subsequently presents the results of the estimation prior to providing the conclusion in the final section.

## 2. Industrial structural upgrading in the era of GVCs

### 2.1. Expansion of GVCs in the 2000s

GVCs have been expanding in the 2000s, as illustrated in Figure 1, where the $x$-axis is the GVC participation index for 1995 and the $y$-axis is the participation index for 2009. These data are derived from the OECD-WTO Trade in Value-Added (TiVA) database. The GVC participation index is calculated as a sum of the forward participation index — the share of exported goods and services used as imported inputs to produce other countries' exports — and the backward participation index — the share of imported inputs in the overall exports of a country. A GVC is an organization of production known as a fragmentation in which different stages of production are divided among different suppliers that are located in different countries. One supplier in one country exports and imports half-finished goods; therefore, the extent of the participation of GVCs can be measured as a sum of forward and backward linkages.

Figure 1 shows that in most countries GVCs participation indices increased during the study period, and it is easily recognized that Asian countries (indicated as white dots) are located far from the

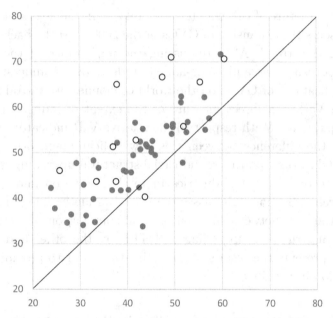

Figure 1. GVCs participation indices for 1995 (*x*-axis) and for 2009 (*y*-axis) for 57 economies (%, white circle dots are for Asian economies).
*Source*: OECD–WTO TiVA database.

45 degree angle, thereby demonstrating that these economies experienced rapid growth of GVCs. Typical examples for the period 1995 to 2009, respectively, include South Korea (38% → 65%), Taiwan (49% → 71%), China (26% → 46%) and the Philippines (48% → 67%). The major driver of the growth of GVCs is the expansion of MNEs through foreign direct investment (FDI), as noted in the OECD *et al.* (2013).

## 2.2. Industrial structural upgrading in Asia and other economies

This chapter focuses on the real side of the economies in the world. With respect to the upgrading of the industrial structure, we first define high-tech industries as target sectors to be promoted. The Eurostat uses the following aggregation of the manufacturing industry according to the technological intensity based on the Nomenclature des Activités Économiques dans la Communauté Européenne

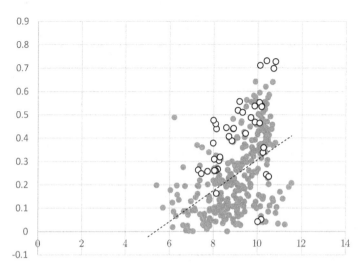

Figure 2. The log of per capita GDP ($x$-axis) and high-tech manufacturing share to total manufacturing ($y$-axis) for 134 economies (white circle dots are for Asian economies) for the years 1995, 2000, 2005, and 2010.

*Source*: UNIDO, INDSTAT2 database and the World Bank, World Development Indicators.

(NACE) Rev. 1.1 at a 3-digit level for compiling aggregates related to high technology, medium high technology, medium low technology and low technology. Based on this classification, this chapter defines high-tech industries as a sum of high technology and medium high technology.[1]

Figure 2 depicts the relationship between per capita GDP ($x$-axis) and high-tech manufacturing share to total manufacturing ($y$-axis) for the years of 1995, 2000, 2005, and 2010 for 134 countries.

---

[1]Aggregations of manufacturing based on the NACE Rev 1.1 are as follows (numbers in parenthesis are NACE codes). High-tech industries are pharmaceuticals, medical chemicals and botanical products (24.4), office machinery and computers (30), radio, television and communication equipment and apparatus (32), medical, precision and optical instruments, watches and clocks (33), aircraft and spacecraft (35.3). Medium-high-tech industries are chemicals and chemical products, pharmaceuticals, medical chemicals and botanical products (24 excluding 24.4), machinery and equipment n.e.c. (29), electrical machinery and apparatus n.e.c. (31), motor vehicles, trailers and semi-trailers (34), other transport equipment (35) excluding building and repairing of ships and boats (35.1) and aircraft and spacecraft (35.3).

*Moving Up the Ladder*

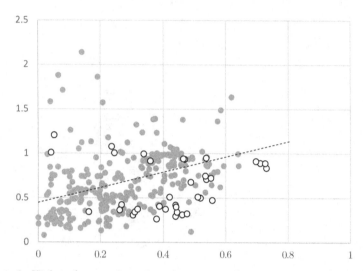

Figure 3. High-tech manufacturing share to total manufacturing (*x*-axis) and TFP (the U.S. TFP in 2005 = 1, *y*-axis) for 134 economies (white circle dots are for Asian economies) for the years 1995, 2000, 2005, and 2010.
*Source*: UNIDO, INDSTAT2 database and the Penn World Table ver. 8.0.

Asian economies (white dots) are located at the top of the samples, which means that their levels of development are relatively low, despite their relatively high high-tech manufacturing shares. This finding gives rise to the question, 'What backgrounds or reasons account for this situation?'

One important clue can be taken from Figure 3, which shows the relationship between high-tech manufacturing shares (*x*-axis) and the TFP of the total industry (*y*-axis) in the same manner as Figure 2. It is evidenced that many of the Asian economies are far below the fitted line. Relatively large shares of high-tech manufacturing cannot result in a high rate growth in Asian economies as it goes against the basic growth theory, a situation that may have important implications.

## 2.3. Gross statistics-based comparative advantage versus net statistics-based comparative advantage

The fact that large shares of high-tech manufacturing are not combined with the improvement in productivity might be closely connected with the present condition of Asian economies that they are typically faced with the rapid expansion of GVCs. As mentioned in the opening section of this chapter, in Asian countries, many labor-intensive MNEs address processing and assembling activities while simultaneously exporting and importing large amounts of half-finished goods. As a result, the amount of added value that is attributed to these economies is relatively small, and the productivity level is inevitably low.

As presented in Figure 1, Asian economies have become deeply integrated into GVCs in the 2000s. Therefore, in this era of GVCs, we should prepare a new indicator to measure the extent of the upgrading of the industrial structure.

Dai (2013) noted that global supply chains changed our understanding of comparative advantage, as we no longer examine official gross export statistics to determine who produces goods for whom. Because of the global fragmentation of supply chains, we must isolate how much value added a nation contributes to the production of a good to illuminate the true comparative advantage of nations.

Based on these recent research interests, several papers have clarified the true industrial structures or true comparative advantages of nations using net-based (value-added) statistics of trade and/or production. According to the analysis of the comparative advantage of the electrical and optical equipment industry, which is classified as a high-tech industry in this chapter, the United States' gross comparative advantage has steadily declined over the past fifteen years from a comparative advantage level of slightly over 1.1 in 1995 to that of less than 0.9 in 2009. In contrast, the value-added comparative advantage shows that the United States' comparative advantage has steadily increased over the 1995 to 2009 period from just below 1.1 to over 1.3. Accordingly, the gross and value-added comparative advantages for the United States illustrate opposite trends over time (Dai, 2013).

The gross comparative advantage, which is larger than that of the value-added comparative advantage, indicates that the economy depends largely on foreign inputs, which is a common trend among Asian economies. This trend can be easily identified by examining macro trade data. In China, for instance, a large difference between gross and net exports has persisted for long periods. The Chinese trade balance GDP ratio was only 2.5%, while the gross export GDP ratio amounted to 26.4% in 2013.

## 2.4. Appropriate indicator to measure industrial structural upgrading in the era of GVCs

On the basis of the preceding analyses of value-added trade data, this chapter introduces an indicator to measure a true industrial structural level of an economy in the GVC era. As previously mentioned, this indicator is the relative VaR of the high-tech industry (defined in Section 2.2).

The relative VaR is defined such that the relative VaR of industry $k$ in country $d$ and the relative VaR of industry $k$ in the world $(w)$ are calculated, respectively, as follows:

$$\frac{\dfrac{V_{dk}}{Y_{dk}}}{\dfrac{V_d}{Y_d}},$$

$$\frac{\dfrac{V_{wk}}{Y_{wk}}}{\dfrac{V_w}{Y_w}},$$

where $V$ is added value and $Y$ is production. In this definition, industry $k$ is a high-tech industry and $V$ and $Y$ with a subscript $d$ or $w$ (variables included in denominators) denote added value and production of total industry, respectively.

We do not use shares of high-tech industries in total added value and/or production but rather use relative VaR to measure upgrading of industrial structures. The concept of this measurement is similar to the comparative advantage of a traditional trade theory that compares productivities of two different sectors in one economy.

The proportion of the relative VaR of one economy to that of the world is equivalent to the proportion of a value-added comparative advantage to that of the gross comparative advantage in the economy as follows:

$$\frac{\frac{V_{dk}}{Y_{dk}}}{\frac{V_d}{Y_d}} \Bigg/ \frac{\frac{V_{wk}}{Y_{wk}}}{\frac{V_w}{Y_w}} = \frac{\frac{V_{dk}}{V_d}}{\frac{V_{wk}}{V_w}} \Bigg/ \frac{\frac{Y_{dk}}{Y_d}}{\frac{Y_{wk}}{Y_w}},$$

where the numerator and denominator on the left-hand side are the ratio of the relative VaR of country d to that of the world and the numerator and denominator on the right-hand side are the value-added and gross comparative advantage indices for country $d$, respectively.[2]

Thus, the relative VaR ratio between one country and other countries for industry $k$ is equivalent to the country's comparative advantage of the industry in terms of added value relative to the country's comparative advantage of the industry in terms of production. The relative VaR ratio (left-hand side of the equation) is low when the country depends largely on foreign inputs and the right-hand side of the equation is low.

This relative VaR ratio can be described as an appropriate indicator to measure the grade of the industrial structure in terms of its technological level. The relative VaR of a high-tech industry is equal to the difference between the value-added and gross comparative advantages of the industry, and the large difference means that the economy depends largely on technology intensive foreign intermediate goods.

Figure 4 shows the relationship between the per capita GDP ($x$-axis) and the relative VaR ratios ($y$-axis) for the years of 1995, 2000, 2005 and 2010 for 134 countries. This figure corresponds to Figure 2, while Figure 5 shows the relationship between the relative VaR ratios ($x$-axis) and the TFP of the total industry ($y$-axis) in the same way as Figure 3. We clearly note that in the relationship

---

[2]Note that variables on the left-hand side are those of production and variables on the right-hand side are those of exports. It is assumed that the right-hand side of the equation (the comparative advantage condition derived from trade data) is empirically equal to the comparative advantage condition derived from the production data.

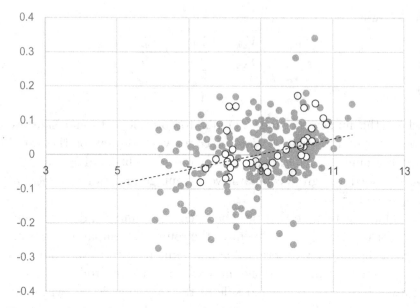

Figure 4. The log of per capita GDP ($x$-axis) and the relative VaR ratio of high-tech manufacturing ($y$-axis) for 134 economies (white circle dots are for Asian economies) for the years 1995, 2000, 2005, and 2010.

*Source*: UNIDO, INDSTAT2 database and the World Bank, World Development Indicators.

between the relative VaR ratio and the per capita GDP and in the relationship between the relative VaR ratio and the TFP, the Asian economies are no longer outliers, as they were in Figures 2 and 3.

## 3. Econometric analysis

### 3.1. International outsourcing and productivity

When we investigate the impact of international outsourcing in GVCs, most research has focused on the implications with respect to domestic labor markets. The relationship between international outsourcing and the relative VaR (measurement of industrial structure upgrades) and the relationship between international outsourcing and the TFP require empirical analyses.

Thus, such analyses are extended from those based on macro and industry level data to those using data at the firm and plant

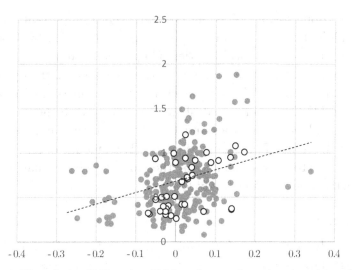

Figure 5. The relative VaR ratio of high-tech manufacturing ($x$-axis) and TFP (the U.S. TFP in 2005 = 1, $y$-axis) for 134 economies (white circle dots are for Asian economies) for the years 1995, 2000, 2005, and 2010.
Source: UNIDO, INDSTAT2 database and the Penn World Table ver. 8.0

level. Furthermore, several recent empirical studies examine specifically the differences between the outsourcing of materials and services inputs. For example, Görg et al. (2008), who investigated the effect of international outsourcing on productivity using plant level data for Irish manufacturing, distinguished the effect of the outsourcing of materials and services inputs.[3] This chapter's empirical study utilizes macro and industry level data and covers not only high-income economies but also low- and medium-income economies, including a number of Asian economies, and argues the differences in the effects of international outsourcing on domestic economies between those of high-income and low- and middle-income economies.

Theoretically, increasing the use of foreign inputs may result in a boost in productivity in any economy because these internationally traded inputs may be available at a higher quality than those

---

[3] A study that focuses on the impacts of outsourcing of service inputs is, for example, Amiti and Wei (2005).

available domestically. This may be particularly important for low- and middle-income economies whose firms are operating far from the international technological frontier (Görg *et al.*, 2008).

In some Asian countries, however, this standard theory might not be applicable. This is because in some Asian countries labor-intensive MNEs continue to deal simultaneously with the processing and assembling of activities and with the exporting and importing of large amounts of half-finished goods. The amount of added value attributable to these economies is, therefore, relatively small and the productivity level is inevitably low.

## 3.2. Data

Two productivity-related variables, the relative VaR of high-tech industry and the TFP, are set as dependent variables. The focal independent variable is an international outsourcing of materials that is defined as the ratio of intermediate goods imported to the GDP. Other control variables include: (1) the log of labor costs per employees to the proxy for human capital, (2) financial depth (M2/GDP), (3) labor market flexibility index to the proxy for production factor mobility.[4] Moreover, we include the log of the averaged value of output per establishment in the high-tech industry and its squared value to measure firm size.

Data of intermediate goods imports are obtained from the UN Comtrade Database under the classification of broad economic categories (BEC). The imported values classified as intermediate goods in this database include natural resource inputs. Given the increase in resource prices in the 2000s, we extracted the imports of 'fuels and lubricants, primary' (BEC code 31) and the imports of 'fuels and lubricants, processed (other than motor spirit)' (BEC code 322) from the intermediate goods imports.

Other data sources are the Penn World Table ver. 8.0 for TFP data; the United Nations Industrial Development Organization (UNIDO), INDSTAT2 Database for data used to calculate

---

[4]Labor market flexibility index is introduced as this variable may have a relationship with the relative VaR index changes or industrial structural changes.

the relative VaR,[5] real wages and averaged firm size; the World Bank, World Development Indicators for financial depth; and the Fraser Institute, Economic Freedom of the World (EFW) Database to obtain data for the labor market flexibility index.[6]

It should be considered, however, that the TFP, financial depth and labor market flexibility data be included on the all-industry basis and that the relative VaR and real wages be included on the high-tech manufacturing basis due to the constraints of available data.[7] Additionally, intermediate goods imports do not include service inputs.

### 3.3. Empirical methodology and estimation results

We use a dataset of 134 countries — 77 high-income countries and 57 low- or middle-income countries — for the years 1995, 2000, 2005, and 2010. The 134 countries includes 10 Asian countries — China, Hong Kong, Macao, Indonesia, Malaysia, the Philippines, South Korea, Singapore, Thailand and Vietnam and among them are the countries categorized as middle-income economies — China, Indonesia, the Philippines, Thailand, and Vietnam. Estimation is performed using the generalized methods of moments (GMM) estimator. This estimation treats the outsourcing variable or intermediate goods import GDP ratio as endogenous. That is, more productive firms might select foreign outsourcing, while alternatively, firms opt to outsource foreign inputs with the objective to improve productivity. We use intermediate goods import GDP ratios for the period $t-1$ (5 years ago) as an instrument.

---

[5]See Section 2.4 regarding data used for calculating the relative VaR.
[6]The EFW database provides a composite measure of labor market flexibility and indicators of labor market flexibility in six policy areas — minimum wage, hiring and firing regulations, centralized collective wage bargaining, mandated cost of hiring, mandated cost of work dismissal, and conscription.
[7]The data for the relative VaR and real wages should be prepared on an all-industry basis. In the case of relative VaR, high-tech industry's added value to production ratio should be calculated relative to other whole industries, rather than to other manufacturing industries. However, the data source, INDSTAT2 database (UNIDO), contains only manufacturing data.

*Moving Up the Ladder*

Table 1. Regression results with the relative VaR as the dependent variable.

|  | (1) | (2) | (3) | (4) |
|---|---|---|---|---|
| Dependent variable | Relative VaR | Relative VaR | Relative VaR | Relative VaR |
| Outsourcing | 0.0877 | 0.0770 | 0.0100 | 0.0675 |
|  | $(0.0292)^{***}$ | $(0.0252)^{***}$ | (0.0195) | $(0.0240)^{***}$ |
| Outsourcing* | 0.2394 | 0.0887 | 0.1041 | 0.2603 |
| Developing_ dummy | $(0.1135)^{**}$ | (0.0747) | (0.0821) | $(0.1110)^{**}$ |
| Outsourcing* | −0.1539 | −0.1207 | −0.1097 | −0.1635 |
| Asian_developing_ dummy | $(0.0752)^{**}$ | $(0.0424)^{***}$ | $(0.0518)^{**}$ | $(0.0895)^{*}$ |
| Human_capital (real | 0.0027 |  |  | 0.0019 |
| labor cost) | $(0.0016)^{*}$ |  |  | (0.0015) |
| Findepth |  | −0.0000 |  | −0.0000 |
|  |  | (0.0000) |  | (0.0000) |
| Labflex |  |  | 0.0098 | 0.0082 |
|  |  |  | $(0.0013)^{***}$ | $(0.0015)^{***}$ |
| Developing_dummy | −0.0753 | −0.0452 | −0.0335 | −0.0692 |
|  | $(0.0155)^{***}$ | $(0.0107)^{***}$ | $(0.0125)^{***}$ | $(0.0135)^{***}$ |
| log(Scale) |  |  |  | −0.0338 |
|  |  |  |  | $(0.0110)^{***}$ |
| log(Scale)^2 |  |  |  | 0.0009 |
|  |  |  |  | $(0.0002)^{***}$ |
| Obserbvation | 163 | 202 | 192 | 148 |
| R-squared | 0.3741 | 0.3640 | 0.3642 | 0.5077 |
| Sargan J $p$-value | 0.8236 | 0.4416 | 0.5010 | 0.7907 |

*Notes*: Developing dummy is created for 57 low- and middle-income economies and Asian developing dummy is created for 10 Asian middle-income economies. The figures in parentheses are $p$-values. *significant at the 10% level, **significant at the 5% level, ***significant at the 1% level.

Table 1 presents the estimation results with the relative VaR of the high-tech industry as the dependent variable, and Table 2 presents the results with the TFP as the dependent variable. A summary of the major findings are as follows:

(1) With respect to the effects of foreign intermediate inputs on the upgrading of the industrial structure in countries excluding Asia, we found positive effects. The size of the effects for middle-income

Table 2. Regression results with TFP as the dependent variable.

|  | (1) | (2) | (3) | (4) |
|---|---|---|---|---|
| Dependent variable | TFP | TFP | TFP | TFP |
| Outsourcing | 0.1992 | 0.0642 | 0.2009 | 0.0686 |
|  | (0.0290)*** | (0.0238)*** | (0.0323)*** | (0.0374)* |
| Outsourcing* | −0.0758 | −0.2601 | −0.4139 | 0.2067 |
| Developing_ | (0.1156) | (0.0410)*** | (0.0425)*** | (0.2211) |
| dummy |  |  |  |  |
| Outsourcing* | −0.5863 | −0.2617 | −0.2470 | −0.7280 |
| Asian_developing_ | (0.0955)*** | (0.0791)*** | (0.0841)*** | (0.1596)*** |
| dummy |  |  |  |  |
| Human_capital (real | 0.0162 |  |  | 0.0127 |
| labor cost) | (0.0026)*** |  |  | (0.0038)*** |
| Findepth |  | 0.0006 |  | 0.0005 |
|  |  | (0.0001)*** |  | (0.0000)*** |
| Labflex |  |  | −0.0028 | −0.0119 |
|  |  |  | (0.0028) | (0.0040) |
| Developing_dummy | −0.3557 | −0.3452 | −0.3398 | −0.3549 |
|  | (0.0132)*** | (0.0146)*** | (0.0109)*** | (0.0346)*** |
| log(Scale) |  |  |  | 0.0993 |
|  |  |  |  | (0.0239)*** |
| log(Scale)^2 |  |  |  | −0.0026 |
|  |  |  |  | (0.0006)*** |
| Obserbvation | 182 | 236 | 234 | 149 |
| R-squared | 0.9615 | 0.9208 | 0.9248 | 0.9300 |
| Sargan J p-value | 0.2502 | 0.2999 | 0.4324 | 0.0706 |

Notes: Developing dummy is created for 57 low- and middle-income economies and Asian developing dummy is created for 10 Asian middle-income economies. The figures in parentheses are p-values. *significant at the 10% level, **significant at the 5% level, ***significant at the 1% level.

Asian countries is smaller than that of other low- and middle-income countries.

(2) With respect to the effects of foreign intermediate inputs on macro TFP improvements, we found positive effects for advanced economies. For middle-income Asian countries, the effects are negative.

(3) With respect to the other controlling variables, labor market flexibility (Labflex) has a positive effect on the upgrading of the industrial structure, an effect that is associated with production

factor movements. Real wages (the proxy for human capital) and financial depth (Findepth) are found to be positively related with TFP improvements.

The relatively weak impact of foreign inputs on the upgrading of the industrial structure and on the productivity of Asian economies are possible attributed to the fact that these economies experienced the rapid growth of GVCs in the 2000s and that they simultaneously export and import intermediate goods. As a result, added values are constrained from strong growth and productivity improvement effects are not observed.

## 3.4. Index to measure industrial structure upgrading

To interpret the above estimation results from a different perspective, we introduce another index to measure the upgrading of the industrial structure.

Figure 1 presents the GVCs participation index, which is based on two types of data or forward and backward participation indices. In this section, we use a new index, the FB index, which is obtained by dividing the forward index by the backward index. The GVCs participation index is obtained by summing these two indices. An increase in the FB index in one country means that the share of its exported goods and services used as imported inputs to produce other countries' exports is becoming larger than the share of imported inputs in the overall exports of the country. Such a phenomenon indicates that the country is advancing to an upstream stage in the production process, which is evaluated as a relatively high value-added, high-productivity production process.

The relative VaR of the high-tech industry is an index that covers only the manufacturing industries. Conversely, the FB index is based on the TiVA database and includes data of all traded intermediate goods and services. Thus, the FB index better corresponds to the TFP or total industry-based productivity index, compared to the relative VaR. The FB index, however, was not used for the aforementioned estimation because the TiVA database covers only

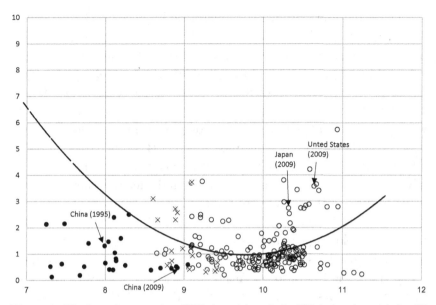

Figure 6. The log of per capita GDP ($x$-axis) and the FB index ($y$-axis) for 57 economies for the years 1995, 2000, 2005, and 2009.
*Source*: OECD-WTO TiVA database and the World Bank, World Development Indicators.

57 countries, while the UNIDO database includes the 134 countries used to develop the relative VaR index.

The FB index is defined as the relative size of exports to imports in technology-intensive intermediate inputs, while the time-series changes of the index indicate the technological or productivity level of each economy. Figure 6 presents the relationship between the per capita GDP ($x$-axis) and the FB ratios ($y$-axis) for the years 1995, 2000, 2005, and 2009 of the 57 sampled countries.[8] White circle dots denote high-income countries and cross-marks denote middle-income countries excluding Asia. Other Asian economies are denoted by black circle dots. The quadratic curve is the fitted line for the sampled countries, excluding the Asian countries.

---

[8]The latest TiVA database for the FB index covers the years 1995, 2000, 2005, 2008, and 2009.

The fitted line is drawn as a quadratic because developing countries begin to develop from points with relatively high FB ratios as they have high comparative advantages in raw materials and low value-added inputs. Then, during the course of development, they experience a decrease in the forward index due to exiting of existing domestic firms from the export markets and an increase in the backward index due to the expanding imports of high value-added inputs, which together leads to a decrease in the FB index. After entering into the group of advanced economies, countries gain comparative advantages in high value-added inputs and increase their exports, which results in the increase of the FB index.

We derive two conclusions from Figure 6. One, it takes a long time for developing countries to advance to the stage where there is notable industrial structure upgrades and improvements in productivity. Two, the FB ratios of Asian countries are relatively low. The estimation results, as reflected on the left side of Figure 6, indicate that the impact of foreign inputs on industrial structure upgrading and on productivity improvements are weak in Asian economies.

## 4. Conclusions

This chapter analyzes the impact that GVCs have on the real side of world economies. GVCs have expanded rapidly in the 2000s, especially in Asian countries. The basic assumption behind this chapter's analysis is that gross trade, including foreign inputs, no longer reflects the country's industrial structure in the era of GVCs. In Asian economies, the share of high-tech industries is extremely high given their levels of development (See Figure 2). As this high share of high-tech industries is due to a great dependence on the importing of intermediate goods, the high share does not result in improvements in domestic productivity. In certain Asian countries, labor-intensive MNEs address processing and assembling activities while simultaneously exporting and importing large amounts of half-finished goods. As a result, the amount of added value attributed to these economies is relatively small, and similarly, the productivity level is inevitably low.

The upgrading of industrial structures is redefined by referring to the new indicator, the relative VaR of high-tech industries, and we analyzed the impact of outsourcing foreign intermediate goods on industrial structural upgrading and productivity improvement. The results reveal that the size of the impact differs between high-income and low- and middle-income economies and that the Asian countries are less affected by outsourcing from abroad than are other countries.

To interpret the estimation results from a different perspective, we introduce the FB index to measure the upgrading of the industrial structure. This index shows the extent to which a country is moving toward an upstream stage of the production process (a relatively high value-added and high productivity production process). This analysis reveals that it takes a considerable amount of time for developing countries to advance to the point where industrial structure upgrades and productivity improve and also observes that the FB ratios of Asian countries are relatively low.

## References

Amiti, M. and S. J. Wei (2005). Fear of service outsourcing: Is it justified? *Economic Policy*, 20, pp. 308–347.

Dai, L. (2013). The Comparative Advantage of Nations: How Global Supply Chains Change our Understanding of Comparative Advantage. Harvard Kennedy School Mossavar–Rahmani Center for Business and Government, M-RCBG Associate Working Paper Series No. 15.

Görg, H., A. Hanley, and E. Strobl (2008). Productivity effects of international outsourcing: Evidence from plant level data. *Canadian Journal of Economics*, 41, pp. 670–688.

OECD, WTO, and UNCTAD (2013). Implications of global value chains for trade, investment, development and jobs. Paper prepared for the G-20 Leaders Summit Saint Petersburg (Russian Federation).

Timmer, M. P., A. A. Erumban, B. Los, R. Stehrer, and G. J. de Vries (2014). Slicing up global value chains. *Journal of Economic Perspectives*, 28, pp. 99–118.

CHAPTER 4

# Financial Development, Openness, and Growth Performance

Wang Chen

*Graduate School of Economics, Kobe University*
*2-1, Rokkodai, Nada-Ku, Kobe 657-8501, Japan*
*tinou3776@yahoo.co.jp*

Takuji Kinkyo

*Faculty of Economics, Kobe University*
*2-1, Rokkodai, Nada-Ku, Kobe 657-8501, Japan*
*kinkyo@econ.kobe-u.ac.jp*

## 1. Introduction

Financial development is essential for economic development because
a well-functioning financial system boosts economic growth by mobi-
lizing savings, allocating funds to investment, and redistributing
risks. A large body of empirical evidence suggests that there is a positive relationship between financial development and economic growth
(King and Levine, 1993; Beck *et al.*, 2000; Loayza and Ranciere, 2006;
Barajas *et al.*, 2013). Moreover, financial development can improve
income distribution by providing better access to credit for individuals and firms that face external financing constraints because of a lack
of collateral, credit history, or connections. Although the existing evidence is mixed, some studies have shown that financial development
can reduce poverty and inequality (Clarke *et al.*, 2006; Hamori and

Hashiguchi, 2012; Inoue and Hamori, 2012, 2013; Chen and Kinkyo, 2015).

While there is a wide consensus on the importance of financial development, there are heterogeneous views on the role of financial liberalization, particularly financial openness in terms of financial development. In fact, the benefits and costs of greater openness in capital accounts have been the focus of policy debates since a series of financial crises in the 1990s. Some have argued that greater financial openness is essential for middle-income countries to upgrade their domestic financial systems and move to high-income status (Fischer, 1998; Summers, 2000). Others have argued that financial openness is harmful for a developing country's macroeconomic stability because volatile global capital flows render these countries more susceptible to financial crises (Stiglitz, 2002). An emerging consensus seems to be that the benefits of financial openness depend on certain threshold conditions, notably the quality of domestic institutions and markets (Kose *et al.*, 2010). A number of studies have found evidence for the existence of threshold conditions. For example, Chinn and Ito (2005) find that financial openness contributes to equity market development only if threshold levels of legal systems and institutions are attained. Fischer and Valenzuela (2013) find that financial openness has a positive effect on the supply of credit if banking sectors are competitive. In sum, the existing studies present evidence for the existence of heterogeneity in the relationship between financial openness and financial development across countries.

In this chapter, we empirically investigate the possible heterogeneity in finance–growth relationships across countries. To this end, we estimate a dynamic panel regression model using the first-differenced GMM estimators developed by Arellano and Bond (1991). Our sample includes 108 countries over the period 1970–2010.

The rest of this chapter is organized as follows. Section 2 reviews the current state of financial development in East Asia. Section 3 describes the econometric method and presents the results. Section 4 concludes.

## 2. The current state of financial development in East Asia

In this section, we provide a brief overview of the current state of financial development in East Asia. In most East Asian economies, banking sectors tend to play a central role in financial intermediation. However, the development stages of these banking sectors vary widely across the region.

Table 1 summarizes the current state of banking sector development in 13 East Asian economies. Banking sector development is evaluated according to four criteria: *depth, access, efficiency,* and *stability*.[1] *Depth* refers to the size of banking sectors, which is measured by the amount of domestic credit to private sectors from deposit money banks as a percentage of GDP. A larger amount of domestic credit relative to GDP implies that banking sectors are deeper. *Access* refers to the ability of individuals and firms to access banking

Table 1. Banking sector development in East Asia.

|             | Depth | Access | Efficiency | Stability |
|-------------|-------|--------|------------|-----------|
| Japan       | 103.7 | 96.4   | 1.2        | 32.9      |
| South Korea | 101.6 | 93.0   | 1.7        | 13.4      |
| Hong Kong   | 152.9 | 88.7   | 4.8        | 33.1      |
| Singapore   | 97.4  | 98.2   | 5.1        | 46.4      |
| China       | 111.1 | 63.8   | 3.1        | 34.8      |
| Malaysia    | 106.3 | 66.2   | 2.8        | 19.6      |
| Thailand    | 93.7  | 72.7   | 4.8        | 4.5       |
| Philippines | 27.2  | 26.6   | 4.8        | 36.8      |
| Indonesia   | 23.8  | 19.6   | 5.5        | 18.3      |
| Cambodia    | 23.3  | 3.7    | —          | 15.2      |
| Lao PDR     | 10.4  | 26.8   | 20.2       | 11.2      |
| Myanmar     | 3.3   | —      | 5.0        | 3.2       |
| Vietnam     | 96.8  | 21.4   | 2.4        | 23.2      |

*Source*: World Bank Global Financial Development Database and World Bank (2013).
*Note*: The data is the average of 2008–2010. The data of *Access* is for 2011.

---

[1]See World Bank (2013) for the details of these criteria.

services, which is measured by the percentage of people with a bank account. A greater number of bank accounts implies better access to banking services. *Efficiency* refers to the cost efficiency of banking services, which is measured by the spread between the lending and deposit rates. A narrower spread implies that banking services are more efficient. *Stability* refers to the resilience of banking sectors against systemic shocks, which is measured by the weighted average of each bank's $z$-score. The $z$-score is the sum of capital to assets and the return on assets divided by the standard deviation of the return on assets. A larger value of this indicator implies that a banking sector has greater buffers against default risks and is thus more stable.

As is evident from Table 1 there is a large developmental gap between the banking sectors among the East Asian economies. On the one hand, there is a group of economies with well-developed banking sectors that rank high on almost all criteria, while on the other hand, there is a group of economies with poorly developed banking sectors that rank low on almost all criteria. Japan, South Korea, Hong Kong, and Singapore are included in the former, while the Philippines, Indonesia, Cambodia, Lao PDR, and Myanmar are included in the latter. The remaining group of economies has moderately developed banking sectors, which rank relatively high on some of the criteria (typically *depth*) but not on all. It appears that the development stage of banking sectors is positively correlated with income level. This casual observation is consistent with the existing empirical evidence that countries with more developed financial systems tend to grow faster over the long run.

By comparison, capital markets remain underdeveloped, particularly in ASEAN countries other than Singapore and Malaysia. Table 2 summarizes the development stages of stock markets in East Asia. The corresponding data are not available for Cambodia, Lao PDR, and Myanmar, in which stock markets are still in very early stages of development. For stock markets, *depth* is measured by stock market capitalization as a percentage of GDP.

A larger amount of market capitalization implies that stock markets are deeper. *Access* is measured by the percentage of market

Table 2. Stock market development in East Asia.

|  | Depth | Access | Efficiency | Stability |
|---|---|---|---|---|
| Japan | 73.4 | 63.1 | 118.9 | 27.7 |
| South Korea | 87.6 | 66.9 | 200.1 | 26.2 |
| Hong Kong | 480.6 | 59.2 | 145.5 | 33.0 |
| Singapore | 147.8 | 67.4 | 87.2 | 24.1 |
| China | 82.9 | 72.4 | 169.1 | 32.9 |
| Malaysia | 126.5 | 62.6 | 30.7 | 14.9 |
| Philippines | 55.0 | 53.1 | 22.4 | 24.6 |
| Indonesia | 34.9 | 53.9 | 60.2 | 27.8 |
| Thailand | 63.0 | 52.5 | 92.7 | 25.5 |
| Vietnam | 16.7 | — | 75.6 | 30.2 |

*Source*: World Bank Global Financial Development Database.
*Note*: The data is for the average of 2008–2011.

capitalization outside of the 10 largest companies. A greater value of this indicator implies a lower degree of concentration and thus better access to stock markets for newer and smaller issuers. *Efficiency* is measured by the ratio of turnover to capitalization in stock markets. A greater value of the turnover ratio implies higher volumes of trade in the market and more liquidity. *Stability* is measured by market volatility, which is defined as the standard deviation of stock prices. A smaller value of volatility implies that stock markets are more stable. As can be seen form the table, stock markets are relatively well developed in Singapore and Malaysia. In fact, these countries' stock market capitalization is well above that of Japan, Korea, and China. In other ASEAN countries, stock markets are shallow and illiquid, and therefore stock prices tend to be very volatile, particularly when there are large fluctuations in foreign capital inflows.

East Asia's bond markets are even less developed than its equity markets. Since the Asian financial crisis, several initiatives have been launched to promote the development of Asian bond markets. Notable examples include the Asian Bond Market Initiatives (ABMI) by ASEAN+3 (Japan, China, and Korea) and the Asian Bond Fund (ABF) initiative by the Executives' Meeting of East Asia and Pacific Central Banks (EMEAP). Although bond markets grew rapidly over the past decade, the majority of Asia's bond markets remain shallow and illiquid. In addition, much of the recent growth in bond markets has come from government bonds, and corporate bonds account for a smaller proportion of the growth. The ABMI's Credit Guarantee and Investment Facility (CGIF) was established in 2010 to facilitate the development of corporate bond markets. The CGIF assists Asian companies in issuing local-currency corporate bonds by providing credit enhancement.

Among policy makers in ASEAN countries, there is shared recognition of the need to develop regionally integrated capital markets. Since the ASEAN capital markets are individually shallow and illiquid, transaction costs are constantly high. Moreover, the varieties of available financial services are limited and the investment base is narrow. Cross-border market integration will increase the depth and liquidity of capital markets and broaden the range of available services across the ASEAN countries. To promote intra-regional market integration, ASEAN finance ministers adopted the Implementation Plan for ASEAN Capital Market Integration in 2009. The Implementation Plan seeks to create an enabling environment for cross-border access by encouraging the mutual recognition and harmonization of regulations and standards as well as by facilitating the alliance of intra-regional stock exchanges. Intra-regional financial integration is also a major goal of the ASEAN Economic Community (AEC). However, the presence of relatively stringent capital controls can be a serious impediment to financial integration in the region. Despite the significant progress on the liberalization of direct investment and portfolio inflows, extensive controls remain on portfolio outflows in many ASEAN countries (Asian Development Bank Institute, 2014).

## 3. Financial development, openness, and growth performance

### 3.1. Econometric method and data

In this section, we examine the relationship among financial development, openness, and growth performance using a dynamic panel regression model. We extend the conventional regression model to include the interaction term between financial development and income levels as well as that between financial openness and income levels to capture the heterogeneity in the finance–growth relationship across countries. The dynamic panel regression models that we estimate are given as follows:

$$G_{it} = \beta_0 + \beta_1 G_{i,t-1} + \beta_2 BD_{it} + \beta_3 BD_{it} \times Y_{it}$$
$$+ \beta_4 CRISIS_{it} + \gamma' X_{it} + \mu_t + \delta_i + \varepsilon_{it}, \tag{1}$$

$$V_{it} = \beta_0 + \beta_1 V_{i,t-1} + \beta_2 FO_{it} + \beta_3 FO_{it} \times Y_{it}$$
$$+ \beta_4 CRISIS_{it} + \gamma' X_{it} + \mu_t + \delta_i + \varepsilon_{it}, \tag{2}$$

where $G$ is the economic growth rate measured by the log-difference of real GDP per capita, $V$ is the annual standard deviation of $G$, $BD$ is the depth of the banking sectors, $FO$ is the degree of financial openness, and $Y$ is the income level. We focus on the banking sectors to gauge the degree of financial deepening due to lower country coverage of data for stock markets. The depth of banking sectors is measured either by domestic credit to private sectors as a percentage of GDP or liquid liabilities as a percentage of GDP. Following Kose *et al.* (2010) and Kim *et al.* (2012), the degree of financial openness is measured by the *de facto* index developed by Lane and Milesi-Ferretti (2007). This index is defined as the sum of a country's foreign assets and liabilities as a percentage of GDP. *CRISIS* denotes the frequency of systemic banking crises; the data source is Laeven and Valencia (2012). $X$ represents a set of control variables that include the initial income level (a lag of GDP per capita), trade openness, government size, the inflation rate, and education attainment.[2] Note that the initial income level is included only in Equation (1). $\mu$, $\delta$, and $\varepsilon$ denote an unobserved country-specific effect, a common time-specific effect, and an error term, respectively. $i$ and $t$ represent the country and time period, respectively. We also add an interaction term between $BD/FO$ and $Y$ to capture the heterogeneity in the finance–growth relationship across income levels. We use the income level as a proxy

---

[2]All the variables are transformed into logarithms. Inflation is defined as: log (1+inflation rate/100).

variable for the quality of institutions and markets because of the
limited availability of data for the latter. The marginal impact of
$BD$ on $G$ and that of $FO$ on $V$ take the forms

$$\frac{\partial G_{it}}{\partial BD_{it}} = \beta_2 + \beta_3 Y_{it}, \tag{3}$$

$$\frac{\partial V_{it}}{\partial FO_{it}} = \beta_2 + \beta_3 Y_{it}, \tag{4}$$

respectively. We anticipate that the marginal effect of $BD$ on $G$ will
be positive and that of $FO$ on $V$ will be negative in higher-income
countries with better institutions and market quality. To estimate
Equations (1) and (2), we use the (one-step) first-differenced GMM
estimators developed by Arellano and Bond (1991). The advantage
of the GMM estimator is that in contrast to traditional estimators, it
can control for unobserved country- and time-specific effects and deal
with the endogeneity of explanatory variables in a dynamic regression
framework. The GMM estimator requires that the number of periods
be small relative to the number of cross-sectional observations and
that there be no autocorrelation in the error term.

The sample data consist of observations for 108 countries over
the period 1970–2010. We use the non-overlapping five-year averages
of the variables to smooth out cyclical variations in growth.[3] See
Appendix 1 for a list of the countries in the samples. Appendix 2
provides the full definitions and sources of all variables.

### 3.2. Estimation results

The estimation results for the growth model specified in Equation (1)
are reported in Table 1. The first two columns correspond to the
case in which domestic credit to private sectors is used as a measure
of the depth of banking sectors, while the last two columns correspond to the case in which liability liquidity is used instead. The
first and third columns correspond to the case that includes only the
initial income level as a control variable, while the second and fourth

---

[3]The first period includes only the data for 1970 and the five-year averaging starts
from 1971.

columns correspond to the case with the full set of control variables. In all four cases, both the Sargan test of over-identifying restrictions and the second-order residual autocorrelation test (AR (2)) reject the null hypothesis, which indicates the absence of misspecification. For the case with full control variables, the estimated coefficient on $BD$, together with that on the interaction term with $Y$, indicates that the marginal effect of banking depth on growth will become positive when the income level drops as low as 2.7 constant 2005 U.S. dollars (which is equivalent to approximately 1.0 in logarithmic terms). In other words, deeper banking sectors will have a positive effect on economic growth across almost all income levels. This is also verified by Figure 1, which shows that the marginal effects of $BD$ on $g$ will become positive when the income level exceeds 1.0 dollars in log terms. Moreover, the positive sign of the estimated coefficient on the interaction term indicates that the benefit of deeper banking sectors will be greater in countries with higher income levels.

The estimation results for the growth volatility model specified in Equation (2) are reported in Table 2. The last column corresponds to the case that includes the full set of control variables, while the other columns correspond to the cases that each excludes one of the control variables. In all five cases, both the Sargan test of over-identifying restrictions and the second-order residual autocorrelation test (AR (2)) reject the null hypothesis, which indicates the absence of misspecification. For the case with full control variables, the estimated coefficient on the $FO$, together with that on the interaction term with $Y$, indicates that the marginal effect of financial openness on growth volatility will be negative when the income level exceeds 2,800 constant 2005 U.S. dollars (which is equivalent to approximately 7.9 in logarithmic terms). In other words, greater financial openness will have a stabilizing effect on growth volatility only when the income level reaches roughly the same income level of Jordan in 2010. This is also verified by Figure 2, which shows that the marginal effects of $FO$ on $V$ will become negative when the income level exceeds 7.9 dollars in log terms. Moreover, the negative sign of the estimated coefficient on the interaction term indicates that

*Moving Up the Ladder*

Table 3. The effect of banking development (BD) on growth.

| | BD: Domestic credit | | BD: Liquid liabilities | |
|---|---|---|---|---|
| | (1) | (2) | (3) | (4) |
| BD | −0.1465*** | −0.1383*** | −0.1490*** | −0.1411*** |
| | (0.0155) | (0.0158) | (0.0122) | (0.0117) |
| BD × GDP per capita | 0.1477*** | 0.1384*** | 0.1544*** | 0.1412*** |
| | (0.0136) | (0.0138) | (0.0125) | (0.0112) |
| Systemic banking crises | −0.0110** | −0.0107** | −0.0121*** | −0.0121*** |
| | (0.0048) | (0.0047) | (0.0037) | (0.0035) |
| *Control variables*: | | | | |
| Initial GDP per capita | −0.1801*** | −0.1692*** | −0.1854*** | −0.1720*** |
| | (0.0111) | (0.0107) | (0.0119) | (0.0095) |
| Trade openness | | 0.0221*** | | 0.0262*** |
| | | (0.0052) | | (0.0054) |
| Government size | | −0.0173** | | −0.0109* |
| | | (0.0082) | | (0.0056) |
| Inflation | | −0.0193*** | | −0.0176*** |
| | | (0.0046) | | (0.0065) |
| Education | | −0.0112 | | −0.0146 |
| | | (0.0406) | | (0.0377) |
| *Time dummy*: | | | | |
| Year 81–85 | −0.0021 | −0.0031 | −0.00464 | −0.0037 |
| | (0.0030) | (0.0029) | (0.0036) | (0.0030) |
| Year 86–90 | 0.0020 | 0.0009 | −0.0010 | 0.0003 |
| | (0.0031) | (0.0030) | (0.0039) | (0.0032) |
| Year 91–95 | 0.0061** | 0.0020 | 0.0026 | 0.0010 |
| | (0.0028) | (0.0033) | (0.0036) | (0.0035) |
| Year 96–00 | 0.0090*** | −0.0006 | 0.0040 | −0.0011 |
| | (0.0035) | (0.0035) | (0.0046) | (0.0038) |
| Year 01–05 | 0.0182*** | 0.0070 | 0.0124** | 0.0058 |
| | (0.0042) | (0.0044) | (0.0052) | (0.0041) |
| Year 06–10 | 0.0155*** | 0.0015 | 0.0080 | 0.0002 |
| | (0.0047) | (0.0051) | (0.0060) | (0.0050) |
| Intercept | 0.2753*** | 0.3277*** | 0.2352*** | 0.2905*** |
| | (0.0761) | (0.0927) | (0.0669) | (0.0951) |
| No. countries/No. observations | 108/711 | 108/692 | 108/647 | 108/634 |
| Sargan test | 0.0574 | 0.0773 | 0.0971 | 0.1715 |
| Serial correlation test | | | | |
| First-order | 0.0003 | 0.0004 | 0.0000 | 0.0000 |
| Second-order | 0.1239 | 0.2418 | 0.0292 | 0.1880 |

*Note*: Standard errors in parentheses. $^{*}p < 0.1$, $^{**}p < 0.05$, $^{***}p < 0.01$.

Table 4. The effect of financial openness on growth volatility.

|  | (1) | (2) | (3) | (4) | (5) |
|---|---|---|---|---|---|
| Financial openness | 4.1852** | 3.7249** | 3.6294* | 4.2210** | 4.1640** |
|  | (1.9181) | (1.4491) | (1.9492) | (2.0133) | (1.9905) |
| Financial openness × GDP per capita | −0.5297** | −0.4783*** | −0.4579** | −0.5309** | −0.5247** |
|  | (0.2269) | (0.1633) | (0.2308) | (0.2379) | (0.2338) |
| Systemic banking crises | 2.3412*** | 2.3366*** | 2.4140*** | 2.4326*** | 2.3897*** |
|  | (0.5572) | (0.5677) | (0.5897) | (0.5707) | (0.5610) |
| *Control variables:* |  |  |  |  |  |
| Trade openness |  | −0.6244 | −0.8973 | −0.7735 | −0.6718 |
|  |  | (0.7579) | (0.9323) | (0.8009) | (0.7997) |
| Government size | −0.8675 |  | −1.5474* | −1.0309 | −0.9209 |
|  | (0.9523) |  | (0.8844) | (1.0226) | (0.9864) |
| Inflation | 1.8072** | 1.8077** |  | 1.6737* | 1.7282* |
|  | (0.8501) | (0.8562) |  | (0.9091) | (0.8825) |
| Education | −1.6178 | −0.8487 | −2.0873 |  | −1.2846 |
|  | (3.7950) | (3.6097) | (3.8963) |  | (3.7797) |
| *Time dummy:* |  |  |  |  |  |
| Year 81–85 | −0.4060 | −0.4834 | −0.4427 | −0.3510 | −0.3645 |
|  | (0.3968) | (0.3676) | (0.4244) | (0.3936) | (0.3945) |
| Year 86–90 | −0.8801*** | −0.9211*** | −0.7786** | −0.8292** | −0.8391** |
|  | (0.3362) | (0.3242) | (0.3786) | (0.3389) | (0.3396) |
| Year 91–95 | −0.8285** | −0.8067** | −0.7527* | −0.7317* | −0.7301* |
|  | (0.4159) | (0.3875) | (0.4511) | (0.4236) | (0.4200) |
| Year 96–00 | −1.2949*** | −1.2313*** | −1.3136** | −1.0942** | −1.1029** |
|  | (0.4384) | (0.4265) | (0.5482) | (0.4741) | (0.4735) |
| Year 01–05 | −1.2292*** | −1.0852** | −1.2137** | −0.9826* | −0.9922* |
|  | (0.4633) | (0.4744) | (0.6113) | (0.5140) | (0.5187) |
| Year 06–10 | −0.5719 | −0.4876 | −0.5310 | −0.2593 | −0.2894 |
|  | (0.4891) | (0.4884) | (0.6628) | (0.5455) | (0.5458) |
| Intercept | −0.0399 | −1.2635 | 14.8204 | 1.0848 | 2.4504 |
|  | (9.4402) | (8.2574) | (9.0574) | (7.3089) | (10.3104) |
| No. countries/No. observations | 108/693 | 108/698 | 108/692 | 108/692 | 108/692 |
| Sargan test | 0.0570 | 0.0415 | 0.0269 | 0.0394 | 0.0526 |
| Serial correlation test |  |  |  |  |  |
| First-order | 0.0034 | 0.0034 | 0.0059 | 0.0037 | 0.0034 |
| Second-order | 0.7178 | 0.6419 | 0.5902 | 0.6984 | 0.7146 |

*Note*: Standard errors in parentheses. $^*p < 0.1$, $^{**}p < 0.05$, $^{***}p < 0.01$.

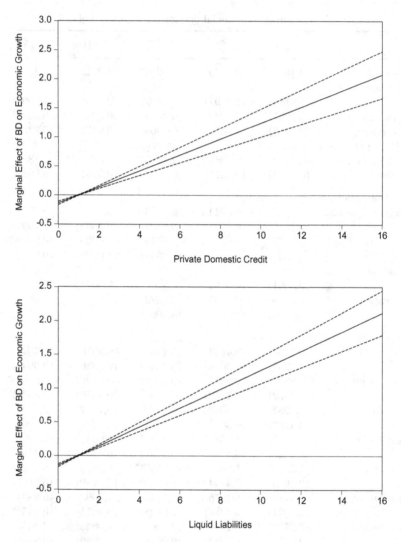

Figure 1. The marginal effect of BD on $G$.

*Note*: The dashed lines represent 95% confidence intervals.


the stabilizing effect of financial openness will be greater in countries with higher income levels.

Figure 3 shows the evolution of the marginal effect of *BD* on *G* (the upper half of the Figure) and that of *FO* on *V* (the lower half of

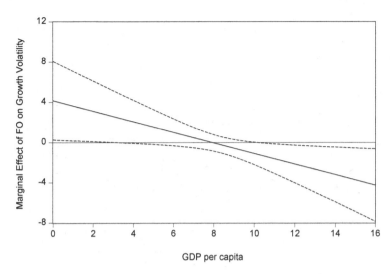

Figure 2. The marginal effect of FO on *V*.
*Note*: The dashed lines represent 95% confidence intervals.

the Figure) in eight Asian countries over the last three decades. Each year's marginal effects are calculated using their respective actual income levels. The marginal effect of BD on G has been positive in all Asian countries throughout the sample period. In addition, the size of positive effects has been increasing with the exception of some set-backs during the period of major crises, such as the Philippines' debt crisis of 1983, the Asian financial crisis of 1997–1998, and the global financial crisis of 2008–2009. In contrast, the marginal effect of *FO* on *V* differs significantly across the countries. While financial openness has a stabilizing effect on growth in a group of higher-income countries that includes Japan and Korea, it has a destabilizing effect in a group of lower-income countries that includes India, the Philippines, and Indonesia throughout the sample period. In the remaining group of countries, there was a switch of signs in the marginal effect at various points during the sample period. Specifically, the positive sign switched to a negative one in Malaysia, Thailand, and China in 1988, 2007, and 2010, respectively. These changes imply that these countries reached the threshold level of income to benefit from financial openness.

*Moving Up the Ladder*

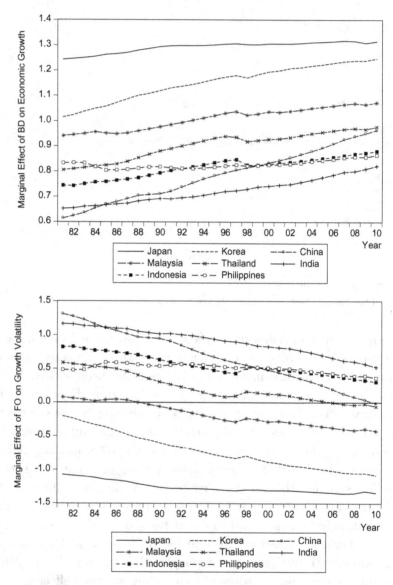

Figure 3. Evolution of the marginal effects of BD/FO on $G/V$.

## 4. Conclusion

In this chapter, we examined the relationship among financial development, openness, and growth performance using a dynamic panel regression model. We extended the conventional regression model to include the interaction term between financial deepening/openness and income levels to capture the heterogeneity in the finance–growth relationship across countries. Our major findings can be summarized as follows. First, deeper banking sectors will have a positive effect on growth across almost all income levels. In addition, the benefit of deeper banking sectors will be greater in countries with higher income levels. Second, greater financial openness will have a stabilizing effect on growth volatility only when the income level reaches approximately 2,800 constant U.S. dollars. Moreover, the stabilizing effect of financial openness will be greater in countries with higher incomes. Third, there is considerable diversity in the development stages of financial systems across East Asian countries. Reflecting this diversity, the effect of financial openness on growth differs significantly across countries. Financial openness decreases growth volatility in higher-income countries and increases it in lower-income countries. However, the effect of financial openness changes over time, and greater openness can be stabilizing once a country reaches the threshold level of income. A group of middle-income countries including Malaysia, Thailand, and China crossed the threshold level at various points during the sample period.

The key policy implication derived from the analysis is that an appropriate sequencing of liberalization is important for financial development. In particular, the threshold conditions must be met before opening up capital accounts. However, once the threshold level is crossed, to gain from greater openness, a country should not delay full capital account liberalization.

## Appendix 1: List of 108 Countries

Albania; Algeria; Angola; Argentina; Australia; Austria; Bahrain; Bangladesh; Belgium; Belize; Brazil; Brunei Darussalam; Canada; Chad; Chile; China; Colombia; Congo, Rep.; Costa Rica; Cote d'Ivoire; Croatia; Czech Republic; Egypt, Arab Rep.; El Salvador; Fiji; France; Gabon; Georgia; Germany; Greece; Grenada; Guatemala; Guyana; Haiti; Honduras; Hungary; India; Indonesia; Iran, Islamic Rep.; Ireland; Israel; Italy; Japan; Jordan; Kazakhstan; Kenya; Korea, Rep.; Kuwait; Lao PDR; Latvia; Lesotho; Libya; Madagascar; Malaysia; Mali; Malta; Mexico; Moldova; Mongolia; Morocco; Mozambique; Namibia; Nepal; Netherlands; New Zealand; Nigeria; Norway; Pakistan; Panama; Papua New Guinea; Paraguay; Peru; Philippines; Poland; Portugal; Romania; Russian Federation; Saudi Arabia; Serbia; Slovak Republic; Slovenia; South Africa; Spain; Sri Lanka; St. Kitts and Nevis; St. Vincent and the Sudan; Swaziland; Sweden; Switzerland; Syrian Arab Republic; Thailand; Tonga; Trinidad and Tobago; Tunisia; Turkey; Uganda; Ukraine; United Arab Emirates; United Kingdom; United States; Uruguay; Vanuatu; Venezuela, RB; Vietnam; Yemen; Zambia; Zimbabwe.

## Appendix 2: Variables and sources

| Variable | Definition | Source |
|---|---|---|
| GDP per capita | Gross domestic product divided by mid-year population. Data are in constant 2005 U.S. dollars. | World Bank National Accounts data, and OECD National Accounts data. |
| BD 1. Domestic credit to private sector (% of GDP) 2. Liquid liabilities (% of GDP) | 1. Domestic credit to private sector refers to financial resources provided to the private sector by financial corporations, such as through loans, purchases of non-equity securities, and trade credits and other accounts receivable, that establish a claim for repayment. 2. Ratio of liquid liabilities to GDP, calculated using the following deflation method: $\{(0.5)*[Ft/P\_et + Ft{-}1/ P\_et{-}1]\}/ [GDPt/P\_at]$ | 1. International Monetary Fund (IMF) International Financial Statistics (IFS), and World Bank and OECD GDP estimates. 2. IMF IFS |

(*Continued*)

(*Continued*)

| Variable | Definition | Source |
| --- | --- | --- |
| | where $F$ is liquid liabilities, P_e is end-of period CPI, and P_a is average annual CPI. | |
| Financial openness | Net foreign asset positions (% of GDP) | Lane and Milesi-Ferretti (2007) |
| Systemic banking crises | Banking crisis dummy (1 = banking crisis, 0 = none) A banking crisis is defined as systemic if two conditions are met: a. Significant signs of financial distress in the banking system. b. Significant banking policy intervention measures in response to significant losses in the banking system. | Luc Laeven and Fabián Valencia (2012) |
| Trade openness | Sum of exports and imports of goods and services (% of GDP) | World Bank National Accounts data, and OECD National Accounts data. |
| Government size | General government final consumption expenditure (% of GDP). General government final consumption expenditure includes all government current expenditures for purchases of goods and services. | World Bank National Accounts data, and OECD National Accounts data. |
| Inflation | Annual growth rate of the GDP implicit deflator (%) | World Bank National Accounts data, and OECD National Accounts data. |
| Education attainment | The number of grades (years) in secondary school. | United Nations Educational, Scientific, and Cultural Organization (UNESCO) Institute for Statistics. |

# References

Asian Development Bank Institute (2014). *ASEAN 2030: Toward a Borderless Economic Community*. Asian Development Bank Institute, Tokyo.

Arellano, M. and S. Bond (1991). Some tests of specification for panel data: Monte Carlo evidence and an application to employment equations. *The Review of Economic Studies*, 58, pp. 277–297.

Barajas, A., R. Chami, and S. R. Yousefi (2013). The Finance and Growth Nexus Re-Examined: Do All Countries Benefit Equally? IMF Working Paper.

Beck, T., R. Levine, and N. Loayza (2000). Finance and the sources of growth. *Journal of Financial Economics*, 58, pp. 261–300.

Chen, W. and T. Kinkyo (forthcoming). Financial development and income inequality: Long-run relationship and short-run heterogeneity. *Emerging Markets, Finance & Trade*.

Chinn, M. D. and H. Ito (2005). What Matters for Financial Development? Capital Controls, Institutions, and Interactions. NBER Working Papers No. 11370, National Bureau of Economic Research, Inc.

Clarke, G. R. G., L. C. Xu, and H. Zou (2006). Finance and income inequality: What do the data tell us? *Southern Economic Journal*, 72(3), pp. 578–596.

Fischer, S. (1998). Capital-account liberalization and the role of the IMF. In *Should the IMF Pursue Capital-Account Convertibility?* Peter Kenen (ed.), Princeton Essays in International Finance, No. 207.

Fischer, R. and P. Valenzuela (2013). Financial openness, market structure and private credit: An empirical investigation. *Economics Letters*, 121(3), pp. 478–481.

Hamori, S. and Y. Hashiguchi (2012). The effect of financial deepening on inequality: Some international evidence. *Journal of Asian Economics*, 23(4), pp. 353–359.

Inoue, T. and S. Hamori (2012). How has financial deepening affected poverty reduction in India? Empirical analysis using state-level panel data. *Applied Financial Economics*, 22, pp. 395–408.

Inoue, T. and S. Hamori (2013). Financial permeation as a role of microfinance: Has microfinance actually been a viable financial intermediary for helping the poor? *Applied Financial Economics*, 23, pp. 1567–1578.

Kim, D. H., S. C. Lin, and Y. B. Suen (2012). Dynamic effects of financial openness on economic growth and macroeconomic. *Emerging Markets Finance & Trade*, 48(1), pp. 25–54.

King, R. G. and R. Levine (1993). Finance, entrepreneurship, and growth: Theory and evidence. *Journal of Monetary Economics*, 32(3), pp. 513–542.

Kose, M. A., E. S. Prasad, and A. D. Taylor (2010). Thresholds in the process of international financial integration. *Journal of International Money and Finance*, 30(1), pp. 147–179.

Laeven, L. and F. Valencia (2012). Systemic Banking Crises Database: An Update. IMF Working Paper 12/163, International Monetary Fund, Washington.

Lane, P. R. and G. M. Milesi-Ferretti (2007). The external wealth of nations mark II: Revised and extended estimates of foreign assets and liabilities, 1970–2004. *Journal of International Economics*, 73, pp. 223–250.

Loayza, N. V. and R. Rancière (2006). Financial development, financial fragility, and growth. *Journal of Money, Credit and Banking*, 38(4), pp. 1051–1076.

Stiglitz, J. (2002). *Globalization and its Discontent*. W. W. Norton and Company, New York.

Summers, L. (2000). International financial crises: causes, prevention, and cures. *American Economic Review*, 90(2), pp. 1–16.

World Bank (2013). *Rethinking the Role of the State in Finance: Global Financial Development Report 2013*. World Bank, Washington, DC.

CHAPTER 5

# Human Resource Development in Asia: Expected Role of Higher Education

Shigesaburo Kabe

*Editorial Bureau, Nikkei Inc.*
*1-3-7 Otemchi, Chiyoda-ku, Tokyo 100-8065, Japan*
*skabe0727@yahoo.co.jp*

## 1. Overview of human resource development and economic development

Economic growth theory supports the accumulation and development of human capital and other factors, such as physical capital, which contribute to economic growth in the long term (Lucas, 1988; Romer, 1990). Human capital is defined as "the ability and efficiency of people to transform raw materials and capital into goods and services" (Son, 2010), and the educational system is expected to help people learn these skills. Many empirical studies have found that education is significantly and positively correlated with economic growth, indicating that education has been a key determinant of economic growth (Son, 2010). As Thant (1999) pointed out, educated people can use physical capital more efficiently, so the more educated a country's population is, the more productive this country becomes. In other words, how human resources are developed in a country determines whether it can achieve economic growth.

When East Asia, including Japan and the newly industrialized economies (NIEs) of Hong Kong, South Korea, Singapore, and Taiwan, attracted world attention because of rapid economic growth in the latter half of the 20th century, the World Bank (1993) argued the importance of primary and secondary, rather than tertiary, education. Barro (1991) also found that primary and secondary school enrolment rates are positively associated with economic development, based on an analysis of 98 countries from 1960 to 1985.

Thus, primary and secondary education have been important for the development of countries in the past, but in the current globalized world, primary and secondary education are not sufficient to meet the challenges each country faces. Instead, higher education is now considered pivotal for development, due to its critical role in expanding the production possibilities of countries (Kimenyi, 2011). The reason higher education is becoming a key factor for economic growth is because the globalized society requires highly educated human resources to compete with advanced countries or to equalize trading and investments in countries with lower levels of development. Thant (1999) explains the mechanisms through which higher education contributes to higher productivity, resulting in economic growth. The contributing factors are: (1) educated people use physical capital more efficiently than less educated people and are more likely to devise new and better forms of production; (2) these benefits spread to co-workers, who learn from their more educated peers and become more productive; and (3) the increase of education causes a rise in the efficiency of all factors related to production.

As Figure 1 indicates, education is strongly correlated with total factor productivity (TFP) (Huang and Szyf, 2011). This is consistent with the argument of Vandenbussche *et al.* (2006) that skilled labour has a higher growth-enhancing effect in countries closer to the technological frontier.

The higher average years of total schooling a population has leads to higher TFP, at current purchasing power parity (PPP). Put another way, longer schooling years (higher education) show higher levels of productivity than shorter schooling years (primary or secondary education).

This chapter focuses on human resource development, which is indispensable for future growth, and discusses what role education, especially higher education, plays in future and long-term economic growth. When discussing the role of higher education, this chapter focuses mainly on middle-income countries in Asia, such as Malaysia, Thailand, China, Vietnam, and India, all of which are attempting to

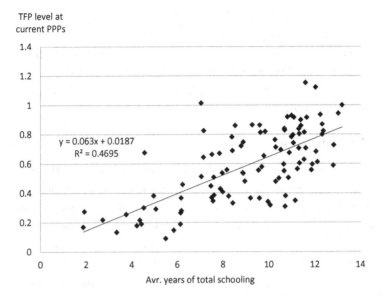

Figure 1. Average years of total schooling and TFP.

*Source*: Penn World Table (8.0), World Bank's World Development Indicators (online).

*Note*: U.S. TFP at current PPP = 1.

shift from a middle-income to high-income economy and place an emphasis on education.

The following section discusses the factors that enhance the significance of higher education in the 21st century. The reasons for the shifting preference towards higher education from primary and secondary education, which was crucial in the 20th century, is explained. The third section of this chapter describes the current situation of higher education in Asia, especially middle-income countries. In the fourth section, the expected role of higher education for achieving economic growth is discussed. Finally, the Section 5 offers conclusions based on each of these discussions.

## 2. Increasing expectations for higher education: Factors enhancing the significance of higher education

In the 21st century, tertiary education has gained importance, while focus on primary and secondary education, which was important during the latter half of the 20th century, has decreased. What facilitated the shift from primary and secondary education to tertiary education? There are three factors that give additional weight to the importance of higher education: globalisation, a rise in the population and economic power (e.g., China and India), and demographic changes such as low fertility and aging populations.

## 2.1. Globalisation

Globalisation provides developing countries with opportunities and risks related to catching-up process. Regardless of development level, each country may be able to compete with other countries, including advanced countries. However, this opportunity accompanies risks that are the opposite side of the same coin, in a globalized society.

Let us consider opportunities first. Kimenyi (2011) argues that world economies are linked together through the various dimensions of globalisation, which means even poor economies must compete with advanced countries. Therefore, low-income countries must continually aim to catch up with technologically advanced nations. If a country with poor human capital fails to develop human resources to match those of advanced countries, the chance of this country being able to compete economically decreases. However, it is worth noting that even a country with poor human capital has advantages, such as enhanced information and free-rider effects that enable it to save money and time due to information spill over and being able to learn from the experiences of advanced countries (Fan, 2014).[1]

Thus, a country may have opportunities to compete with advanced countries if it fully utilizes free-rider effects and improves human capital, with the assistance of an education system. A simple question then arises: What kind of education should be emphasized? The answer is higher education, as the globalized society requires people with higher education to deal with a complicated and rapidly changing environment.

---

[1]Fan (2014) takes the example of China, comparing it to the NIEs, and points out that Chinese companies began to catch up to more advanced countries, mainly due to the changing tradability of knowledge and technological regimes and the global economic environment.

Next, let us turn to the risks of a globalized economy. While developing or poor economies may be able to compete with advanced economies due to free-rider effects, developing economies can catch up with poorer countries due to the same free-rider effects. This is often the case with Asia's middle-income countries, if they want to become high-income countries. If a country misses opportunities to catch up with advanced countries and is at risk for catching up with less-developed countries, economic development might become difficult. Put another way, Asia's middle-income countries may fall into a sandwich situation, in which they are pressed between advanced countries and lower-income countries. This outcome is a likely eventuality for middle-income countries. Countries with lower technology or poorer human capital often follow imitation-based development strategies, which do not require the same type or amount of investment in advanced education as countries close to the technological frontier (OECD, 2014).

Middle-income economies that attempt to advance cannot rely on low costs to the same extent hereafter. Therefore, innovation, that is the capacity to create new and better products and services, as well as new business models are increasingly needed to sustain productivity growth and for effective competition in global markets (OECD, 2014).

Vandenbussche *et al.* (2006) argues that human capital affects innovation and imitation differently. Unskilled human capital imitates or diffuses existing technology; in other words, the "imitation of technologies is the main engine" of TFP growth. On the contrary, skilled human capital innovates new technology in an advanced country that "relies more and more on innovation." Thus, in a globalized society, higher education grows increasingly important to obtain innovative capabilities.

## 2.2. Increasing populations and economic power: China and India

The influence of China and India, in terms of their population power, is becoming increasingly significant, and China, as an economic giant, has a considerable impact on the world economy. Rapid advances by

China and India are found, not only in their economies but also in technology. Table 1 shows that both countries are approaching the technology frontier, based on increasing trends of numbers related to patents granted by the U.S. Patent and Trademark Office (PTO) to different countries. A patent represents something newly developed and is regarded as a proxy for innovative capability. China and India were ranked in the 30s for the total number of patents granted by U.S. PTO before 2000 but moved up to the 20s in 2000. In 2013, China ranked in the top ten and India was ranked 12th. This indicates that China and India are now moving to an economic stage requiring innovation and people with higher educations and away from imitation and people with primary and secondary education.

   This rapid increase in patents granted by the U.S. PTO may raise questions regarding how both countries have improved their technology level.[2] Marukawa (2014) pointed out the recent variety of paths towards technological development, arguing that catching up with advanced countries is not the only way for developing countries to develop technology. Marukawa (2014) assumes that a large country has a domestic market with domestic industrial technology infrastructures, and if so, it is likely to generate a variety of technological development paths.

## 2.3.  Low fertility and aging populations

East Asia's economic spike in the latter half of the 20th century occurred, in part, due to demographic changes, including a demographic bonus in this area (Bloom and Williamson 1998). A demographic bonus stage is defined as a period when the dependency ratio[3] decreases. The higher this dependency ratio is, the higher the burden of sustaining children and the elderly on the working-age population (15–64 years old). As Kabe (2013) explains, in the past, many Asian countries faced substantial increases in populations, which led

---

[2]Some patents may be derived from subsidiaries of multi-national enterprises or their joint venture with local enterprises.
[3]Dependency ratio = (population of children ($\sim$14) & the elderly (65$\sim$))/working age (15–64) population.

Table 1. Number of patents granted by the U.S. PTO (1963–2013).

| Pre 2000 | | | 2000 | | | 2013 | | |
|---|---|---|---|---|---|---|---|---|
| Rank | Total | 2,923,919 | Rank | Total | 157,494 | Rank | Total | 277,835 |
| 1 | The United States | 1,784,960 | 1 | The United States | 85,068 | 1 | The United States | 133,593 |
| 2 | Japan | 421,445 | 2 | Japan | 31,295 | 2 | Japan | 51,919 |
| 3 | Germany | 221,098 | 3 | Germany | 10,235 | 3 | Germany | 15,498 |
| 4 | The United Kingdom | 97,986 | 4 | Taiwan | 4,670 | 4 | South Korea | 14,548 |
| 5 | France | 85,400 | 5 | France | 3,819 | 5 | Taiwan | 11,071 |
| 6 | Canada | 53,887 | 6 | The United Kingdom | 3,659 | 6 | Canada | 6,547 |
| 7 | Switzerland | 43,315 | 7 | Canada | 3,419 | 7 | France | 6,083 |
| 8 | Italy | 32,431 | 8 | South Korea | 3,314 | 8 | China | 5,928 |
| 9 | Sweden | 28,286 | 9 | Italy | 1,714 | 9 | The United Kingdom | 5,806 |
| 10 | Netherlands | 26,689 | 10 | Sweden | 1,577 | 10 | Israel | 3,012 |
| 11 | Taiwan | 19,992 | 21 | Singapore | 218 | 12 | India | 2,424 |
| 12 | South Korea | 14,854 | 23 | Hong Kong | 176 | 21 | Singapore | 797 |
| 27 | Hong Kong | 1,329 | 24 | India | 131 | 23 | Hong Kong | 540 |
| 31 | China | 798 | 26 | China | 119 | 30 | Malaysia | 214 |
| 32 | India | 772 | 32 | Malaysia | 42 | 37 | Thailand | 77 |
| 33 | Singapore | 747 | 43 | Thailand | 15 | 51 | Philippines | 27 |
| 43 | Philippines | 195 | 54 | Indonesia | 6 | 57 | Indonesia | 15 |
| 46 | Malaysia | 170 | | | | | | |
| 51 | Indonesia | 125 | | | | | | |
| 54 | Thailand | 97 | | | | | | |

*Source:* U.S. PTO.

to the burden of feeding children, and this left little capacity for economic growth. However, when those children become adults and part of the working-age population, and if fertility rates decrease, the dependency ratio also decreases because the denominator (working-age population) of this ratio increases, while the numerator (children) decreases.[4] If the dependency ratio continues to decrease, it indicates that the burden on the working-age population to sustain children and the elderly has decreased, and the economy is likely to be energized (Komine and Kabe, 2009).[5] This defines the demographic bonus phase. Japan enjoyed a demographic bonus until 1990, and the NIEs and most of the middle-income countries in Asia entered a demographic bonus phase between 1960 and 1970 and remain in this phase now (Figure 2).

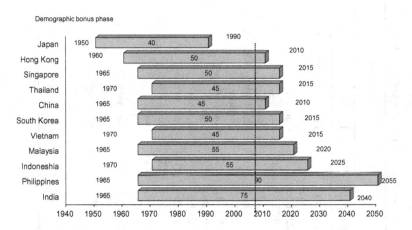

Figure 2. The demographic bonus phase.

*Source*: Kabe (2014).

*Notes*: 1. A demographic bonus phase is defined as a time when the dependency ratio of a country is increasing. This is measured at five-year intervals.

2. Figures are based on the United Nations' World Population Prospects: The 2012 Revision.

---

[4]At this stage, the percentage of the aged population is not yet very high.
[5]On the contrary, if this burden is large, the economy is likely to be inactivated (demographic onus).

For many countries in Asia, especially middle-income countries, it will not be long until this phase comes to an end, with countries successively moving from the demographic bonus phase to demographic onus phase.[6] As Komine and Kabe (2009) point out, the demographic structure of Asia is expected to change rapidly between 2020 and 2050, and Asian countries will witness a further decline in birth rates and aging populations. Table 2 shows that Japan faces low fertility and aging populations, which is similar to other Asian countries. These factors result in a society with a smaller future working population, a greater burden on the working-age population to sustain the non-working population, including the elderly, and a reduction in the total population. It is clear that the mechanism that contributed to East Asia's economic spike in the 20th century is no longer available. Currently, economic growth requires other contributing factors than a demographic bonus. If the number of people in the work force is not expected to grow, then finding ways to improve the quality of the work force will be crucial. It is a matter of great importance to determine ways to effectively develop human capital, and education is currently attracting attention.

Asia's demographic changes have two characteristics. One is the speed with which these changes have occurred, and the other is the substantial scale of the aging population. To compensate for the faster and more substantial scale of low fertility and aging populations, a higher quality of human capital is required, if a country is aiming to achieve sustainable economic development. Consequently, higher education is likely to be needed.

## 3. The current situation of high education in Asia

Table 3 shows the percentage of the population with the highest level of completed primary, secondary, and tertiary education, among the population 15 years old and over. Most advanced countries in Asia, including Japan and NIEs, show a higher percentage for completion of tertiary as well as secondary education in their populations, when

---

[6]Demographic onus phase is defined as a period when the dependency ratio increases.

Table 2. Timing of key events in the population structures of Asian countries.

| Year | Period when the TFR falls below 2.1 | Period when ratio of those aged 65 and over to the total population reaches 14% | Period when the labor force begins to decrease | Period when the population begins to decrease |
|---|---|---|---|---|
| 1960–1965 | Japan | | | |
| 1965–1970 | | | | |
| 1970–1975 | | | | |
| 1975–1980 | Japan, Singapore | | | |
| 1980–1985 | Hong Kong | | | |
| 1985–1990 | South Korea | | | |
| 1990–1995 | China, Thailand | Japan | | |
| 1995–2000 | | | | |
| 2000–2005 | Vietnam | | Japan | |
| 2005–2010 | Malaysia | | | |
| 2010–2015 | | Hong Kong | | Japan |
| 2015–2020 | | South Korea | China, Hong Kong, South Korea, Thailand | |
| 2020–2025 | | Singapore, Thailand | Singapore | |
| 2025–2030 | Indonesia | China | | Thailand |
| 2030–2035 | India | Vietnam | Vietnam | China |
| 2035–2040 | | | | South Korea |
| 2040–2045 | | Malaysia, Indonesia | | |
| 2045–2050 | | | Malaysia | Hong Kong, Vietnam |

*Source*: Kabe (2014).

*Notes*: 1. The total fertility rate (TFR) and rates of change in the labor force and population are measured as five-year averages. The ratios of those 65 years old and older are not averaged, but the levels for the end of a period. For example, if for a particular country, the ratio reached 14% in 1995, then the period in which the country is considered to have reached this ratio is 1990–1995.

2. Figures after 2005–2010 are based on the United Nations' World Population Prospects: The 2012 Revision.

Table 3. Educational attainment levels of the population
15 years old and over, for 2010.

|  | Highest level completed | | |
|---|---|---|---|
|  | Primary | Secondary | Tertiary |
| Country | (% of population aged 15 and over) | | |
| The United States | 2.0 | 36.2 | 26.8 |
| France | 15.3 | 38.2 | 10.6 |
| Germany | 2.9 | 54.8 | 13.1 |
| Sweden | 8.6 | 48.3 | 14.9 |
| The United Kingdom | 11.8 | 47.3 | 15.3 |
| Japan | 9.1 | 41.0 | 18.9 |
| South Korea | 8.8 | 35.5 | 30.0 |
| Singapore | 4.1 | 30.0 | 29.7 |
| Taiwan | 11.7 | 32.5 | 8.2 |
| Hong Kong | 14.8 | 43.7 | 15.2 |
| Malaysia | 11.2 | 39.8 | 5.8 |
| Thailand | 27.8 | 19.0 | 10.5 |
| Indonesia | 29.3 | 22.1 | 3.7 |
| Philippines | 17.0 | 23.8 | 5.5 |
| Vietnam | 14.3 | 19.4 | 3.3 |
| China | 14.8 | 22.9 | 2.7 |
| India | 15.2 | 25.0 | 4.9 |
| Brazil | 25.6 | 26.4 | 5.6 |
| South Africa | 6.2 | 53.9 | 0.3 |

*Source*: Barro and Lee (2014).

compared to middle-income countries, which show higher completion
levels for primary education. Among these countries, only Thailand's
completion level for tertiary education amounts to 10%.[7]

The gross school enrolment ratio in tertiary education[8] during 2012 reveals a contrast between advanced countries and Asian
middle-income countries. The ratio of the former was 50–90%, while
the ratio of the latter was 20–40%, except for Thailand, where the
ratio was 51%.

---

[7]Thai has high completion level of primary level (27%) as well as tertiary level.
[8]World Bank's World Development Indicators (online). Gross enrollment ratio is
the ratio of total enrollment, regardless of age, to the population of the age group
that officially corresponds to the level of education shown.

Table 4. Educational attainment levels of the population 25 years old and over, by sex.

| Country | Reference year | Upper secondary (%) | | Tertiary (%) | |
|---|---|---|---|---|---|
| | | Male | Female | Male | Female |
| The United States | 2012 | 47.1 | 46.9 | 40.2 | 41.1 |
| France | 2012 | 41.2 | 34.5 | 25.6 | 26.3 |
| Germany | 2012 | 51.9 | 48.6 | 30.3 | 21.2 |
| Sweden | 2012 | 45.2 | 41.0 | 25.4 | 33.3 |
| The United Kingdom | 2011 | 53.4 | 52.7 | 34.3 | 31.9 |
| Japan | 2010 | 38.3 | 41.4 | 32.2 | 27.8 |
| South Korea | 2010 | 38.8 | 36.1 | 40.8 | 30.1 |
| Singapore | 2012 | 17.3 | 20.6 | 43.0 | 36.4 |
| Hong Kong | 2011 | 33.6 | 35.5 | 21.3 | 16.5 |
| Malaysia | 2010 | 35.0 | 34.0 | 17.0 | 15.7 |
| Thailand | 2010 | 16.2 | 12.4 | 11.0 | 12.5 |
| Indonesia | 2011 | 24.6 | 17.6 | 8.2 | 7.5 |
| Philippines | 2008 | 35.3 | 34.9 | 22.4 | 25.9 |
| Vietnam | 2009 | 16.1 | 11.3 | 7.6 | 5.9 |
| China | 2010 | 15.4 | 11.6 | 4.1 | 3.0 |
| Brazil | 2011 | 27.5 | 28.3 | 10.1 | 12.6 |
| South Africa | 2012 | 48.3 | 46.2 | 7.0 | 5.8 |

*Source*: UNESCO.

It is worth noting that the educational attainment levels illustrated in Table 4 show a gender gap for secondary education in Asia, with China showing males at 15.4% and females at 11.6% in 2010, Vietnam showing males at 16.1% and females at 11.3% in 2009, and Thailand showing males at 16.2% and females at 12.4% in 2010.[9]

## 4. Expected role of higher education

If a country has a large percentage of the population with a higher education, it is not likely to experience an economic slowdown (Eichengreen *et al.*, 2014), because people with higher educations

[9]This does not necessarily mean that there is no gender gap in tertiary education in other Asian countries, because the percentage of tertiary education may not be sufficiently high to highlight the gender gap.

are able to utilize technology to a higher degree. As Ang *et al.* (2011) stressed, higher education is more appropriate for innovation, whereas primary and secondary education are more suitable for imitation. This means that low-income countries are more likely to imitate higher technology than develop their own. It is important for them to realize economic growth and primary and secondary education is required to increase technological imitation. Innovative ability is necessary for middle-income countries to compete with more highly developed countries, and in this situation, higher education is crucial. Knowing how to promote innovation through higher education is an important issue. The imitation process involves acquiring, assimilating, and improving mature technology from advanced countries, while the innovation process involves an indigenous innovative capability and the ability to generate emerging technologies (Kim, 1997; Fan, 2014).

To increase human capital at individual and social levels requires many processes, such as researching new or not fully utilized technology and related knowledge, learning and applying new technology, and absorbing its essence. This process is not at all linear but rather complicated in a spiralling manner, as shown in Figure 3, and takes both time and energy to accomplish. This is the case at both the individual and social levels of developing human capital.

Figure 3 shows that the more the level of human capital increases, the wider the circle becomes, reflected on a two-dimensional surface consisting of three processes (research capacity, technological and innovative performance, and absorptive capacity), during a spiralling process. This suggests that higher human capital contains a rich capacity for and experience in research, learning, applying, and absorbing new technology, and therefore, an increasingly stable and flexible capability to deal with complicated and fast-changing environments.

This development path may seem to consume too much time and energy. A country may want to drastically increase its current level of human capital in a linear manner, instead of spiralling upwards, by buying the latest technology. For example, technological license agreements on the latest technology from foreign companies

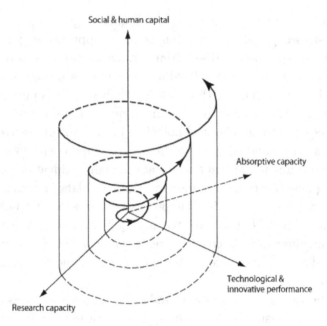

Figure 3. The development path of human capital.
*Source*: This modified figure was taken from Soete (2007, p. 35).[10]

in advanced countries may provide up-to-date technology and knowledge on specific industries and products.

However, after increasing human capital in a linear way, this
country will once again face the same issue related to improving
human capital, but without the support of its own capacity for and
experience of research, learning, applying, and absorbing the new
technology. Saving time and money by buying new technology does
not always lead to innovative capacity.

Figure 3 illustrates how important it is for an economic entity,
individual, or society to have the capacity to absorb and generate new ideas. Above all, the initial spiralling process is most fundamental and important for cultivating innovation; therefore, this

---

[10]The original two-dimensional figure from Soete (2007) was modified into a three-
dimensional figure, by treating social and human capital as an axis with three
dimensions.

process should be guided and supported by higher education. In later processes, it is desirable for this supporting and guiding role to involve collaboration between business training and higher education. Such collaboration allows for the 'combining [of] the capabilities of the workforce in innovative and productive ways' (ADB, 2014).

Even though higher education plays an important role in supporting and guiding the initial spiral process of developing human capital, whether higher education and business training can collaborate efficiently also has an influence on the extent to which human capital increases. The experiences of NIEs indicate the importance of industrial-academic cooperation in education, and there is another reason this cooperation is required. Upon careful examination of Figure 3, it is clear that the development path of human capital is a long-term process. In other words, if a country wants to increase the level of human capital, it should provide life-long education so that individuals can continue to develop themselves. Entering into and graduating from a university in youth is not one's only opportunity to experience education. After beginning a job, there are many additional opportunities to experience higher education, by attending graduate school, collaborating with universities, and accepting academic training or instruction in technology frontiers.

It is worth emphasising that the diffusion of secondary or primary education is a prerequisite to expanding higher education. People who have completed primary education can receive secondary education, and those who complete secondary education can go on to study at a higher level. Therefore, the creation of an effective and high-quality tertiary education system reveals a critical need to increase the quality of education and student attainment at the secondary level (ADB, 2014).

Reaffirming the importance of secondary education directs our attention once again to the gender gap in Asia, shown in Table 4. People completing secondary education move on to higher education, but the reality in Asia's middle-income countries is that men have a lower attainment level in secondary education than high-income countries, and females have a lower attainment level than their male counterparts. It is necessary to reduce the gender gap to enhance the general attainment level of secondary education.

## 5. Conclusion

Asia's middle-income countries aim to move to a high-income stage while facing globalisation, low fertility, and an aging population. Globalisation provides these countries with opportunities to economically catch up to high-income counties by utilising free-rider effects, but it also creates risks for becoming sandwiched or pressed between advanced countries and lower-income countries. Additionally, demographic changes, such as low fertility and an aging population, create a shift from demographic bonus periods, when a country's economic development accelerates due to a high proportion of the population being working-age, to a demographic onus period, when a country suffers from an increasing burden on the working-age population to support children and the elderly.

Fang (2012) argues that it is important to upgrade the pattern of economic growth from one driven by production factor inputs to one driven by improvements in TFP, underlining that improvements in TFP are the only source of maintaining sustainable economic growth. Enhancing productivity requires people with higher education who are able to utilize technology. Even though there is support and guidance in higher education for developing human capital, it takes time due to a spiralling process, in which new technology is researched, learnt, applied, and absorbed. Therefore, a higher level of human capital can flexibly find solutions to problems brought about by a rapidly changing environment. Higher education is expected to play a key role in maintaining sustainable economic growth, especially in the initial development process of human capital. However, this is a long-term process, and individuals should be provided with various opportunities for educational development.

Finally, three things should be mentioned. First, it is important to diffuse secondary or primary education, and second, the gender gap that appears in the attainment of secondary education should be reduced. These are prerequisites to expanding higher education systems and increasing the benefits this can have for economies. The third factor is innovative capacity. As Figure 3 indicates, the higher the level of human capital, the more innovative capacity increases. However, the source of innovative capacity is not limited to technology or new knowledge. Drucker (1985) highlighted the unexpected as one source for innovation, saying that far more often, and unexpected success is simply not seen at all and to exploit the opportunity for innovation offered by unexpected success requires analysis. Put another way, existing, but not fully utilized, technology and knowledge may also become sources or opportunities for innovation, if such opportunities are sought out and exploited systematically.[11] In this sense, Asian middle-income countries have sufficient opportunities to achieve innovative capacity through higher levels of human capital.

## References

Ang, J. B., J. B. Madsen, and M. R. Islam (2011). The effects of human capital composition on technological convergence. *Journal of Macroeconomics*, 33, pp. 465–476.

Asian Development Bank (ADB) (2014). *Innovative Asia: Advancing the Knowledge-Based Economy*. Asian Development Bank, Manila.

Barro, R. and J. W. Lee (2014). *A New Data Set of Educational Attainment in the World, 1950–2010*, version 2.0.

Barro, R. J. (1991). Economic growth in a cross section of countries. *The Quarterly Journal of Economics*, 106(2), pp. 407–443.

Bloom, D. E. and J. G. Williamson (1998). Demographic transitions and economic miracles in emerging Asia. *The World Bank Economic Review*, 12(3), pp. 419–455.

Drucker, P. F. (1985). *Innovation and Entrepreneurship — Practice and Principles*. Harper & Row, Publishers, Inc., New York.

Eichengreen, B., D. Park, and K. Shin (2014). Growth slowdowns redux. *Japan and the World Economy*, 32, pp. 65–84.

Fan, P. (2014). Innovation in China. *Journal of Economic Surveys*, 28(4), pp. 725–745.

---

[11]There may remain another issue, that is, how to establish educational system which provides better opportunities for creative thinking and problem solving *outside the box*. Huang and Szyf (2011) pointed out that even high-income countries should deal with it while Asian countries suffer from creative thinking deficit. Even though this seems interesting issue, it is beyond this chapter.

Fang, C. (2012). Is there a "middle-income trap"? Theories, experiences and relevance to China. *China & World Economy*, 20(1), pp. 49–61.

Huang, Y. and Y. A. Szyf (2011). Driving productivity and growth. In *Asia 2050 — Realizing the Asian Century*, H. S. Kohli, A. Sharma, and A. Sood (eds.), 99–127, Asian Development Bank, Sage Publication India Pvt. Ltd., New Delhi, India.

Kabe, S. (2013). Can south-south trade be a driving force for future economic growth? In *Global Linkages and Economic Rebalancing in East Asia*, T. Kinkyo, Y. Matsubayashi and S. Hamori (eds.), pp. 139–158, World Scientific Pub. Co. Pvt. Ltd, Singapore.

Kabe, S. (2014). To what extent is population size in ASEAN? In *Illustrated Brief Introduction of ASEAN* (Zukaide Zakkuri Wakaru ASEAN), R. Ushiyama and S. Kabe (eds.), pp. 27–32. (In Japanese)

Kim, L. (1997). *Imitation to Innovation — The dynamics of Korea's Technological Learning*. Harvard Business School Press, Boston.

Kimenyi, M. S. (2011). Contribution of higher education to economic development: A survey of international evidence. *Journal of African Economies*, 20, AERC Supplement 3, pp. 14–49.

Komine, T. and S. Kabe (2009). Long-term forecast of the demographic transition in Japan and Asia. *Asian Economic Policy Review*, 4(1), pp. 19–38.

Lucas Jr, R. E. (1988). On the mechanics of economic development. *Journal of Monetary Economics*, 22, pp. 3–42.

Marukawa, T. (2014). "Catch-down" innovations in developing countries. *Ajia Keizai*, 55(4) (in Japanese)

Organisation for Economic Co-operation and Development (OECD). *Perspective on Global Development 2014: Boosting Productivity to Meet the Middle-Income Challenge*. Organisation for Economic Co-operation and Development, Paris, pp. 57–101.

Romer, P. (1990). Endogenous technological change. *Journal of Political Economy*, 98(5), Part 2, pp. S71–S102.

Soete, L. (2007). Notes on UIL-related policies of national governments. In *How Universities Promote Economic Growth*, S. Yusuf and K. Nabeshima (eds.), The World Bank, Washington.

Son, H. H. (2010). Human Capital Development. ADB Economics Working Paper Series No. 225, Asian Development Bank, Manila.

Thant, M. (1999). Lessons from East Asia: Financing human resource development. In *Human Capital Formation as an Engine of Growth: The East Asian Experience*, J. L. H. Tan (ed.), Institute of Southeast Asian Studies, Singapore.

Vandenbussche, J., P. Aghion, and C. Meghir (2006). Growth, distance to frontier and composition of human capital. *Journal of Economic Growth*, 11, pp. 97–127.

World Bank (1993). The *East Asian Miracle: Economic Growth and Public Policy*. Oxford University Press for the World Bank.

# Part III

# Case Studies: Current State and Challenges of Five Asian Countries

CHAPTER 6

# Affirmative Action and Transformation in Malaysia

Hwok-Aun Lee

*Faculty of Economics and Administration,*
*University of Malaya, 50603 Kuala Lumpur, Malaysia*
*halee@um.edu.my*

## 1. Introduction

Malaysia's pursuit of high income, fully developed status, with an advanced economy and mature society, must find a passage away from its current majority-favoring affirmative action regime. The rhetoric, logic and practice of transformation encompass various, fundamental changes, including reforms of the country's extensive Bumiputera-favoring preferential programs. These reforms are imperative from two perspectives. First, affirmative action ultimately aims to be effective, successful and as a result redundant and unnecessary. This general tenet is especially pertinent to Malaysia, where the interventions have been more extensive and intensive than in any other country. Second, perpetual affirmative action risks undermining a country's continual development toward being advanced and fully developed in a multidimensional sense. While countries may pass high income thresholds without necessarily undertaking fundamental reforms, as Malaysia may do in the coming years, graduating further into the ranks of fully developed and advanced nations will require shifts away from the current modes of affirmative action, which in significant ways attenuate the development of capability, competitiveness and confidence of the majority population.

This chapter examines the state of affirmative action and its inter-relationships with Malaysia's multiple transformation projects. We first conceptualize affirmative action, to set out a systematic understanding of the policies' objectives and instruments, and to help maintain clarity and consistency in evaluating policy outcomes and alternatives. We then critically evaluate recent policy reform agendas, drawing out incoherence and inadequacies of view that "need-based affirmative action" provides a systemic replacement for affirmative action based on ethnicity. A credible and effective transformation platform, this chapter argues, must first address the inefficacies of current affirmative action programs and formulate transition plans, instead of posing misguided alternatives.

## 2. Affirmative action: Concept and Malaysia context

### 2.1. Defining affirmative action

No standard definition of affirmative action prevails, but it can be defined as preferential policies to redress the under-representation of a disadvantaged population group in socially esteemed and economically influential positions (Weisskopf, 2004; ILO, 2007; Fryer and Loury, 2005). These policies respond to a specific problem: under-representation of a population group — categorized by race, ethnicity, gender, disability, region, and so on — in socio-economic positions that affect the collective esteem and stature of the group. Visible and persistent absence of group members among university students, professionals, managers and business owners causes the group as a whole to be viewed negatively, both from outside and within the group. Such conditions may also discourage their upward mobility, and are compounded by socioeconomic disadvantages of the group on the whole — inferior schooling, shortage of work experience, and lack of capital ownership or access to credit. Moreover, entry into high level positions must overcome various barriers: university entry grades, higher education qualifications for professional jobs, work experience and network connections for managerial positions. Thus, marginalization of a disadvantaged group may perpetuate across generations.

In view of these specific problems and obstacles as well as the objective of affirmative action to accelerate upward mobility, the vital role of group preference becomes clearer. Affirmative action intervenes in such a way because conventional criteria of need, formal qualifications or "merit" will not sufficiently facilitate upward educational and occupational mobility or capital ownership. A socioeconomically disadvantaged group will continually struggle to enter the high level positions targeted by affirmative action unless conferred some degree of preference — that is, being given opportunities even though they may not formally meet the full qualifications. Because affirmative action inherently grants preference based on group identity and hence can breed dependency and complacency or risk political manipulation, it is imperative that such policies be effective, capability-building and transitory.

Undoubtedly, the policy is complex and controversial, presenting both benefits and costs, to the beneficiary and non-beneficiary groups, and to the nation as a whole, in terms of integration and unity. These broader, multidisciplinary debates are important and interesting, but will be reserved for other spaces. This chapter acknowledges that affirmative action is established and entrenched in Malaysia and maintains for on its immediate, direct and principal objective: Bumiputera representation in high level positions. We also take the position that completion of Malaysia's transformation aspirations requires that Bumiputera capability and confidence be attained to an extent that the current Bumiputera preferential policy regime may be phased out.

## 2.2. The new economic policy (NEP)

Affirmative action in Malaysia is most closely identified with the NEP, introduced in 1971. The associated is tightly knit by the fact that Bumiputera preferential policies massively expanded under the NEP, and transformed Malaysia's economy and society, although affirmative action had existed in smaller scope and scale since Independence in 1957. However, the NEP judiciously differentiated poverty alleviation and affirmative action — a distinction that should be maintained, to maintain clarity and coherence in analyzing Malaysia's policies.

The NEP was built around a two-pronged mission. First, it set the goal of eradicating poverty *irrespective of race*. Second, it laid the groundwork for interventions to *accelerate social restructuring* to reduce and eventually eliminate the identification of race with economic function. This second prong encapsulated the fundamental problems addressed by affirmative action policies. Gross underrepresentation of Bumiputeras in university and among professionals and managers and capitalists, was a socio-politically unacceptable state, particularly when the socioeconomically disadvantaged constituted the politically dominant major ethnic group. Moreover, this structure would persist, although some Bumiputera advancement could be expected over time through poverty alleviation programs, as increased provision of basic education, with improved health services and infrastructure, widened the scope for Bumiputera upward mobility. Nonetheless, while social restructuring may occur as an indirect result of general development policies, direct and proactive interventions were deemed necessary to push the process at a faster pace — arguably, in line with socio-political pressures and expectations for visible and meaningful change. As explained above, the package of interventions involved giving preference to Bumiputeras, who were on the whole disadvantaged in their capacity to gain upward educational and occupational mobility, and to begin to own and operate businesses.

The broader context behind the NEP's formulation also warrants a brief note. From Malayan independence and into the 1960s, the Malay community remained mired in widespread poverty, and confined to agricultural activities. This ethnic division of labor, translating into ethnic disparities in opportunity and income that also curtailed cross-cultural social interaction, created schisms and tensions in Malaysian society and polity (Andaya and Andaya, 2001). Malay upward mobility in the educational and occupational ladders, and in access to credit and ownership of capital, were severely constrained.[1] The early post-Independence government was characterized by relative *laissez faire* approach toward inter-ethnic inequalities, with some notable interventions through Malay reservation in civil service employment and scholarships. By the late 1960s, there were increasing calls for more policies promoting the growth of a Bumiputera capitalist class. The May 13, 1969 inter-ethnic violence and social unrest thrust Malaysia onto a different trajectory, driven by assertion of Malay political primacy, centralization of state power and dominance of the executive (Ooi, 2013). As a result, Malaysia's policy regime uniquely features discretionary exercise of executive power, ethnic quotas or Bumiputera-exclusive programs, and highly centralized administration, in contrast to other countries with affirmative action, notably South Africa where affirmative action also favors a politically dominant majority but through a more legislative and democratically governed manner (Lee, 2014b). Pressures for more wealth transfers and business opportunities conceived the high priority Bumiputera Commercial and Industrial Community (BCIC), as introduced in the NEP. The circumstances prevailing on affirmative action gave wide scope and a forceful mandate for the policy to make a difference, while presenting challenges toward effective and in some ways restrained implementation, and enormous hurdles to reform and transformation.

## 2.3. Affirmative action and transformation

Affirmative action interacts with Malaysia's transformation pursuits, which have aspired to attain the status of high income economy and fully developed country. Equitable distribution of capabilities and benefits, for fair and equal participation in economic life, without conspicuous absence of a particular group, constitute key ingredients

---

[1] In 1957, the poverty rate among Malays was 70.5%, compared to 27.4% for Chinese and 35.7% for Indians. The disparity persisted through 1970, as poverty remained considerably higher for Malays (64.8%) than for Chinese (26.0%) and Indians (39.2%) (Leete, 2007). In Peninsular Malaysia in 1967, the Chinese: Malay household income ratio was recorded at 2.47, and 1.95 for Indian per Malay households (Anand, 1981).

of these development visions. The policy, if successful, renders itself
redundant and unnecessary. Affirmative action depends on economic growth for opportunities to be generated then distributed,
but is also mandated to contribute vitally to economic growth
and transformation by cultivating capabilities of a disadvantaged
population.

The desirable impermanence of affirmative action has found
expression in Malaysia, but in mellow and fleeting moments. The
policies have generally averted commitments to deadlines or sunset
clauses. Although the NEP (1971–1990) originally set a two decades
long timeframe, with suggestions that preferential selection would
be transitional, there was no explicit and binding commitment to
dismantle the policy in 1990. Moreover, the clearest articulation of
the policy's passage over time — for 30% of equity to be under
Bumiputera ownership within one generation — was specific to one
policy area, and not the totality of affirmative action programs,
and was expressed as a sunset clause or trigger point for policy
change (Malaysia 1976). Vision 2020, pronounced by Prime Minister
Mahathir in 1991, projected bolder aspirations for Malaysia, around
the overarching theme of becoming a fully developed country. Vision
2020 pronounced the "need to ensure the creation of an economically
resilient and fully competitive Bumiputera community so as to be at
par with the non-Bumiputera community." This statement can be
read to mean a proper levelling of the playing field, but again, this
suggestion of dismantling Bumiputera-favoring handicaps was specific to the BCIC, without touching on education, employment and
other spheres of affirmative action.

In recent years we have witnessed sentiments for Malaysia to transition away from ethnicity-based affirmative action toward "need-
based affirmative action," as part of transformations to lift Malaysia
out of the middle income trap and become a developed and competitive economy. In 2010, the New Economic Model was launched, with
high income economy, inclusiveness and sustainability as a troika
of national goals. Although the NEM itself has become eclipsed in
practice by reactions that neutered its transformative instruments,
notably rescinding an original plan to set up an equal opportunity

commission, it marked a turning point by establishing these policy platforms.

However, this rhetoric misleads; the notion of need-based affirmative action is flawed and incoherent; it ultimately offers very marginal replacement for race-based affirmative action. The vast bulk of affirmative action programs remain firmly in place, with no attention to possible reforms and transitions toward more competition and effective capability building. It largely reacts to the most glaring abuses of the policy — concentration of wealth in the hands of politically connected individuals, wasteful award of opportunities to unproductive rent-seekers — but omits the less obvious, yet in some ways more disempowering effects of affirmative action in higher education. We return to a discussion of the coherence and efficacy Malaysia's policy discourse and implementation, after the following overview of programs and their outcomes and implications.

## 3. Affirmative action programs

Malaysia's affirmative action programs span four main spheres: higher education, high level employment, managerial and enterprise development, and equity and wealth ownership. Deriving from the definition provided above — preferential section in designated areas of Bumiputera under-representation — major programs are described next, and summarized in Table 1.

### 3.1. Higher education

A few institutions have been created and reserved for Bumiputeras, in secondary schooling and early post-secondary education. At the secondary level, $MARA^2$ junior science colleges (MRSM) have provided for Bumiputera students, ideally those from rural communities whose schools lag in quality of instruction and facilities. Superior facilities to Bumiputera students, especially from rural communities. At the post-secondary level, matriculation colleges offer a one-year preparatory course prior to university entry, a shorter and evidently

---

[2]MARA derives from *Majlis Amanah Rakyat*, or Council of Trust for the People.

Table 1. Malaysia's affirmative action system: spheres, programs and notable features.

| Sphere | Programs/Agencies | Notable features |
|---|---|---|
| Education | • MARA junior science colleges (MRSM)<br>• Post-secondary matriculation colleges<br>• MARA University of Technology (UiTM); MARA scholarships<br>• Public university admissions quotas<br>• Government scholarship quotas | • Exclusively Bumiputera until 10% non-Bumiputera quota from 2000<br>• Exclusively Bumiputera, until 10% non-Bumiputera quota from 2002. From late 1990s, predominant route for Bumiputera university entry.<br>• Exclusively Bumiputera<br>• Centrally administered by federal government. Since 2002, "meritocracy" declared, but questionable in view of differences in duration and difficulty of matriculation and Higher Education School Certificate (STPM) examinations<br>• Ethnic allocations publicized from mid-2000s |
| High level occupations | • Bumiputera representation among professionals and management | • *De facto* quota in public sector, though largely ad hoc in implementation |
| Managerial and Enterprise development | • BCIC<br>• Government investment agencies<br>• Public procurement/contracting and licensing<br>• Small enterprises | • Agencies engaged in direct employment of Bumiputeras and enterprise support through upstream/downstream linkages, predominantly large and medium scale:<br>• SEDCs (since 1970s); Petronas, national petroleum agency (since mid-1970s); Takeover of previously foreign companies through government investment agencies (since late 1970s); Heavy Industries (1980s); Privatization (1980s – 1997–1998 AFC; GLCs — Renationalized privatization entities, corporations held through government investment agencies |

*(Continued)*

Table 1. (*Continued*)

| Sphere | Programs/Agencies | Notable features |
|---|---|---|
| | | • Financial and advisory support for GLCs |
| | | • Small contracts reserved for Bumiputera contractors, price handicaps favoring Bumiputera contractors, for medium to large contracts |
| | | • Loans and business support by MARA, PUNB, and other agencies |
| Equity and wealth ownership | • ICA 1975<br>• Foreign Investment Committee regulations<br>• Government investment funds<br>• Privatization | • 30% Bumiputera allotment in new and existing medium to large manufacturing forms; waiver to export-oriented. Conditions relaxed over time, ended by 2004.<br>• 30% Bumiputera requirement in public listing and foreign investment. FIC closure, investment liberalization, reduced public listing requirements in 2009.<br>• Bumiputera quotas<br>• Massive transfer of previously state-owned assets, creation of new rights |

*Source*: Lee (2014a).

easier path, compared to the two-year Malaysian Higher School Certificate (STPM). These institutions were exclusively for Bumiputera students until about 2001, when 10% non-Bumiputera quotas were introduced.

At the university level, affirmative action has taken the form of ethnic quotas for admissions — reportedly 55% Bumiputera, and centrally administered by the federal bureaucracy (Aihara, 2009; Faridah, 2003). MARA's technical institute, recently upgraded to University Technology MARA (UiTM), and MARA scholarships, have remained exclusive Bumiputera domains. Government-sponsored scholarships have also undertaken the affirmative action mandate, with Bumiputeras comprising the vast majority of recipients. Since 2002, a portion of Public Service Department scholarships have been designated for Bumiputera, and another portion opened to competitive, merit-based selection.

## 3.2. High level occupations

In contrast to higher education, Malaysia's interventions promoting Bumiputera representation in the occupational sphere have been less extensive. The NEP laid a general guideline that "employment patterns at all levels and in all sectors must reflect the racial composition of the population" (Malaysia, 1971: 42). Affirmative action, facilitating Bumiputera entry to professional and managerial positions were the group has been under-represented, has predominantly operated in the public sector and state-owned enterprises. This process has proceeded mostly without a particular code of practice, and over time acquired an inertia and self-perpetuating momentum. The number of non-Bumiputera entrants and employees has severely dwindled, to the point of effectively precluding need for preferential measures.[3] Conspicuous absence of non-Bumiputeras in top administrative posts in spite of availability, notably in public universities, suggests a significant exercise of group reservation. Senior officials in the public sector also tend to transition to high level positions in state-owned enterprises.

## 3.3. Managerial and enterprise development

This arm of affirmative action — to cultivate Bumiputera participation in managing and starting commercial enterprises, or the BCIC, as distinct from public administration — has received tremendous attention and resources. Malaysia has deployed various instruments toward developing the BCIC, with state agencies supporting these endeavors through loans, direct employment and procurement, importantly through the State Economic Development Corporations

---

[3]Puthucheary (1978) notes that, in post-Independence Malaya, four fifths of recruitment into the Malayan civil service was reserved for Malays (cited in Khoo, 2005).

(SEDCs) and Government-linked Companies (GLCs). The main instruments and priorities have shifted over time, from a big push into Heavy Industries in the 1980s to privatization of state-owned enterprises from the mid-1980s until the 1997–1998 Asian Financial Crisis (AFC), after which the GLCs took up the mantle (see Table 1). A large part of the reason for the changing configuration of policy instruments is the government's practical and necessary responses to underachievement or failure, which are more momentous in this area than in the education and employment spheres of affirmative action. Most spectacularly, collapses of privatized entities in the aftermath of the AFC resulted in their rescue and reconstitution as GLCs.

The role of government-linked investment agencies (GLICs) also consolidated in the post-AFC era. Through the GLICs, particularly *Khazanah Nasional*, *Permodalan Nasional* (National Corporation) and Ministry of Finance, Inc., the state exercises control over GLCs, thus in partnership promote the BCIC agenda. More recently, the government established *Ekuinas* and *Teraju* to cultivate new Bumiputera ventures, with emphasis on high growth potential. Public procurement, contracting and licensing play a major role in promoting Bumiputera enterprise development, given the leverage the government holds in disbursing such rights and rents. The public procurement system reserves the smallest class of contracts for Bumiputera contractors, while medium to large contracts (except for the largest category) offer price handicaps. Bumiputera small businesses, another category of beneficiaries, are offered financial and advisory assistance through agencies such as MARA and PUNB (*Perbadanan Usahawan Nasional*, the National Entrepreneurial Corporation).

## 3.4. Equity and wealth ownership

The NEP cast the spotlight on the negligible Bumiputera ownership of share capital, 2.4% in 1970, and ushered in various interventions to address this disparity. The Industrial Coordination Act (ICA) of 1975 required medium- to large-scale manufacturing firms to allocate at least 30% of existing and new equity to Bumiputera interests. The drastic measure provoked fierce reactions. Subsequently, this requirement was waived for export-oriented firms, and revisions were made to also exempt more domestic, predominantly Chinese-owned, companies. In response to the mid-1980s recession and the 1997– 1998 AFC, Malaysia further liberalized investment conditions, and by 2004, equity requirements in manufacturing were effectively vestigial. Bumiputera preferential conditions, administered by the Foreign Investment Committee, have applied to foreign investments in general, as well as mergers and acquisitions, property purchases and public listings, adopting the conventional 30% Bumiputera holdings as a benchmark. These regulations were significantly rolled back in 2009.

Privatization, discussed above in the context of promoting managerial and enterprise development, also functioned as a conduit for transferring ownership to individual Bumiputera capitalists. Bumiputera ownership also derives from institutional sources. Government investment funds, such as unit trusts managed by *Permodalan Nasional*, have continually fostered equity participation and wealth accumulation, with offerings in part or whole reserved for Bumiputera investors. In response to the preponderance of passive ownership, from the late 2000s the Malaysian government has increasingly prioritized active equity participation, as well as commercial property ownership.

## 4. Affirmative action outcomes

Our evaluation of policy outcomes maintains focus on the framework and set of programs outlined above. For the most part, literature on Malaysia's development record has not zoomed in on affirmative action, but has incorporated the subject into broader overviews of development policies, especially the NEP. Hence, achievements in economic growth, structural change, poverty reduction and inter-ethnic disparities tend to be blended together (Faaland, Parkinson and Saniman, 2001; Snodgrass, Yusof and Shari, 2003; Chakravarty and Roslan, 2005; Jamaluddin, 2003; Jomo and Gomez, 1999;

Salih and Yusof, 1989; Jomo, 2004). These outcomes are certainly inter-related and in some ways interdependent, but one ramification of such general analyses is that the immediate and specific objectives and instruments of affirmative action may get appraised indirectly, such as by reference to inter-ethnic household income gaps, or be conflated with other development programs, such as poverty alleviation.

The discourse has also been shaped by data availability — rather, the lack of information disclosed from official sources and prohibitive access to the original national survey datasets. For instance, inter-ethnic household income inequality is one of very few inter-ethnic inequality indicators that Malaysia, through the five-year Malaysia Plans, has tracked and reported over time. Nonetheless, while narrowing inter-ethnic household income would be consistent with the execution of affirmative action, the primary outcome that demands precedence are ethnic compositions in higher education, high level employment and asset ownership, and the benefits and costs of policies promoting Bumiputera representation in the particular fields. A few works have specifically probed affirmative action outcomes, but with uneven coverage of all policy spheres and adequate, critical consideration of the achievements and deficiencies (Lee, 2005; Yusof, 2013).

The analysis presented here, drawing on Lee (2012) and Lee (2014a), seeks to concisely survey available evidence of affirmative action outcomes across the four main spheres of intervention. As emphasized in this chapter, affirmative action, as one distinct mainstay of the NEP, and warrants specific empirical analyses consistent with its objectives and mechanisms: increasing Bumiputera representation in specific positions, by according the group's members preferential treatment. This chapter analyzes direct policy outcomes and immediate implications, engaging with contemporary issues and synthesizing current, available data.

## 4.1. Higher education

The educational profile of the Bumiputera population steeply rose, bolstered by extensive affirmative action programs. In public universities, the share of Bumiputeras in enrollment jumped from 40% in 1970 to 63% by 1985, and stabilized at that level until 2003 (Khoo, 2005; Sato, 2005). Current data on ethnic composition of university student bodies are difficult to obtain, but preferential policies undeniably sustain Bumiputera entry to a considerable degree. In 2009, UiTM, which is reserved for Bumiputera students, accounted for 140,000 out of a total 590,000 among all public universities.

Affirmative actions at the secondary and post-secondary levels have also expanded. MRSMs have maintained their role as conduit for Bumiputera educational advancement, and continually enjoy curricular and instructional upgrades. However, MRSMs and MARA overseas scholarships have arguably contributed less than before toward inter-generational mobility, since disproportionate shares of these opportunities are taken by Malay middle and upper classes (Lee, 2013). The vast majority of Bumiputera students reach university through the matriculation colleges, whose enrollment grew from about 15,000 in 1995 to over 55,000 in 2005.

The above education achievements are borne out in labor force statistics, which can be compiled from published documents (Figure 1). By 2010, the Malay labor force registered the highest share with tertiary (degree, diploma, or certificate) qualifications.

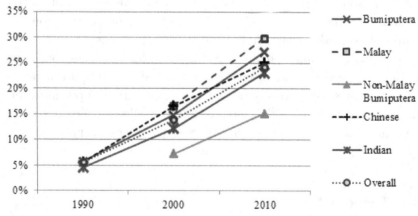

Figure 1. Malaysia: Share of labor force with tertiary education, by ethnic group.
*Source*: Labour Force Survey Report (various years).

Importantly, while the Malay labor force profile exceeds all others in this regard, non-Malay Bumiputeras are considerably lagging. Beyond these quantitative outcomes, and applicable to all Bumiputeras, quality shortfalls warrant attention. An official "meritocracy" policy practiced since 2002 commits false equivalence by appraising matriculation grades on par with the STPM, when the latter is demonstrably less rigorous. Matriculation's lighter program is evidenced by the lesser preparedness of its graduates for university study (Tan and Raman, 2009). This putatively ethnicity-blind policy is thus illusory, since it treats predominantly Bumiputera matriculation graduates on par with non-Bumiputera STPM holders. By paving easier paths instead of adequately equipping students for university, is ultimately does a disservice to the Bumiputera community. It also curtails the scope for post-secondary programs to bridge primary and secondary schooling gaps, since the residential matriculation colleges serve many students from socioeconomically disadvantaged backgrounds.

Problems of pre-university institutions recur at the post-graduation stage, where Bumiputera youth experience relatively greater challenges in securing employment. Bumiputera graduates of public universities gravitate more to the public sector, which partly captures preferences and choices but also indicates deficits in achieving the affirmative action goal of equipping beneficiaries to be mobile and competitive across public and private sector employment (Lee, 2012). The need for the government's considerable efforts to provide basic technical and inter-personal skills and to enhance Bumiputera graduates' employability also reflect the deficiencies of affirmative action in public higher education.[4]

## 4.2. High level occupations

A similar story of quantitative gains and qualitative shortfalls emerges when we assess affirmative action outcomes in occupational advancement. Bumiputera representation in high level positions rose

---

[4]The government spent RM415 million over 2001–2005 to retrain 40,000, predominantly Bumiputera, graduates (Cheong *et al.*, 2011).

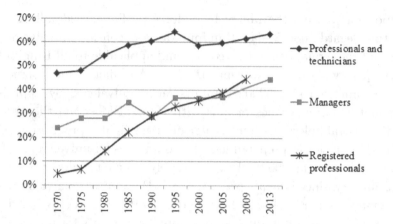

Figure 2. Malaysia: Share of bumiputera in high level occupations.

*Sources*: Malaysia Plans (various years), Labor Force Survey Report (2013).

*Notes*: 1970 and 1975 for Peninsula only; occupational classifications changed in 1980 and 2000.

over the 1970s toward the 1990s. However, the momentum apparently waned from the mid-1990s, reflected in slower increases in the Bumiputera share of professional and managerial positions, and in registries of select professions (Figure 2). It should be noted that Bumiputera proportions in registered professionals vary across jobs, with higher shares among lawyers and lower shares among engineers. The public sector has played a vital role in facilitating upward mobility and growing a Malay middle class, particularly over the 1970s and 1908s (Torii, 2003; Embong, 1996). Bumiputeras, especially Malays, are heavily over-represented in the bureaucracy; dependency on the public sector employment persists (Lim, 2013).[5] In 2005, the share of teachers and lecturers (predominantly in the public sector) among total professionals was 52.5% for Bumiputera, 22.4% for Chinese and 30.8% for Indians.[6]

Confinement of ethnic preferential policies to the public sector entails that Bumiputera representation in high level occupations in

---

[5] In 2009, Malays comprised 79% of top management and 75% of professional and management positions (Lim, 2013).

[6] Author's calculations from Malaysia (2006).

the private sector hinges on the capability and mobility of graduates. Deficiencies in Bumiputera empowerment through education, discussed above, have thus extended to the employment sphere, where the community reportedly faces more acute graduate unemployment problems. At the same time, perceptions of Bumiputera, especially Malay, graduates and possible biases against them, may also limit opportunities and perpetuate schisms between the private and public sectors.

### 4.3. Managerial and enterprise development

Bumiputera representation is consistently lower in managerial positions. The statistics presented in Figure 2 include both public and private sectors, and we can expect the Bumiputera share in private sector management to be lower. Accordingly, the barriers to entry to top, decision-making and sometimes ownership-linked positions are substantially higher than to other occupation groups. At the same time, Malaysia's policies in this sphere have registered checkered results, arguably underachieving on the whole. State-owned enterprises performed poorly over the 1970s and 1980s (Jesudason, 1989). Nonetheless, in particular sectors, notably finance and banking, plantations, and mining, a significant Malay presence has prevailed since the 1980s (Kamal and Zainal, 1989). The 1990s saw a bump in formation of the BCIC, as privatization catapulted Malays into management of corporations across many sectors.

However, systemic collapses in the aftermath of the AFC ushered in momentous reconfiguration of the government-business nexus, thrusting renationalized, formerly privatized entities, renamed GLCs, as the hub of the BCIC agenda. In terms of small and medium scale industries, progress in building a corps of dynamic and independent Bumiputera companies, especially in manufacturing, remains sluggish (Gomez, 2013). Affirmative action through public procurement and licensing have continually disbursed state largesse to Bumiputera contractors, but fallen short on the further aim of fostering dynamic, competitive enterprise. The program is beset by poor selection, inadequate monitoring for efficiency and technical progress, and ineffective checks against corruption, political patronage and cronyism.

## 4.4. Equity and wealth ownership

Bumiputera equity ownership has probably been the most vigorously discussed affirmative action targets, and one of the more visibly tracked, ever since the 30% threshold was set under the NEP. Official estimates show substantial progress in the Bumiputera share over 1971–1990, but slow progress since 1990 (Figure 3). The data have been disputed, with reference to the opacity of shares held through nominees, the application of par value instead of market value, and the omission of government ownership through the government-linked investment companies (Jomo, 2004; CPPS, 2006). Alternate estimates have obtained significantly higher figures — in other words, Bumiputera ownership in excess of 30% — but have been ignored or dismissed. Apparently, vested interests prevail on retaining estimation methods that show low Bumiputera ownership, which legitimates the perpetuation of privileged access and Bumiputera reservations.[7]

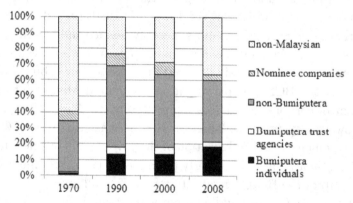

Figure 3. Equity ownership (at par value), percentage of total.
*Source*: Malaysia Plans (various years).

---

[7]Abu Samad (2002) concluded that the 30% target was passed by 1997. The Center for Public Policy Studies (CPPS) (2006) traced 45% of equity in 2005 as representing Bumiputera-owned — assigning 70% of government holdings, omitted in the official estimation exercise, as representing Bumiputera interest.

The above debates aside, evidence points to pervasive profiteering and rent-seeking, compounded by Malaysia's poor track record in monitoring efficiency and enforcing performance standards (Gomez and Jomo, 1999). Mandated equity allocations have overwhelmingly been sold off for profit; available data on financial asset ownership indicate that the vast majority of Bumiputera have scarcely been impacted by preferential wealth redistribution measures. *Amanah Saham Bumiputera* unit trust holdings are exceedingly skewed, with a top crust taking a mammoth share, and recent issues have been undersubscribed. In sum, these developments warrant a return to more basic objectives of developing capabilities and earnings capacity — above all, re-emphasizing effective affirmative action in education.

## 5. Current policy discourses

The problems, deficiencies and discontent arising from the ethnicity basis of affirmative action, and the ways it is implemented in Malaysia, have elicited searches for alternatives — especially, the notion of "need-based affirmative action." This reform-sounding rhetoric is also a part of Malaysia's transformation agenda; sustaining progress toward an advanced and mature economy, society and polity depends on the Bumiputera majority attaining sufficient capability, competitiveness and confidence. However, the stance that need-based affirmative action should be pursued as a systemic replacement for ethnicity-based affirmative action, while popular, fails to comprehend the fundamental distinction and separation between need-based policies of the NEP's poverty alleviation prong and the ethnicity-based policies of the affirmative action prong. The underlying logic and structure of this relationship needs clarity and coherence. Malaysia's existing, specific and entrenched pro-Bumiputera programs cannot be simply replaced with pro-poor preferential selection, although they can serve as complements.

Unfortunately, contemporary views on the matter are largely muddled — furthermore, cemented by a bipartisan consensus. From 2008, both federal government and opposition alliances articulated

122 *Moving Up the Ladder*

reform agendas along the lines of implementing need-based affirmative action in place of ethnicity-based affirmative action with need-based affirmative action.[8] The argument is appealing but flawed. It holds that, instead of assisting on the basis of being Bumiputera, giving help on the basis of socioeconomic need will result in the Bumiputeras being helped the most, since the community constitutes an overwhelming majority of the poor. Hence, targeting based on ethnicity can be abolished and replaced with targeting based on need, while concurrently avoiding troublesome and polarizing ethnic identification. After closer scrutiny, this argument is deeply misguided.

Need-based and ethnicity-based policies both involve preferential selection — respectively, favoring the poor and favoring an ethnic group — and correspond with the NEP's two prongs, which pursue different objectives through different instruments. Poverty alleviation programs principally deliver basic needs such as schooling, healthcare, infrastructure and social assistance. Undoubtedly, Bumiputeras immensely benefit from such programs, in proportion to their representation among the poor. However, they will benefit principally in the form of poverty alleviation, which has no direct impact on upward mobility. There are steep limits to the extent that need-based policies can be utilized or recast to attain affirmative action goals. For instance, providing basic rural schooling to the poor is plainly an incoherent and ineffective means for cultivating Bumiputera lawyers and managers.

Giving preference to socioeconomically disadvantaged can complement affirmative action in some aspects, possibly reinforcing intergenerational mobility. It is desirable and legitimate that those

---

[8]*Pakatan Rakyat Policies*, released in December 2009, contained a section headlined "Need-based Affirmative Action," which resolved to provide economic assistance and fair distribution to all races based on need, to avail scholarships based on need and merit, and to utilize savings from curbing corruption toward poverty alleviation. Barisan Nasional's (BN) *New Economic Model* (Part 1) in April 2010 committed to continue and revamp affirmative action, to remove rent-seeking and market distorting features and to "consider all ethnic groups fairly and equally as long as they are in the low income 40% of households" (NEAC, 2009).

with greater socioeconomic need within the Bumiputera community receive more help. However, this principle is only applicable in a few, quite narrow, areas — again, it cannot systemically replace existing ethnicity-based programs. In higher education, the case for weighing need-based considerations is firmest, particularly in university admissions and scholarships, where socioeconomic background can be a legitimate criterion, and taking into account that the disadvantages borne by such young beneficiaries are mainly due to circumstances outside of their control. Family background also can feasibly and reasonably be considered university selection processes, although it also comes with limits and drawbacks, most importantly the reality that students from lower socioeconomic backgrounds are on average less equipped for university-level study.

Need-based preferential selection presents exceedingly limited practical alternatives in other spheres of affirmative action. In public sector employment, the implication of need-based preference is that persons from lower income backgrounds should be given priority in recruitment or promotion. This is plainly unworkable; at this stage of an individual's life, family background should drastically diminish as a basis for preferential treatment. Conferring preference on those from lower socioeconomic rungs in employment, as well as public procurement, licensing or other similar allocation of opportunity, also potentially imperils quality of delivery, for this entails privileging persons or companies with lower earning, lesser capability or poorer performance. Policy discourses, therefore, will do well to avoid the notion of need-based preferential treatment *as a systemic alternative* for ethnicity-based affirmative action. In the contemporary context, however, Malaysia is virtually locked in to this flawed notion, and leaves untouched the vast bulk of ineffective affirmative action programs, emphatically in higher education.

## 6. Conclusion

Affirmative action has contributed immensely to reshaping the landscape of opportunities and socioeconomic outcomes of Malaysia's ethnic groups, specifically in narrowing the gap between Bumiputera

and non-Bumiputera participation in high level positions. The policy
has delivered on various quantitative outcomes, but more challenging transformations lie ahead. Its external contribution to Malaysia's
progress to high income, fully developed and advanced country status demands more qualitative changes; beyond producing numbers of
graduates, professionals and managers, the next stage requires quality graduates, competent professionals and competitive managers.

Affirmative action programs must also undergo internal transformation to arrive at a point where overt, direct Bumiputera preference
is no longer necessary. The popular notion of need-based affirmative
action as a systemic alternative is misguided and unhelpful; moving forward requires clarity and coherence. The fading momentum of
progress and declining efficacy of various programs in recent decades,
as discussed above, call for affirmative action to be made more effective — in order that Bumiputera preferential treatment in its current forms can be rolled back. Only then can the majority be sufficiently empowered and transformational aspirations of inclusiveness
be realized.

## References

Abu Samad, M. F. (2002). *Bumiputeras in the Corporate Sector: Three
    Decades of Performance, 1970–2000.* CEDER Research Reports Series,
    No. 1.
Aihara, A. (2009). Paradoxes of higher education reforms: Implications
    on the Malaysian middle class. *International Journal of Asia-Pacific
    Studies,* 5(1), pp. 81–113.
Anand, S. (1981). *Inequality and Poverty in Malaysia: Measurement and
    Decomposition.* Oxford University Press, Oxford.
Andaya, B. W. and L. Y. Andaya (2001). *A History of Malaysia.* University
    of Hawai'i Press, Honolulu.
Centre for Public Policy Analysis (CPPS) (2006). *Corporate Equity Distri-
    bution: Past Trends and Future Policy.* CPPS, Kuala Lumpur.
Chakravarty, S. P. and R. Abdul-Hakim (2005). Ethnic nationalism and
    income distribution in Malaysia. *The European Journal of Development
    Research,* 17(2), pp. 270–288.
Cheong, K.-C., V. Selvaratnam, and K.-L. Goh (2011). Education and
    human capital formation. In *Malaysian Economy: Unfolding Growth*

*and Social Change*, R. Rasiah (ed.), Oxford University Press, Petaling Jaya, pp. 159–184.

Department of Statistics (various years). *Labour Force Survey Report*. Government Printer, Kuala Lumpur.

Embong, A. R. (1996). Social transformation, the state and the middle classes in post-independence Malaysia. *Southeast Asian Studies*, 34(3), pp. 56–79.

Faaland, J., J. R. Parkinson, and R. Saniman (1990). *Growth and Ethnic Inequality: Malaysia's New Economic Policy*. Hurst, London.

Fryer Jr, R. G. and G. Loury (2005). Affirmative action and its mythology. *Journal of Economic Perspectives*, 19(3), pp. 147–162.

Gomez, E. T. and K. S. Jomo (1999). *Malaysia's Political Economy: Power, Profits, Patronage*. Cambridge University Press, Cambridge.

Guan L. H. (2005). Affirmative Action in Malaysia, *Southeast Asian Affairs 2005*, pp. 211–228.

Guan L. H. (2013). Racial citizenship and higher education in Malaysia. In *The New Economic Policy in Malaysia: Affirmative Action, Ethnic Inequalities and Social Justice*, E. T. Gomez and J. Saravanamuttu (eds.), NUS Press, ISEAS and SIRD, Singapore and Petaling Jaya, pp. 235–261.

International Labour Organization (ILO) (2007). *Equality at Work: Tackling the Challenges*, ILO Conference 96th Session, Report I(B), ILO, Geneva.

Jamaludin, F. (2003). Malaysia's new economic policy: Has it been a success? In *Boundaries of Clan and Color: Transnational Comparisons of Inter-Group Disparity*, W. Darity and A. Deshpande (eds.), Routledge, London and New York, pp. 152–174.

Jesudason, J. V. (1989). *Ethnicity and the Economy*. Oxford University Press, Singapore.

Jomo, K. S. (2004). *The New Economic Policy and Interethnic Relations in Malaysia*. Identities, Conflict and Cohesion Programme Paper No. 7, UNRISD, Geneva.

Lee, H.-A. (2012). Affirmative action in Malaysia: Education and employment outcomes since the 1990s. *Journal of Contemporary Asia*, 42(2), pp. 230–254.

Lee, H.-A. (2014a). Affirmative action: hefty measures, mixed outcomes, muddled thinking. *Routledge Handbook on Contemporary Malaysia*, Meredith L. Weiss (ed.), New York, Routledge, pp. 162–176.

Lee, H.-A. (2014b). Affirmative action regime formation in Malaysia and South Africa. *Journal of Asian and African Studies*. Published online 5 October 2014. DOI: 10.1177/0021909614550895.

Leete, R. (2007). *From Kampung to Twin Towers: 50 Years of Economic and Social Development.* Petaling Jaya, Oxford Fajar.

Lim, H. H. (2013). Public service and ethnic restructuring under the new economic policy. In *The New Economic Policy in Malaysia: Affirmative Action, Ethnic Inequalities and Social Justice*, E. T. Gomez and J. Saravanamuttu (eds.), NUS Press, ISEAS and SIRD, Singapore and Petaling Jaya, pp. 175–203.

Malaysia (1971). *Second Malaysia Plan, 1971–1975.* Government Printer, Kuala Lumpur.

Malaysia (1996). *Seventh Malaysia Plan, 1996–2000.* Government Printer, Kuala Lumpur.

Malaysia (2001). *Eighth Malaysia Plan, 2001–2005.* Government Printer, Kuala Lumpur.

Malaysia (2006). *Ninth Malaysia Plan, 2006–2010.* Government Printer, Kuala Lumpur.

Malaysia (2010). *Tenth Malaysia Plan, 2011–2015.* Government Printer, Kuala Lumpur.

National Economic Advisory Council (NEAC) (2009). *New Economic Model — Part 1.* NEAC, Putrajaya.

Ooi, K. B. (2013). The new economic policy and the centralisation of power. In *The New Economic Policy in Malaysia: Affirmative Action, Ethnic Inequalities and Social Justice.* E. T. Gomez and J. Saravanamuttu (eds.), NUS Press, ISEAS and SIRD, Singapore and Petaling Jaya, pp. 317–334.

Puthucheary, M. (1978). *The Politics of Administration: The Malaysian Experience.* Kuala Lumpur, Oxford University Press.

Salih, K. and Z. A. Yusof (1989). Overview of the NEP and framework for a post-1990 economic policy. *Malaysian Management Review*, 24, pp. 13–61.

Sato, M. (2005). Education, ethnicity and economics: Higher education reforms in Malaysia, 1957–2003. *Nagoya University of Commerce and Business Journal of Language Culture and Communication*, 7(1), pp. 73–88.

Snodgrass, D., Z. A. Yusof, and I. Shari (2003). *Managing Economic Growth and Ethnic Diversity: Malaysia, 1970–1990.* Harvard Institute for International Development, Cambridge, MA.

Tan, J. (2008). *Privatization in Malaysia: Regulation, Rent-seeking and Policy Failure.* Routledge, London and New York.

Tan, Y. S. and S. R. Raman (2009). The Transformation from Elitist to Mass Higher Education in Malaysia: Problems and Challenges. CenPRIS Working Paper 101/09, Universiti Sains Malaysia.

Teik K. B. (2005). *Ethnic Structure, Inequality and Governance in the Public Sector: Malaysian Experiences.* Democracy, Governance and Human Rights Programme Paper No. 20, UNRISD, Geneva.

Torii, T. (2003). The mechanism for state-led creation of Malaysia's middle classes. *The Developing Economies*, 41(2), pp. 221–242.

Weisskopf, T. E. (2004). *Affirmative Action in the United States and India: A Comparative Perspective.* Routledge, London.

Yusof, Z. A. (2012). Affirmative action in Malaysia: An overview of progress and limitations. In *Affirmative Action in Plural Societies: International Experiences*, G. Brown, F. Stewart and A. Langer (eds.), Palgrave Macmillan, Basingstoke, pp. 128–150.

CHAPTER 7

# Vietnam: New Doi Moi: Strategy and Priorities of Development Policies for Lower Middle Income Country

Nguyen Cao Duc

*Vietnamese Academy of Social Sciences*
*14th floor, VASS Building No. 1, Lieu Giai St.,*
*Ba Dinh Dist., Hanoi, Vietnam*
*ngcaoduc@yahoo.com*

## 1. Overview of current economic situation in Vietnam

### 1.1. Current macroeconomic situation of Vietnam: 2007–2014

Although the global financial crisis occurred in 2007, it has its long-term negative effects on many countries' economic growth and particularly their macroeconomic stability. IMF (2012) showed that overcoming the serious consequences of this crisis through the process of restructuring the global economy generally and enhancing the capacity building of the effectively macroeconomic management in particular has been slow. In fact, many countries have been still faced with their rising risks of macroeconomic instability and financial instability as well as economic stagnation.

Although Vietnam had been one of the fastest economic growth countries (with its growth rate of 8.8% per year in the period of 1992–1997) all over the world, Vietnam is not an exception in this post-global financial crisis because its macroeconomic instability in

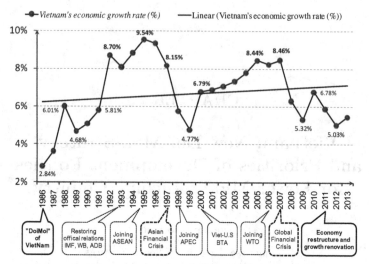

Figure 1. Overview of Vietnam's economic growth rate since 1986 of "Doi Moi."

*Source*: GSO (2014) Statistical Yearbook of Vietnam 2013, Statistical Publishing House, Hanoi; GSO (2013) Statistical Yearbook of Vietnam 2012, Statistical Publishing House, Hanoi.

company with the low economic growth has been done seriously since the year of 2007 (Figure 1).

In reality, Vietnam's economy has not only its declining tendency in the economic growth rate (on average from 7.63% per year in the period of 2001–2007 to 5.87% per year in the period of 2008–2012) but also comes with its rising trends of the seriously macroeconomic instability in the same period. For example, the ratio of the budget deficit to GDP and the ratio of the trade deficit to GDP in Vietnam were recorded respectively at 5.48% and 8.68% per year in the whole period of 2007–2012 (compared with 4.87% and 5.35% per year in the 2001–2006 period) (GSO, 2004, 2010, 2012, and 2014). Besides, the inflation rate was still high reaching double digits of 12.62% per year in the 2007–2012 period (compared with 5.38% per year in the period of 2001–2006) (Duc, 2014b). The most noteworthy point here is that the relative volatility of Vietnam's fundamentally macroeconomic indicators in the post-World Trade Organization (WTO) period has become much higher than that of the previous periods (the standard deviation of Vietnam's economic growth rate, the ratio of budget deficit to GDP, the ratio of the trade deficit to GDP, and inflation rate rose quickly from 0.63; 0.07; 2.25; and 3.35 in the 2001–2006 period to higher levels of 1.24; 0.91; 7.42; and 5.57 in the 2007–2012 period, respectively) (Duc, 2014a; GSO, 2006, 2008).

## 1.2. Brief introduction of three biggest challenges of Vietnam

Since joining WTO (in November 2006), Vietnam has already faced three biggest challenges, namely the low labor productivity, the low economic efficiency, and the low competitiveness compared with that of many Asian countries in the same period. Thus, it is necessary and urgent for Vietnam to restructure the economy and renovate the economic growth model to address these seriously structural weaknesses, overcome such biggest challenges, and avoid the middle-income trap in the future (Duc, 2012, 2014a, 2014b).

## 2. The process of Doi Moi policy and its evaluation and challenges

## 2.1. The objective and content of Doi Moi policy in Vietnam

First of all, the Doi Moi policy since 1986 should be reviewed thoroughly in order to draw some useful lessons for effectively restructuring the economy and renovating the economic growth model in the post-global financial crisis period. The overall objective of the Sixth Congress Party of Vietnam consists of the two key parts, namely (i) to stabilize the real situation in all social-economic aspects in the first stage of Vietnam's transition road to the socialism, (ii) and establish the necessary precondition for the promotion of Vietnam's industrialization in the next stage. After that, the Sixth Congress determined its five socio-economic specific objectives as follows: (i) Domestic production mainly for enough consumption and partly for accumulation, (ii) Initial creation of a suitable economic structure to develop production, (iii) Construction and completion of a new production relations in line with the nature and development level of the productive forces, (iv) Creation of some good changes in social aspect, (v) Consolidation of the need to strengthen national defense and security (CPV, 1987, 1991).

The Sixth Congress of the Communist Party of Vietnam (CPV) mapped out Renovation policy in 1986. The content of Vietnam's Renovation policy had six main parts, namely (i) Economic renovation policy; (ii) Social policy implementation; (iii) Defense and security; (iv) Foreign Affairs; (v) Implementation of Socialist democracy and improvement of the operation of the State and the people's organizations; (vi) Communist Party in the renovation. In this research paper, we would like to focus totally on analyzing the Economic renovation policy or "Doi Moi" policy only in the economic aspect.

The economic renovation policy consists of the four main parts, namely (1) Rearrangement of the (economic) production structure, and adjustment of investment structure as well as implementation focused mainly on the objectives of the three economic programs (Food Production Programme, Consumer Goods Production Programme and Export Commodities Production Programme); (2) Implementation of the multi-sector economic policy; (3) Renewal of economic management mechanism; (4) Expansion and improvement of the efficiency of foreign economic activity (CPV, 1987 and 1991).

## 2.2. Performance of Doi Moi policy in Vietnam

— *Renovation of economic development thinking of the CPV*: One of the most important factors of Vietnam's Doi Moi policy was that the renovation of the economic development thinking of the Vietnamese Communist Party has moved from the old perception of "*the centrally-planned economy*" to the new conception of "*Vietnam's multi-sector economy is a typical characteristic of the transition period*" at Vietnam's 6th National Congress, and further confirmed at Vietnam's 7th National Congress "*initially formed a multi-sector commodity economy under a market mechanism with the State management.*" One of the typical examples of the renovation of economic development thinking is the official enactment of Vietnam's Company Law (issued January 2, 1991) and Law on Private Enterprises (issued January 2, 1991). The renovation of the economic development thinking of the Vietnamese Communist Party from the centrally-planned economy to the market-oriented economy has played a key role not only in enhancing the resource mobilization efficiency, allocation efficiency, and utilization efficiency but also in forming the necessary legal grounds in effective support of transition from the state-dominated commodity economy to the multi-sector commodity economy under a market mechanism with the State management (Duc, 2012, 2014a, 2014b, 2015a).

— *Liberalization of the prices*: The official enactment of Decision No. 217-HDBT (on November 14, 1987) on planning renovation policy and socialist business accounting for SOEs gave the production and business autonomy for state enterprise in the direction that SOEs must implement the cost accounting, take account of the self-financing and had no state subsidies to cover their business losses. Basically, this Decision forced the majority of SOEs to adjust the official prices of their products to reflect their production real cost and thereby became closer to the market prices (mainly on the basis of the market-oriented price mechanism under the State management). Moreover, the official enactment of Decision No. 209A-HDBT (on November 3, 1987) on the activity transformation of the current food industry to Socialist business accounting clearly became a turning point for enhancing the liberalization of the domestic prices of the food commodities with the aim of better reflecting the production real cost as well as closer to the free market prices.

In particular, the official enactment of Decision No. 231/HDBT (on December 31, 1987) relating to shifting the material branch to the accounting of business cost and reorganization of the materials business helped Vietnam's multi-sector economy to move from the subsidized price of the material branch (based on the administrative pricing system) to business price of taking account of enough real cost on the basis of the market-oriented price mechanism. Besides, the official enactment of Decision No. 90-HDBT on 24 May in 1988 limited significantly the necessary product list with their officially basic price or the basic price frame determined completely by the

Table 1. Official retail "business" prices, and free market prices: 1988–1989 (in VND).

|  | Official "Business" prices | | Free market prices | |
| --- | --- | --- | --- | --- |
|  | June 1988 | June 1989 | June 1988 | June 1989 |
| Rice* (kg) | 50 | 530–550 | 450 | 550 |
| Pork (kg) | 3,500 | 5,200–5,300 | 4,300 | 5,500 |
| Sea Fish (kg) | 1,200 | 2,200 | 1,200 | 2,200 |
| Kerosene* (liter) | 180 | 600–700 | 240 | 600–700 |
| Gasoline** (liter) | 360 | 750 | 450 | 800 |
| Cement** (kg) | 110 | 200–210 | 120 | 210–220 |
| Steel** (6 mm) | 500 | 1,200 | 800 | 1,200 |

*Source*: World Bank (WB) (1990).
*Notes*: (*) Official business prices shown for these products are the ration prices for periods when the items were still subject to ration. The ration system was eliminated in January 1989 for all items except rice and kerosene. The ration system for kerosene was eliminated in June 1989. (**) Official business prices shown for these items are the prices for sales to farmers.

State in the whole economy (these limited product number was really necessary for the people's life and production). As a matter of fact, the domestic prices of almost all of the agricultural and industrial commodities as well as services have been basically liberalized since 1989 (except for some goods specified clearly in the Decision No. 90-HDBT) (Table 1).

The space of Vietnam's price liberalization had obtained a greater progress than that of many socialist countries in Eastern Europe during the transitional process to the market-based economy. Basically, the liberalization of the price in the year of 1989 helped Vietnam's economy to improve significantly the resource mobilization efficiency, allocation efficiency, and utilization efficiency in line with the market mechanism under the management of the State (Duc, 2012, 2014a, 2014b, 2015a).

— *Liberalization of the distribution and circulation*: The performance of Doi Moi policy in Vietnam had been done gradually through many small economic reforms. For example, one of them was the official enactment of Decision No. 80-CT (on March 11, 1987) to eliminate all the established control checkpoints of goods and services on the roads and rivers. This Decision helped Vietnam to positively open the liberalization of the distribution and circulation of commodity in the whole country and resulted in the significant increase in Vietnam's retail sales of goods and services from 0.33 billion of VND in 1986 to 7,233 billion of VND in 1988 (equivalently 21,918 times higher than that in 1986). In other words, there was a remarkable achievement on the rising growth rate of Vietnam's retail sales of goods and services (at current prices) from −48.7% in 1986 to 397.6% in 1988. In fact, this Decision No. 80-CT helped all the multi-sector economy to expand the retail sales of goods and services (the retail sales growth of both the State sector and the Non-State sector rose extraordinarily from −48.3% and −49.2% in 1986 to 322.1% and 481.1% in 1988, respectively). In general, this Decision made a vital contribution to increasing the domestic trade, thereby improving the domestic demand significantly.

— *International economic integration with trade and investment liberalization*: On the one hand, the government had taken the initiative to implement the open-door economic policy to help transform Vietnam's economy from a heavily self-sufficient economy to a multi-sector commodity economy" under a market mechanism with the State management. For example, Vietnam established its diplomatic relations with the European Union (EU) in October 1990, normalized its relations with China in May 1991, signed its cooperative economic and trade agreements with EU in December 1992, restored and normalized its relations with IMF, WB and ADB in October 1993, became a full member of ASEAN in July 1995, joined Asia-Pacific Economic Cooperation (APEC) in November 1998, signed its Bilateral Trade Agreement (BTA) with the United States in July 2000, and became the official member of the WTO in November 2006. In fact, Vietnam's deeper and more comprehensive international economic integration has played a key role not only in promoting the trade liberalization but also in enhancing the investment liberalization as well as in putting higher pressure on the domestic economic reforms. On the other hand, Vietnam's trade liberalization since Doi Moi had been done not only by removing the constraints on the trade outside the Council of Mutual Economic Assistance

(CMEA) but also by loosening the State's controls on the export and import activities to the reasonable levels of the tariff-based trade management according to the market mechanism. In fact, the trade liberalization had been clearly reflected by the issuance of Decision No. 193/HDBT on 23 December in 1988 *"on commercial and services business in the domestic market"* and Decision No. 64/HDBT on 10 June in 1989 *"on the organization of managing the export-import business activities."* Thereby, almost all of the domestic enterprises had been encouraged officially to perform their commodity and services export to the convertible area in line with their financial choice in the year of 1989. Moreover, after deciding to unify the multiple exchange rate system in the year of 1989, the State Bank of Vietnam had decided to carry out devaluating the exchange rate of VND against USD with the aim of being closer significantly to the free market exchange rate. This great devaluation of VND against USD in 1989 helped Vietnam to improve remarkably its trade balance of goods and services. Besides, Vietnam's investment liberalization had been first initiated by the open-door policy and next by the official enactment of the Law on Foreign Investment in Vietnam (December 29, 1987). The open-door policy, international economic integration as well as liberalization of trade and investment has helped Vietnam expand its trade and investment, enhance technology transfer, increase the resources mobilization-allocation-utilization efficiency, improve the labor productivity and competitiveness, while help to improve the balance of payments and reduce the key macroeconomic imbalances.

— *Agricultural reform*: On the one hand, the agricultural reform had started with the enactment of the Land Law in the year of 1987. This is the first step in the institutional reform in the agricultural sector. One of the most important features of this Land Law is that it helped to setup the long-term legal ground for unifying the State's management of Vietnam's land areas. However, it had not resulted in the expected outcomes as the policy makers in the process of carrying out this Law in the whole country. Next, the enactment of Resolution No. 10-NQ/TW (on April 5, 1988) on renovation of management in agriculture has created a turning point in transforming Vietnam from a country that had to import a lot of rice (on average 0.220 million tons of rice per year in the period of 1986–1988) to become a major rice exporter in the world (the average export 1.338 million tons of rice per year in the period of 1989–1991). There are two fundamental reasons for Vietnam's obtaining the great achievement in the agriculture reform generally and in the rice export particularly. The first reason is that Resolution No. 10-NQ/TW gave both the co-operatives and farming families the more flexibly economic freedom in the direction of firstly recognizing the new basic economic unit of the farming family rather than the old one of the co-operatives. Therefore, it had already encouraged almost all of the farmers in the rural areas to make their special effort to invest in and produce the agricultural products in line with the market mechanism under the management of the State. The second reason is that Resolution No. 10-NQ/TW had become to perform much more effectively in the market-based economy than that in the centrally-planned economy. Before that, the Directive No. 100 (on January 13, 1981) on piecework contracting to laborers' groups and individual laborers in agricultural co-operatives had been not successful when it had done totally in the centrally-planned economy. In reality, the market mechanism in the market-based economy of Vietnam regularly become much more effectively in enhancing the resource mobilization efficiency, allocation efficiency, and utilization efficiency than that of the State at the same periods.

— *State-owned enterprises (SOEs) reform*: The reorganization, innovation and improvement of the efficiency of Vietnam's SOEs in the period 1986–1989 had focused on implementing the business accounting, and establishing higher autonomy in the production organization and business activities as well as decentralizing the SOEs management between the local and central authorities. For example, the official enactment of Decision No. 217-HDBT (on November 14, 1987) *"on planning renovation policy and socialist business accounting for state-run enterprises"* gave these enterprise the bigger autonomy of the production and business in implementing the cost accounting and taking account of the self-financing as well as covering their full business losses on the basis of the market-oriented mechanism under the management of the State. Although the SOEs reform in this period had been seen to be one of the important issues related to liberating the labor force to further concretize the Renovation policy of our Party initiated since 1986, the SOEs reorganization, innovation results in the period 1986–1989 were considered as unsuccessful. The number of Vietnam's SOEs in 1989 rose by almost 2 times (up to 12,084 SOEs) as compared to that of 1986 and operated with their very low efficiency (Duc, 2015b).

In the period of 1990–1991, Vietnam's SOEs reform was done in the way of the "pilot" equitization of *"just try it, just to correct"* to continue to reform the SOEs management mechanism and overcome the widespread establishment phenomenon of SOEs at the local level in the same period. For instance, Decision No. 144/HDBT *"on regulating the financial management of state-run enterprises"* was officially issued (on May 10, 1990) to continue to improve the management mechanism of Vietnam's state-run enterprises, and overcome the basic weaknesses in the financial management of these state-run enterprises under the market-oriented mechanism. In addition, Decision 315-HDBT was issued on September 1, 1990, on correcting and reorganization of production and business in the State economic sector to gradually establish the market-based competition environment and improve the efficiency of the state-run enterprises. Of which, it gave an emphasis that the state-run enterprises made their consecutive losses in the long run, did not perform their business tasks, and had no real ability to pay their full debt as well as cannot be overcome by the recommended measures such as shifting the production direction, changing the main commodity, as well as correcting and reorganizing the production and business with the support of their superiors could be officially declared closed down in line with the stipulated procedure of this Decision. Also, Decision 143-HĐBT (issued on May 10, 1990) mentioned to research and try the "pilot" equitization model by transforming some selected SOEs into the joint stock companies in Vietnam. Besides, Decree No. 388/HĐBT was issued (on November 20, 1991) about regulating the establishment and dissolution of State enterprises to continue implementing the policy of reorganization and innovation of these

State enterprises in transition to market mechanism under the State management. As a result, it had rapidly reduced the number of SOEs to 9,832 enterprises on December 31, 1991, (or decreased by 2,465 enterprises compared with that of in 1990) and focused mainly in the key economic sectors (Duc, 2015b).

Vietnam's SOEs reform in the period 1992–1993 had been actively shifted to focus on innovating the SOEs management mechanisms associated with reorganizing the SOEs quantity and scale (to overcome the widespread establishment of the SOEs in the period 1986–1991, especially the local SOEs), and the "official" equitization of SOEs was done in 1992. For example, in order to amend some weaknesses of the Decree No. 388/HĐBT, the Decree No. 156/HĐBT was officially issued (on May 7, 1992) on regulations of the establishment and dissolution of Vietnam's State enterprises. In particular, the Decree No. 196/CT was issued (on June 5, 1992) to help significantly limits the discretion to allow the new establishment of Vietnam's state enterprises but having not sufficient condition under the tighter evaluation process. Additionally, the official enactment of Decision 202-CT (issued on June 8, 1992) on continuing the pilot transformation of some selected state enterprises into joint-stock companies in Vietnam made a contribution to reorganizing and innovating these State enterprises in line with the market mechanism under the State management. Consequently, the number of Vietnam's SOEs decreased rapidly from 9,300 enterprises on December 31 (1992) to 6,055 enterprises on December 31 (1993).

The reorganization, innovation and improvement of the efficiency of Vietnam's SOEs in the period of 1994–1997 had focused not just on the "pilot" equitization (mostly small-scale SOEs number) and reorganization of medium and large-scale SOEs, but more importantly, focused primarily on improving the business corporate governance with the aim of enhancing the economic efficiency of SOEs, boosting the competitiveness of SOEs, strengthening the state management role of SOEs, the first step to distinguish the SOEs with the social SOEs operating public utility, and actively expanding the SOEs equitization since 1996. For example, the official enactment of the Decision No. 90/TTg on restructuring of SOEs (dated March 7,

1994) and the Decision No. 91/TTg on experimental establishment
of the number of State corporations (dated March 7, 1994) as well
as the Law on State Enterprises (dated April 20, 1995) helped to
set up the consistently legal framework for reorganizing, innovating
and improving the efficiency of Vietnam's SOEs, particularly State
corporations. Consequently, the number of Vietnam's SOEs reduced
slowly from 6,264 enterprises in 1994 (in which the local SOEs number accounted for 68.8% of the total number of Vietnam's SOEs in
the same period) down to 6,020 enterprises in 1996 (Duc, 2015b).

## 2.3. Evaluation of Vietnam's Doi Moi policy

*Firstly, Doi Moi policy has a significantly positive impact on reduc-
ing Vietnam's macroeconomic instability.* In the period of 1986–1991,
Vietnam's macroeconomic instability index obtained its highest average value of 0.49 per year (0.59 per year in the period of 1986–1988).
Of which, the ratio of the budget deficit to GDP and the ratio of
the trade deficit to GDP as well as inflation rate in Vietnam were
recorded respectively at 5.75% and 8.9% as well as 253% per year in
the period of 1986–1991 (its unemployment rate of 13.8% per year
in the same period). However, Vietnam's macroeconomic instability index decreased quickly to average value of 0.3 per year in the
period of 1992–1997. Of which, the ratio of the budget deficit and
trade deficit to GDP as well as inflation rate in Vietnam were respectively at 3.33% and 8.4% as well as 253% per year in the period of
1992–1997 (its unemployment rate of 8.27% per year). Thus, Doi Moi
policy played a key role in helping Vietnam transform from it's the
most seriously macroeconomic instability in the period of 1986–1991
to the low macroeconomic instability in the period of 1992–1997.
More importantly, it helped Vietnam obtain the volatility of these
key macroeconomic indicators in 1992–1997 much lower than that of
the previous period.

   *Secondly, Doi Moi policy has a great and positive impact on
improving Vietnam's economic growth.* In the period of implementing Doi Moi policy (1986–1991), Vietnam's economy had not only
the lowest average annual GDP growth rate of about 4.68% per year
but also had the highest volatility value of approximately 1.243 per

year (however, the difference value between the maximum and minimum values is relatively small, about 1.129 in the same period). In the period of 1992–1997, Vietnam's economy had obtained both the highest average annual GDP growth rate of 8.77% per year and the lowest volatility value of about 0.598 per year (the difference value between the maximum and minimum values is relatively reasonable, about 1.462 in the same period). It means that Doi Moi policy had helped Vietnam became one of the most successful countries with its highest economic growth all over the world in the period of 1992–1997 (Duc, 2012).

*Thirdly, Doi Moi policy has made an important contribution to shifting swiftly Vietnam's economic structure towards industrialization and modernization.* In reality, the share of agriculture, forestry and fishing sector in Vietnam's gross domestic product (GDP) at current price decreased significantly from 41.75% per year in the period of 1986–1989 to 28.66% per year in the period of 1992–1997, while the share of services sector in its GDP increased quickly from 32.22% per year to 42.08% per year in the same periods, respectively.

*Fourthly, Doi Moi policy has resulted in great achievements in Vietnam's social progress and poverty reduction particularly.* Doi Moi policy helped Vietnam obtained high economic growth, thereby stimulating its social progress and reducing poverty quickly. According to the WB's World Development Indicators (WDI), Vietnam's life expectancy at birth (years) increased significantly from 69.2 years in 1986 to 72.8 years in 1997 (and quickly to 75.6 years in 2012). Besides, according to UNDP, Vietnam's human development index (HDI) value also rose remarkably from 0.463 point in 1980 to 0.563 point in 2000 (and to 0.635 point in 2012). Besides, Vietnam's adjusted net enrollment rate at primary education (% of primary school age children) increased from 90.13% in 1990 to 97.9% in 1998 (and to 98.2% in 2012). Furthermore, Vietnam's percentage of population with access to improved water sources rose remarkably from about 61.6% in 1990 to 72.8% in 1997 (and sharply to 95% in 2012). In particular, Vietnam's poverty headcount ratio at $PPP 1.25 a day (% of population) decreased significantly from 63.76% in 1993 to 49.36% in 1998 (and to 2.44% in 2012).

## 2.4. Challenges of Doi Moi policy under Vietnam's new context

Although Vietnam has achieved great success to become a lower middle-income country since 2009 (WB, 2014), the GDP per capita growth of Vietnam have not been improved significantly and even lagged behind many Asian countries in the post-global financial crisis phase (a significant fall from 6.50% per year in the period of 2001–2007 to 4.77% per year in the period of 2008–2012 at constant price of 1994) (GSO, 2004, 2013). According to WB's WDI, Vietnam's GDP per capita was about 4.912 thousand \$PPP in 2012 (at constant 2011 international \$PPP). Hence, it was 15.2 times lower than that of Singapore, about 4.46 times lower than Malaysia's, 2.80 times lower than in Singapore's, and 1.80 times lower than Indonesia's, as well as 1.22 times lower than Philippines'. One of the most important reasons for Vietnam's relatively low GDP per capita lagged behind many ASEAN countries is that Vietnam has faced three biggest challenges since joining WTO (in November 2006), namely the low labor productivity, and the low economic efficiency, as well as the low competitiveness (Table 2).

## 3. New renovation policy: its objectives, contents, and evaluation

### 3.1. Vietnam's new renovation policy

So as to address the seriously internal structural weaknesses and overcome the biggest long-term challenges as well as avoid the middle-income trap risk in the future, the 11th National Congress of the CPV in January 2011 showed clearly that *"the renovation of the growth model and the restructuring of the economy"* has been regarded as one of the most important solutions of Vietnam's economic development strategy in the period of 2011–2020. The renovation of the economic growth model and the restructuring of the economy can be considered as the beginning of Vietnam's "new" economic renovation policy.

Afterwards, this very important subject of the renovation of the growth model and the restructuring of the economy were discussed

Table 2. Vietnam's productivity, competitiveness, and ICOR in the 2007–2012 period.

| | Productivity (at constant 1990 $PPP) | Productivity (times, Vietnam = 1) | GCI (value) | GCI (rank) | ICOR$_t$ | I/GDP (%) | Economic growth rate (%) |
|---|---|---|---|---|---|---|---|
| Singapore | 48,031 | 8.32 | 5.58 | 2 | 4.80 | 27.25 | 5.68 |
| Malaysia | 24,253 | 4.20 | 5.00 | 23 | 5.16 | 23.97 | 4.65 |
| Thailand | 15,894 | 2.75 | 4.54 | 37 | 6.30 | 21.79 | 3.46 |
| Indonesia | 10,454 | 1.81 | 4.37 | 44 | 4.04 | 24.20 | 5.99 |
| Philippines | 8,278 | 1.43 | 4.09 | 71 | 3.71 | 18.54 | 5.00 |
| Vietnam | 5,785 | 1.00 | 4.15 | 69 | 6.75 | 42.52 | 6.30 |

*Source*: Author's estimates from the data of: WB (2015); World Economic Forum — WEF (2015).
*Notes*: Labor productivity is calculated by GDP per person employed at constant 1990 $PPP (according to the data of WDI by WB, 2015); and GCI is the global competitiveness index (WEF, 2015); and ICOR$_t$ is the incremental capital-output ratio at the year of $t$; and $I$ is the capital formulation of each country at that constant LCU; and ICOR$_{(t)} = [(I/\text{GDP})_t]/g_{(t)}$; and $g_{(t)}$ is the annual economic growth rate (Vietnam's economic growth rate $g_{(t)}$ and the gross capital formation at the constant 1994 price), and all are on average in the whole period of 2007–2012.

carefully in the third Conference of the 11th Party Central Committee in October 2011. After taking careful consideration, the third Conference of the 11th Party Central Committee had a firm decision: *"have to restructure the economy associated with renovating the growth model. These tasks are very large and complex, requiring the synchronization implemented in all economic industries and fields in the whole country and in local areas as well as in grassroots units for many years."*

To concretize the Party's guidelines on the renovation of the growth model and the restructuring of the economy, Prime Minister had issued Decision No. 339/QD-TTg on February 19, 2013 about *"Approving the overall scheme on restructuring the economy in association with transforming the growth model towards improving quality, efficiency and competitiveness during the 2013–2020 period."* This is a very important turning point in the process of implementing Vietnam's new renovation policy.

The overall objectives of Vietnam's new renovation policy is demonstrated clearly in Decision No. 339/QD-TTg as follows: *"To implement the restructuring of the economy in association with the transformation of the growth model under the suitable roadmap and steps so that by 2020, Vietnam basically form its economic growth model in depth, ensure the quality of growth, enhance the efficiency and competitiveness of the economy."* Of which, three specific objectives of Decision No. 339/QD-TTg are as follows:

(i) *"To complete socialist-oriented market economy institutions; to create a suitable, stable, and long-term incentives system, especially tax priorities and other measures to promote investment; to promote the allocation and use of the essential social resources under market mechanism in industries and products with their competitive advantages; to raise the labor productivity, total factor productivity as well as competitiveness.*

(ii) *To form and develop a rational economic structure on the basis of improving and upgrading the development level of economical industries, fields, regions; to develop economical industries and fields using high technology, creating high added value, and step by step replacing industries with low technology and low added value to become the key economic industries.*

(iii) *To step by step consolidate the internal forces of the economy; to take initiative in international integration and consolidate the national position in the international arena; to maintain politic stability;to assure national security as well as social order and security"* (*Decision No. 339/QD-TTg*).

The general contents of Vietnam's new renovation policy was first demonstrated by the 11th Party Congress of the CPV as follows: *"To transform the growth model from mainly the width development to harmonious development between the width and depth; combine the scale expansion with the emphasis on improving the quality, efficiency, and sustainability. To implement the restructuring of the economy, focusing on restructuring the economic industries and services suitable for the regions; to promote the restructuring of enterprises and the adjustment of business strategy; to quickly increase the domestic value, added value, and competitiveness of products, businesses and the whole economy; to develop the knowledge economy.*"

As regards the restructuring of the economy, the third Conference of the 11th Party Central Committee in 2011 showed the main contents of Vietnam's new renovation policy: *"In the next 5 years, need to focus on three most important areas: Restructuring the investment with a focus on public investment; Restructuring the financial markets with a focus on restructuring the commercial banking system and financial institutions; Restructuring the state enterprises with a focus on economic groups and state corporations."*

In particular, the main contents of Vietnam's new renovation policy had been described in detail in Decision No. 339/QD-TTg in 2013 about *"Approving the overall scheme on restructuring the economy in association with transforming the growth model towards improving quality, efficiency and competitiveness during the 2013–2020 period."* In addition to the transformation of the growth model under the reasonable roadmap and steps in order to basically form its economic growth model in depth by 2020, Decision No. 339/QD-TTg had showed clearly three most important focuses of the restructuring of Vietnam's economy, namely the restructuring of the investment with a focus on public investment,[1] the restructuring of the financial markets with a focus on restructuring the commercial banking

---

[1]With three following important contents: (i) *To mobilize the rational resources for development investment; to keep total investment of about 30–35% GDP; to maintain the key balances of the economy at a suitable level such as: balance between saving and investment and consumption, fiscal balance, trade balance, balance of payment, public debts and foreign debts of nation, etc.* (ii) *To maintain a suitable state investment ratio of 35–40% total investment; to gradually raise the annual saving from the State budget for investment; to spend about 20–25% of the total budget expenditure on development investment. To renovate basically mechanism of capital allocation and utilization management; to overcome the spread, dispersed, and wasteful investments; to raise the state investment efficiency.* (iii) *To expand the utmost scope and chance for the investment of the private sector, particularly the domestic private sector. To encourage and facilitate for the private investment in the field of the infrastructure development and in the development of industries and products with their competitive advantages, development potential, and dynamic economic areas (Decision No. 339/QD-TTg).*

system and financial institutions,[2] the restructuring of the enterprises with a focus on economic groups and state corporations in Vietnam.[3]

---

[2]With four main contents: (i) *In the period of 2013–2015, to concentrate on making the financial situation of credit institutions to become healthy; before of all, to make a concentration on handling bad debts of the credit institutions system and each credit institution; to concentrate on developing main business activities, ensuring solvency and payment, and sustainable development; to concentrate on handling cross-ownership status and increasing the transparency in the business activities of the credit institutions.* (ii) *To basically, thoroughly, and comprehensively restructure the system of credit institutions so that by 2020 to develop multifunction credit institution system in the direction of modernization, safe operation, sustainable efficiency with diversified structure on ownership, sizes, and types, more competitiveness based on the technological foundation and advanced banking governance in line with the international practices and standards to better satisfy the demand for financial and banking services of the economy.* (iii) *To enhance the role, dominant position, and market leadership of Vietnam's credit institutions; to ensure state commercial banks and commercial banks with the dominant state shares are really a key and fundamental force in the system of Vietnam's credit institutions. To strive for establishing at least from one to two state commercial banks or with the dominant state shares have regional qualification on its sizes, governance, technology, and competitiveness by the end of 2015.* (iv) *To recheck, assess, classify all credit institutions so as to have rational measures to handle jont-stock commercial banks, financial companies, finance leasing companies, and other credit institutions; of which to concentrate first on the weak credit institutions or credit institutions with their serious violation of the law regulations; to strictly supervise the process of making and implementing the approved restructuring plan of credit institutions. To strengthen the safety regulations; reorganize the operations of people's credit funds and micro credit institutions; to consolidate and handle the weak organizations; to create favorable conditions for these credit institutions to conduct their normal business operations; to continue to develop the sizes, governance capacity, and liquidity safety. To create favorable conditions for foreign credit institutions to conduct a fair competition in Vietnam; to encourage these foreign institutions to have cooperation and linkage with Vietnam's credit institutions in new product development, the governance renovation, and the banking modernization, and especially in handling the difficult issues of Vietnam's credit institutions in the process of restructuring the credit institutions (*Decision No. 339/QD-TTg*).

[3]With three key contents as follows: (i) *To implement the classification and reorganization of SOEs in the direction of concentrating on the main fields including the defense industry, the natural monopoly industries and fields or industries providing essential goods and services, the hi-tech and basic industries with their great pervasiveness; to accelerate the equitization, and diversify the ownership*

## 3.2. Evaluation of Vietnam's new renovation policy

*Firstly, Vietnam's new renovation policy has played a fundamental role in effectively fighting against the seriously macroeconomic instability so as to establish the solid macroeconomic stability foundation in the medium term.* In fact, the process of restructuring the economy and renovating the economic growth model in Vietnam *has a positive and significant impact on reducing* the seriously macroeconomic instability quickly. For example, the annual value of Vietnam's macroeconomic instability index had decreased quickly from 0.576 in 2008 to 0.492 in 2011 and to 0.433 in 2013 (Duc, 2014b). In particular, Vietnam's new renovation policy made a significant contribution to establish and ensure the key macroeconomic balance of the whole economy. For instance, the annual inflation rate of Vietnam declined significantly from its double digit of 19.89% in 2008 to 18.13% in 2011 and sharply to 6.04% in 2013 (Duc, 2014a, 2015). Besides, the ratio of the balance trade to GDP diminished remarkably from −15.21% in 2008 to −4.22% in 2011 and to +4.88% in 2013. Moreover, the WEF had a similar remark in relation to Vietnam's macroeconomic stability index in the same period. For example, Vietnam's macroeconomic stability index value increased quickly from 3.864 in 2008

---

*of state enterprises that the State does not need to hold 100% ownership. For each economic group and state corporation, to implement the restructuring of the investment portfolio and business lines with a focus on the main business lines; to accelerate the implementation in conformity with the market principles in the divestments of the state capital for investing in business lines that are not main business lines or not relate directly to main business lines and the state capital in joint-stock companies which the state does not need to hold itsdominant shares. (ii) To renovate, develop, and proceed to fully apply the modern governance framework in conformity with the good practices of the market economy for economic groups and state corporations. To strictly implement the law, state administrative rules, and market disciplines; to renovate the incentives system to encourage the SOE to operate in conformity with market mechanism and have a fair competition with different enterprises of the other economic sectors. (iii) To further accelerate the restructuring of and the improvement of the quality, efficiency, competitiveness of private enterprises; to encourage the establishment and development of private economic groups with their strong potential and competitiveness in overseas and domestic markets (Decision No. 339/QD-TTg).*

(ranking 112) to 4.164 in 2011 (ranking 106) and to 4.658 in 2013 (ranking 75).

*Secondly, Vietnam's new renovation policy has made a great contribution to improving the labor productivity generally and the total factor productivity particularly.* On the one hand, according to *"Vietnam Productivity Report: 2014"* by Vietnam National Productivity Institute, the process of restructuring the economy and renovating the economic growth model helped Vietnam to significantly improve its labor productivity growth rate from 3.06% in 2012 to 3.84% in 2013 and to 4.35% in 2014. On the other hand, according to *"Vietnam Productivity Report: 2014"* by Vietnam National Productivity Institute, of Vietnam's economic growth rate of about 6.24% per year in the year of 2011 (at constant 2010 price), the $K$ capital stock contributed 60.61%, the $L$ labor factor contributed 25.37%, and the TFP total factor productivity contributed 14.01%. In 2014, of Vietnam's economic growth rate of 5.98% per year, the contribution of K, L and TFP per year is 47.74%, 15.46%, and 36.81% respectively. Thus, in spite of the fact that Vietnam's economic growth model is basically the width growth model, the growth quality has been improved significantly in the process of restructuring the economy and renovating the growth model.

*Thirdly, Vietnam's new renovation policy has made a great contribution to its global competitiveness index.* In addition to the significant labor productivity improvement and TFP, Vietnam's incremental capital-output ratio ($ICOR_t$ based on the gross capital formulation and GDP at constant 2010 price) decreased quickly from 5.80 in 2012 to 5.62 in 2013 and to 5.23 in 2014. It means that Vietnam's investment efficiency has been basically improved in the process of implementing the new renovation policy. The significant improvement of the labor productivity and TFP as well as the investment efficiency has contributed much to enhancing Vietnam's competitiveness. According to the WEF, Vietnam's competitiveness index value had been improved from 4.03 in 2008 (ranking 75) to 4.18 in 2012 (ranking 70) and to 4.23 in 2013 (ranking 68). Therefore, the process of restructuring the economy and renovating the economic growth model helped Vietnam to improve its competitiveness.

### 3.3. Challenges of the new renovation under the new context

In the real process of implementing the new renovation policy, Vietnam has faced three most important challenges in the deeper and more widespread globalization context. The first fundamental challenge is that the annual public debt to GDP ratio in Vietnam has its quickly rising tendency, from 50.8% in 2012 to 54.2% in 2013 and sharply to 60.3% in 2014. According to Vietnamese government's public debt report to the Congress in 2015, this annual public debt to GDP ratio will be likely to obtain the forecasted level of 64% in 2015 and even to 64.9% in 2016, relatively nearest to Vietnam's public debt threshold of 65% of GDP, thereby having significantly negative impacts on the macroeconomic stability foundation, the government's credibility, and the adjustment room of the fiscal policy.

The second vital challenge in the performance process of New Doi Moi policy in Vietnam is that the real performance pace of restructuring of the economy (including the restructuring of the investment with a focus on the public investment, the restructuring of the financial markets with a focus on restructuring commercial banking system and financial institutions, as well as the restructuring of the enterprises with a focus on economic groups and state corporations) has been taken place slowly. Moreover, the pace of restructuring of the economy seems to be not well in line with that of renovating the economic growth model in the deeper and more widespread globalization context.

The third central challenge is that the slow renovation of modern economic development thinking of effectively handling the relationship between the state role and the market role in the socialist-oriented market economy. One of the most obvious examples is the government's slowly thinking renovation of reforming the SOEs in line with the full market mechanism with the aim of improving significantly the resource mobilization efficiency, the allocation efficiency, and the technique efficiency as well as the competitiveness.

### 3.4. Perspectives of the new renovation to avoid middle-income trap

In fact, because of being so clearly aware of these fundamental challenges in implementing the new renovation policy, Vietnam's government has been making its special effort to readjust its macroeconomic policies and structural reform pace since the middle of 2014. For example, the government has been paying much more attention to enhancing the current repayment ability and improving the efficiency of the public investments in line with the Law on Public Investment (on June 18, 2014) in all sectors of the whole country. In reality, although the annual public debt to GDP ratio in Vietnam in 2013–2016 is relative high, it is still below the public debt threshold of 65% of GDP set by the Congress. According to Vietnam's government report, these measurement will help to reduce the annual public debt to GDP ratio since 2017 and will reach the level of 60.2% in 2020. Moreover, the government has been making its special effort to accelerate the equitization of the SOEs attached closely with their modern corporate governance principles, especially transparency of information on SOEs since 2014. Besides, the government has been strengthening the faster pace of restructuring commercial banking system and financial institutions. Basically, the faster pace of restructuring the economy attached to the renovation of the economic growth model on the basis of the relatively macroeconomic stability foundation will enhance the long-term growth dynamics and improve the growth quality in the efficiency-driven stage of development, thereby help Vietnam's economy to maintain the sustainable economic growth prospects of about 6.5–7.0% per year in the period of 2016–2030 with the aim of avoiding the middle-income trap in the future.

### 4. Conclusion

Vietnam's Doi Moi policy since 1986 has been successful with the high economic growth and fast significant poverty reduction as well as higher HDI improvement under the market mechanism with the State management. On the one hand, the Doi Moi policy helped Vietnam to successfully transform from the centrally-planned economy to the multi-sector commodity economy under market mechanism with the State management in line with socialist orientation. On the other hand, the Doi Moi policy helped Vietnam to take advantage of its economic growth model that has been mainly on the basis of the width-based growth pattern with low-skilled and low-cost labor advantage as well as the natural resources-intensive inputs (only suitable for the *"factor-driven stage of development"*). Although the Doi Moi has helped Vietnam's economy to successfully transform from a low-income to a lower middle-income economy since 2009, the key dynamics of the renovation policy have been limited significantly. Therefore, the new renovation policy (considered as "new Doi Moi" policy) has been first mentioned in 2011 and really carried out since 2013 in the deeper and more widespread globalization context with the aim of creating the new economic growth model towards its higher efficiency, productivity, competitiveness based on the high-skilled labor, technology innovation, and inclusiveness (especially suitable for Vietnam's economy in transition to the *"efficiency-driven stage of development"*).

Thanks to the significantly positive impacts of really carrying out Vietnam's new renovation policy since 2013, the economy has gradually recovered and come to bounce back to the new and stable economic growth trajectory of about 6.5–7% per year in the period of 2016–2020. In fact, the process of restructuring the economy and renovating the economic growth model since 2013 has helped Vietnam reduce significantly the rising concerns over the falling TFP growth, the growing reliance of the growth model on the too high capital accumulation, and the seriously internal structural weaknesses, as well as these biggest challenges. Since 2014, under the significantly positive impacts of the new renovation policy, Vietnam's economy has created its important turning point in the *"transitional stage of development"* from the *"factor-driven stage of development"* to the *"efficiency-driven stage of development"* because the GDP per capita of Vietnam in 2014 is about 2.050 U.S. $ (on the basis of the WEF's international classification criteria). Therefore, the restructuring of the economy and the renovation of the growth model will not only helped Vietnam transform its economy from the lower middle-income economy to the upper middle-income economy in the long term but more important to help Vietnam to successfully avoid the middle-income trap risk in the future.

## References

Communist Party of Vietnam — CPV (1987). *Documents of the Seventh Party Congress.* The Truth Publishing House, Hanoi.

CPV (1991). *Documents of the Seventh Party Congress.* The Truth Publishing House, Hanoi.

Decision No. 339/QD-TTg of Prime Minster (2013). *Approving the overall scheme on restructuring the economy in association with transforming the economic growth model towards improving quality, efficiency, and competitiveness during the 2013–2020 period.* Available at http://www. chinhphu.vn/portal/page/portal/chinhphu/hethongvanban?class_id= 2&mode=detail&document_id=165844. (Accessed 2 February 2015).

General statistical Office — GSO (2004). *Statistical Yearbook of Vietnam 2003.* Statistical Publishing House, Hanoi.

GSO (2006). *Statistical Yearbook of Vietnam 2005.* Statistical Publishing House, Hanoi.

GSO (2008). *Statistical Yearbook of Vietnam 2007.* Statistical Publishing House, Hanoi.

GSO (2010). *Statistical Yearbook of Vietnam 2009.* Statistical Publishing House, Hanoi.

GSO (2012). *Statistical Yearbook of Vietnam 2011.* Statistical Publishing House, Hanoi.

GSO (2013). *Statistical Yearbook of Vietnam 2012.* Statistical Publishing House, Hanoi.

GSO (2014). *Statistical Yearbook of Vietnam 2013.* Statistical Publishing House, Hanoi.

International Monetary Fund — IMF (2012). *World Economic Outlook: Coping with High debt and Sluggish Growth.* International Monetary Fund, Washington, DC.

Nguyen Cao Duc (2012). Renovating the growth model in Vietnam in 2011–2020. *Vietnam Social Sciences,* Vietnamese Academy of Social Sciences, 150, 20–27.

Nguyen Cao Duc (2014a). Empirical relationship between macroeconomic instability and economic growth in Vietnam over the period 1986–2012. *Vietnam's Socio-Economic Development Review*, 78, 22–35.

Nguyen Cao Duc (2014b). Vietnam's macroeconomic instability after nearly 30 years of "DoiMoi" (Renewal). *Vietnam's Socio-Economic Development Review*, 79, 3–16.

Nguyen Cao Duc (2015a). Sources of Vietnam's economic growth after nearly 30 years of "DoiMoi" and policy implications. *Vietnam's Socio-Economic Development Review*, 80, 3–15.

Nguyen Cao Duc (2015b). Vietnam's state owned enterprises reforms since the year of 1986. *Vietnam's Socio-Economic Development Review*, 81, 3–10.

Vietnam National Productivity Institute (2014). *Vietnam Productivity Report: 2014*. Available at http://vnpi.vn/Desktop.aspx/News/Tin-noi-bat-topmenu/Bao_cao_Nang_suat_Viet_Nam_2014/ (accessed 1 March 2015).

World Bank — WB (2014). *Country and Lending Groups*. Available at http://data.worldbank.org/about/country-and-lending-groups (accessed 2 October 2014).

World Bank (WB) (1990). *Vietnam Stabilization and Structural Reforms: An Economic Report*. WB, Washington, DC.

World Bank (2015). World Development Indicators (WDI). Available at http://data.worldbank.org/products/wdi (accessed 10 March 2015).

World Economic Forum — WEF (2015). Competitiveness Dataset (XLS), Available at http://reports.weforum.org/global-competitiveness-report-2014–2015/economies/ (accessed 10 March 2015).

CHAPTER 8

# Thailand: How to Consolidate Social Security Systems: Universal Healthcare/Pension Systems

Worawan Chandoevwit

*Faculty of Management Science, Khon Kaen University*
*Thailand Development Research Institute*
*123 Mitraphab Rd., Muang 40002, Khon Kaen*
*cworaw@kku.ac.th,*
*worawan@tdri.or.th*

Tirnud Paichayontvijit* and Yos Vajragupta[†]

*Thailand Development Research Institute*
*565 Ramkhamhaeng Soi 39, Wangthonglang*
*Bangkok 10310, Thailand*
*\*tirnud@tdri.or.th*
*[†]yos@tdri.or.th*

The public health insurance and pension policies development in Thailand has developed in the shorter period compared to the other developing countries. The country's economic, employment environment and the bureaucracy have shaped Thailand's public health insurance and pension for elderly to the fragmented inefficient and unfair systems. Three public healthcare schemes provide unequal basic benefits package, receive unequal subsidy per head from the government, and pay to service providers using different mechanisms. People were treated according to the type of health insurance they are entitled to which could lead to unfair health treatments and outcomes.

The pension systems cover only one-third of working age population. The delay of an implementation of the new National Saving Fund and lack of portability of pension systems could make elderly end up with very low amount of pension. In this chapter, we recommend the harmonization of public health insurance and an implementation of saving for retirement policy. These policies will benefit Thailand during the anticipated demographic transition and improve its capital accumulation in the long-run.

## 1. Overview of the current economic situation in Thailand

Thailand is a middle-income country with a 10-year average GDP of 917 billion of $PPP and per capita income of $PPP 13,199. Thailand experienced the high growth rates of 8–13% annually in 1987–1995. It was the period that Thailand benefited from supportive external factors. In particular, the 1985 Plaza Accords effectively devalued USD and Thai Baht with respect to other major currencies that stimulated Thai export as well as the Foreign Direct Investment. The high growth also stemmed from the domestic factors such as high public and private investment. The government invested heavily on basic infrastructure. The investment by the private sector was shown from the boom in the real estate and stock exchange markets. Such environment down played the agriculture sector which used to share 23% of GDP in 1971–1980, but the share reduced by half in the following ten years (Table 1).

The high growth without strong institutions and economic foundations could not be sustained, especially when Thailand experienced with a series of shocks in terms of economic, political, and environmental. The economic shocks started with the Asian financial crisis in 1997, followed by the oil price shock in 2005, and the global financial

Table 1. Thailand's GDP and growth, 1980–2013.

|  | 1971–1980 | 1981–1990 | 1991–2000 | 2001–2010 | 2004–2013 |
|---|---|---|---|---|---|
| Real GDP (2011 prices): $PPP billion |  | 360 | 557 | 851 | 917 |
| Economic growth rate: % | 6.7 | 7.9 | 4.6 | 4.4 | 3.8 |
| Per capita income ($PPP) |  | 6,263 | 8,771 | 12,270 | 13,199 |
| GDP share by sector |  |  |  |  |  |
| Agriculture | 23.24 | 12.50 | 9.02 | 12.39 | 11.99 |
| Manufacturing | 21.51 | 27.20 | 33.59 | 35.62 | 32.94 |
| Construction | 4.44 | 6.24 | 3.06 | 2.66 | 2.64 |
| Service | 50.81 | 54.06 | 54.32 | 49.32 | 52.43 |

*Source*: CEIC.

crisis in 2008. The political shocks included a series of political conflicts, the violent in the three southern-most provinces, and the coup d'état in 2006. The political conflicts continued for many consecutive years involving riots, firearms and a closure of international airports for more than a week. Thailand was under a State of Emergency in 2008. Conflicts led to protest camps on the streets of downtown Bangkok that ended with killing and arson attack in 2011. The situation was close to a civil war. Political demonstration and disputes were followed by another coup d'état in 2014.

The environmental shocks included natural disasters in many occasions, for instance in 2004 Tsunami hit the Southern coasts of Thailand, drought that hit 70 provinces, and in 2011 uncommon heavy rainfall together with water resources mismanagement results in severe flooding in Bangkok and other 64 provinces. Therefore, to achieve as high growth rates as before the mid-1990, there is a need of sound macroeconomic policies, political accords, and public administrations.

The high growth rates in 1990s did not result in an equal distribution of wealth among all Thai citizens. Between 1980 and 1990, the poverty headcount ratios reduced from 67% of the population to 58% of the population (Table 2). The average growth rate in 1991–2000 was 4.6%, much lower than the previous decade, but the poverty headcount ratio was reduced by 15 percentage points.

Table 2. Poverty rates and income distributions.

|  | 1980 | 1990 | 2000 | 2010 | 2013 |
|---|---|---|---|---|---|
| Poverty: % of population | 67.30 | 57.97 | 42.33 | 16.37 | 10.94 |
| Gini coefficient | 0.43 | 0.44 | 0.43 | 0.40 | 0.36 |
| Share of household expenditure |  |  |  |  |  |
| — quintile 1 (20% lowest) | 5.90 | 6.00 | 6.15 | 6.58 | 7.33 |
| — quintile 2 | 9.57 | 9.37 | 9.60 | 10.40 | 11.37 |
| — quintile 3 | 14.00 | 13.25 | 13.65 | 14.73 | 15.64 |
| — quintile 4 | 21.46 | 20.10 | 20.86 | 21.61 | 22.44 |
| — quintile 5 (20% highest) | 49.08 | 51.29 | 49.74 | 46.68 | 43.22 |

*Source*: TDRI (Calculate using household expenditure in the Socio-Economic Survey).

The average growth rates were even lower in the next decade (2001–2010) meanwhile the poverty headcount ratio was reduced further by 22 percentage points.

Possible explanations behind a reduction of the poverty rate could be that many social and economic policies were imposed and took effect in 2001–2010. In the 2000s, the government has introduced a number of social and economic policies that aim to help the low and middle income groups. These policies include the universal healthcare coverage (UHC), debt suspension for farmers, village revolving fund, unemployment insurance, one-tambon-one-product (the government supports each sub-district to produce local products), people bank project, scholarship for poor students, and cash benefit for elderly. These policies did not only help the poor, but also improved the economic well-being among the rich. However, the rich gained from these policies relatively less than the poor since the income share of the top quintile reduced by about 3% points each decade after 1990. Income share of the top quintile earners reduced at the highest speed in the last three-year period (2011–2013). The Gini coefficients changed only marginally.

The structure of employment in Thailand has changed together with the sectoral development. As the manufacturing sector has been gaining more shares of the country's GDP, more workers were transferred to that sector. In 1980, the manufacturing sector employed 8.2% of the labor force and the agricultural sector employed up to 70% of the labor force. In 2010, employment share of the agricultural sector reduced by approximately 30% points and of the manufacturing sector increased by 6% points. The employment share of the construction sector was doubled between 1980 and 2010 although the share of construction to GDP reduced by 1.8% points (Table 3).

In 2013, the value added per worker in service sector is about USD 10,000 per worker while it is about USD24,000 in the manufacturing sector.[1] This implies that the service sector is unproductive relative to the manufacturing sector. The major components of the service

---

[1]Hour of work and the number of worker are from Thailand's Labor Force Survey.

Table 3. Thailand's labor force.

|  | 1980 | 1990 | 2000 | 2010 | 2013 |
|---|---|---|---|---|---|
| Labor force (million) | 22.6 | 30.8 | 33.8 | 39.1 | 39.5 |
| By education: % | | | | | |
| Primary | 90.4 | 83.2 | 67.9 | 54.2 | 51.1 |
| Secondary | 8.8 | 13.5 | 24.9 | 34.1 | 36.2 |
| Tertiary | 0.8 | 3.3 | 7.2 | 11.7 | 12.8 |
| By sector: % | | | | | |
| Agriculture | 70.4 | 63.4 | 48.3 | 40.5 | 41.8 |
| Manufacturing | 8.2 | 10.4 | 14.8 | 13.6 | 14.0 |
| Construction | 2.0 | 3.4 | 4.1 | 5.4 | 5.8 |
| Service | 19.4 | 22.8 | 32.7 | 40.5 | 38.4 |
| By work status: % | | | | | |
| Government and SE employee | 5.3 | 6.1 | 8.2 | 9.6 | 9.0 |
| Private employee | 16.9 | 22.9 | 32.1 | 33.2 | 31.3 |
| Employer & self-employed | 31.4 | 31.4 | 33.2 | 34.5 | 35.8 |
| Unpaid family worker | 46.3 | 39.6 | 26.5 | 22.6 | 22.5 |
| Others | 0.0 | 0.0 | 0.0 | 0.1 | 1.5 |
| Unemployment rate (%) | 0.9 | 2.2 | 2.4 | 0.9 | 0.8 |

*Source*: TDRI (Calculate from Labor Force Survey Quarter 3).

sector are retail and wholesale trade. With a small investment, any worker can participate in such trades. It is quite common to see family members of the retail trade family helping in the business without paid.

The level of education of the labor force has changed significantly in the past three decades (Table 3). Approximately 90% of the labor force obtained only primary education in 1980 however this percentage has been decreasing and dropped to 51% in 2013. On the other hand, employees with tertiary education increased by 10 percentage points in the past three decades. This is because the compulsory education was raised from 6 years to 9 years in 1999, along with free basic education of 12 years policy which is guaranteed by the constitution.

As more people obtained a tertiary degree, there is an increasing share of workers employed by the government and private sectors, from 22% in 1980 to 40% in 2013. Number of workers in the unpaid family business has been declining. The proportion of the unpaid family workers was 46% of the labor force in 1980. However the share dropped to 23% in 2010.

Thailand has experienced very low unemployment rate. The highest unemployment rate was in 1999 during the Asian financial crisis. The high unemployment rate was temporarily as the informal sectors absorbed the unemployed into their labor pools. Despite the fact that Thailand has relatively stable number of labor force of 39 million in 2013 and a low unemployment rate of about 1%, the country faces with shortage of labor, particularly the low-skilled labor. This results in an inflow of low-skilled migrants from the neighboring countries. The number of low-skilled migrants was 1.1 million in 2015 (Department of Employment, 2015).

## 2. Challenges for further development of the Thai economy

The main challenge relating to the development of healthcare and social security systems in Thailand is a changing population structure to an ageing society. The number of birth has been declining and therefore the labor force has been increasing very slowly. Chandoevwit and Chawla (2011) shows that Thailand's first demographic dividend was exhausted in 2010.

In 1980, about 40% of the population was in the age group 0–14 years old. The share of the population in this age group has been reducing continuously and reached 18% in 2013 (Table 4). We also observed that Thai people get married older. About 25% of the adults between 25 and 30 years old were single in 1980. However, in 2013, about 35% of the same age group were single. Moreover, the total fertility rate (TFR) reduced from 2.95 in 1980 to 1.36 in 2013. Family size reduced by half. These altogether imply a changing population structure.

The UN population projection (UN, 2013) reports that Thailand's population will reach the maximum of 67.9 million by 2025. By that period, the share of the working age population will decline to the same proportion as in 1990. But, the number and the share of the elderly will be higher than the children age groups (Figure 1). Given that Thailand's has not yet proposed an effective policy to encourage higher fertility rates, only 54% of the population will be in the working age group by 2040. The elderly will account for 34%

Table 4. Demographic transition.

|                                | 1980   | 1990   | 2000   | 2010   | 2013   |
|--------------------------------|--------|--------|--------|--------|--------|
| Population: thousand[a]        | 47,369 | 56,583 | 62,343 | 66,402 | 66,480 |
| Population share[a]            |        |        |        |        |        |
| Age group 0–14                 | 39.4   | 30.2   | 24.2   | 19.3   | 18.3   |
| Age group 15–59                | 55.0   | 62.6   | 65.9   | 67.7   | 67.9   |
| Age group 60+                  | 5.6    | 7.1    | 9.9    | 12.9   | 13.8   |
| Male                           | 50.1   | 49.5   | 49.1   | 49.0   | 49.0   |
| TFR[a]                         | 2.95   | 1.99   | 1.60   | 1.41   | 1.36   |
| Family size[b]                 | 5.20   | 4.02   | 3.53   | 3.12   | 2.95   |
| Proportion of 25–30 years old population who are single[b] (%) | 24.9 | 27.3 | 31.3 | 34.6 | 35.1 |

*Source*: [a]United Nations, Department of Economic and Social Affairs, Population Division (2013). [b]TDRI data from the Labor Force Survey Quarter 3.

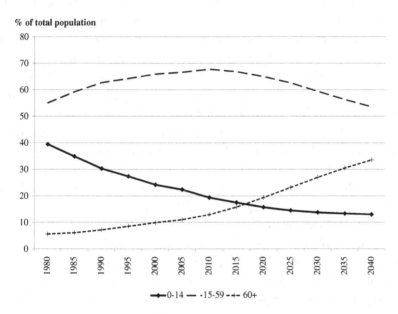

Figure 1. Thailand's population estimates.

*Source*: United Nations, Department of Economic and Social Affairs, Population Division (2013). World Population Prospects: The 2012 Revision. DVD Edition.

*Note*: Using medium fertility assumption.

of the population. With this projected age structure, there are many
more actions to be taken to improve individual's well-being. Policies
related to public health insurance and pension are among the most
important ones.

In 2012, Thailand's National Statistical Office (NSO) conducted a
nation-wide life satisfaction survey covering 54,100 individuals.[2] The
survey asks individuals to provide score out of 10 on the following
life aspects: education, residence, work, family, quality of life, health
and society. The top three scores were health (average score of 8.75),
family (average score of 8.66) and quality of life (average score of
8.60). The self-reported results imply that there is a need for sound
policies on healthcare along with other policies which aim to improve
family well-being and quality of life.

Chandoevwit (2006) reports that the social security systems in
Thailand classify Thai population into 5 different groups as follow: (1) the private employees in non-agricultural sector, (2) private
school teachers, (3) civil servants, (4) state-enterprise employees, and
(5) the rest which includes private employees in the agricultural sector, self-employed, other work-cohorts, and people not in the labor
force (Table 5). This chapter does not discuss the health insurance
and pension systems for private school teachers and state-enterprise
employees which cover only 1.5% of the total population. Table 6
shows the budget allocation on healthcare and income security for
elderly. Government employees and retirees have received a large
share of government budget for healthcare, pension;[3] and contribution to their pension fund, the Government Pension Fund (GPF).[4]
The number of government employee and retiree is about 5 million.
In 2003, they received 9% of the government budget for the benefits
and increased to 13% in 2013. Private employees received about 3%
of the government budget and the last group received about 7% of the
government budget for their benefits. There were about 11 million
private employees.

---

[2]http://service.nso.go.th/nso/nsopublish/themes/files/Satis-Excec55.pdf.
[3]A non-contributory pay-as-you-go defined benefit system.
[4]A defined contribution system.

Table 5. Social security by type of coverage.

| | Health care | Invalidity | Death, old age and survivor | Child allowance | Child education | Unemployment |
|---|---|---|---|---|---|---|
| Private employees in non-agricultural sectors | √ | √ | √ | √ | | √ |
| Private school teachers | √ | √ | | √ | √ | |
| Government employees or civil servants | √ | √ | √ | √ | √ | Permanent employment |
| State-enterprise employees | √ | √ | √ | √ | √ | Permanent employment |
| Private employees in the agricultural sector, self-employed, other work-cohorts, and people not in the labor force. | √ | | | | | |

*Source*: Chandoevwit (2006).

The following subsections explain the background of the UHC and pension policies and their policy related issues. The pension policy is an important social security scheme (SSS) that needs more attention because of the population transition into a complete ageing society. The current state of this policy has lacked behind the demographic changes.

## 3. Universal health care coverage

Thailand had a major healthcare reform in 2001. Before the reform, about 70% of Thai populations were insured under a pluralistic

Table 6. Public expenditure on healthcare and pension.

| Types of public expenditure | 2003 Millions of THB (% of total expenditure) | 2013[2] Millions of THB (% of total expenditure) |
|---|---|---|
| Beneficiary: government employees and dependents (approximately 8% of the population) | | |
| Healthcare expenditure for civil servant | 22,679 (2.27%) | 59,828 (2.49%) |
| Pension and payment to government retirees | 49,693 (4.97%) | 93,737 (3.91%) |
| Contribution to the GPF | 17,562 (1.76%) | 156,928 (6.54%) |
| Beneficiary: private employees (approximately 17% of the population) | | |
| Contribution to Social Security Fund (SSF) | 11,208 (1.12%) | 34,848 (1.45%) |
| Contribution to SSF for child allowance | 5,656 (0.57%) | 25,118 (1.05%) |
| Beneficiary: population not in the first two groups | | |
| UHC (approximately 75% of the population) | 30,538 (3.05%) | 108,744 (4.53%) |
| Cash benefit for elderly (approximately 12% of the population) | 1,449 (0.5%) | 58,347 (2.43%) |

*Sources*: Comptroller's General Office, Social Security Office, and National Health Security Office (NHSO).
*Note*: *The elderly who received cash benefit are covered by the UHC.

health insurance systems (HISRO, 2001: 16) and the rest of the population were uninsured. About 11% of the population, who was the government employees, civil servant retirees, and dependents of civil servants, receive benefit from the Civil Servant Medical Benefit Scheme (CS). Another 9% and 10% were insured under the SSS for private non-agriculture employees and the private health insurance. About 37% and 12% of population were insured under the Medical Welfare Scheme (MWS) for Low-Income and Disadvantages and Voluntary Health Card Scheme (VHCS) (see Figure 2 in Section 3.1). The pluralistic systems have been separately developed such that one could be insured by multiple schemes. Table 7 shows the gaps of the benefit and financing of these schemes that could lead to unequal healthcare subsidies and treatments. For example, approximately 20 million people were uninsured by any healthcare scheme, which

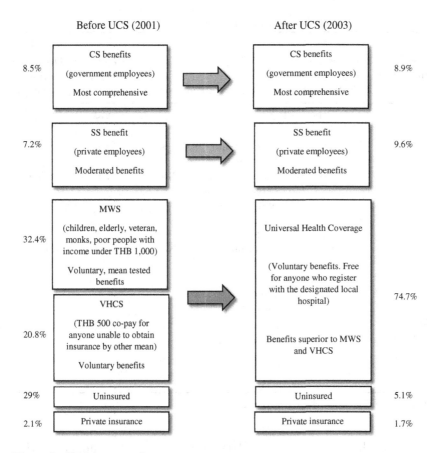

Figure 2. Health care reforms.

*Source*: Chandoevwit and Wibulpolprasert (2014).

means that they have to pay for their own healthcare costs. The systems were heavily criticized for inequity and inefficiency.

## 3.1. Moving from targeting programs to an entitlement program

Public health insurance system development in Thailand started 40 years ago. In the 1970s, Thai government launched a number of social security policies focusing on an improvement of healthcare system. A medical assistance scheme — MWS, was initiated to help low-income groups. In 1975, the MWS covered the rural population

Table 7. Health insurance schemes in Thailand before 2001.

| Public health Insurance schemes | Government Expenditure (THB/head) | Choice of hospital | Cash compensation | Maternal/ child delivery | Disease control/ prevention |
|---|---|---|---|---|---|
| CS | ~2,000 | Public hospital | No | Yes | Yes |
| SSS | 1,060 | Public/private hospital | Yes | Yes | Limited |
| MWS | 244 | Visit primary care unit and refer to public hospital | No | No | Limited |
| VHCS | 446 | Visit primary care unit and refer to public hospital | No | Maybe | Maybe |
| Uninsured: approximately 20 million people | | Pay out-of-pocket | | | |

*Source*: revised from HISRO (2001).

with monthly income below THB 1,000 Baht.[5] The budget for the scheme was targeted to support 7–8 million people or about 0.2% of the population. Eligibility was determined at the point of service with the discretion of hospital's staffs (Gajeena *et al.*, 2000: 18).

In 1984–1995, MWS offered free medical care cards to eligible low-income families (with monthly income below THB 2,000) and individuals (with monthly income below THB 1,500). Card holders can visit public hospitals under administration of the Ministry of Public Health (MOPH), the Bangkok Metropolitan Administration, the Red Cross Society, Pattaya City, and municipalities. The MWS card was valid for 3 years. In 1995, income cut-off points were

---

[5] Approximately USD 50 in 1975.

raised to THB 2,800 for a family and THB 2,000 for an individual. Moreover, the program was expanded to cover children aged 12 and below, people aged 60 and older, disabled, veterans and their family, and monks and other religious priests. More public hospitals belonging to the public universities and some government organizations were included in the program.

Subsidies provided to hospitals that accepted the MWS card were under-funded. Government allocated global budget to the MOPH based on the expected number of the eligible population, past records of healthcare services, and the subsidy per unit of card holder. The allocation of budget to each hospital was decided by a committee appointed by the head of MOPH. The number of low-income families and individuals was determined by the National Economic and Social Development Board (NESDB). The budget per MWS card holder was proposed by the MOPH. However, the actual amount paid to the hospitals was always below the proposed amount by the MOPH.

The allocated budget per MWS card was THB 68 in 1984, increased to THB 163 in 1992, and increased to THB 244 in 1995.[6] Empirically, it was shown that allocated budgets were far below the actual healthcare costs. In 1991, the community hospital's[7] outpatient cost per visit was THB 85 and inpatient cost per episode was THB 1,200. Healthcare costs at the general and regional hospitals were much higher. A hospital in Nan province received THB 10.5 million to treat patients who were eligible for this scheme, but the actual cost of providing care was THB 16.8 million. A hospital in Samutprakarn province received THB 2.3 million, but the actual cost of providing care was more than doubled at THB 5.8 million (Khoman, 1997: 187).[8]

---

[6] Using the official annual average exchange rates, they are equal to USD 2.5, 6.4, and 9.8 in 1984, 1992, and 1995 respectively.

[7] Community hospital is the hospital at the district level. Higher level hospitals are general hospital and regional hospital. These two hospitals have more beds, better equipment and all other resources.

[8] One might wonder how the hospitals survived given such loss. It should be noted that public hospitals receive government budget to cover wages and salary,

Beside subsidization under the MWS scheme, public hospitals also provide free medical treatment to many of the poor who did not have the MWS cards. In 1987, there were 7.6 million MWS card holders but the public hospitals provided free medical treatment to 13.7 million people. Additionally, many of the uninsured were charged at a lower favorable price when they received medical treatments at the public hospitals (Rojvanit, 1993: 8).

Poor targeting strategy is a controversial issue of the MWS. It was shown that a large proportion of the poor had no access to the free medical card (Khoman, 1997; Gajeena *et al.*, 2000). About 20% of MWS card holders were not poor (Khoman, 1997: 187). Another important issue is sub-standard quality of care because of insufficient funding. It has been observed that patients were reluctant to show the MWS card at the admission check-in and they choose to provide the card details after they have received the medical care (Gajeena *et al.*, 2000: 24). With limited resources and financial supports, MWS could not be extended to cover all Thai citizens.

The MOPH introduced a VHCS project in 1983. The VHC pilot project was started in seven provinces (18 villages), focusing only maternal and child health, health promotion, disease control, and health education. The project aimed to develop the primary healthcare system, referral system, and encourage the contribution of people in the local communities. The VHC scheme was expected and has the potential to expand to a universal coverage scheme.

The government encouraged each village to set up their own healthcare insurance system by establishing a Village Health Card Fund (VHC). There was no government contribution at the beginning. In 1985–1987, the price of joining VHC or the premium was 300 Baht for a family of four, covering up to 6 episodes per year. The deductible for each episode was 2,000 Baht with no co-insurance or co-payment (MOPH, 1990: 4). Later, there is an introduction of the co-insurance system up to 90%. However this deductible and

---

operating and investment expenses regardless of service performance. Wages and salary was about 50% in 2001 of the budget. Loss usually caused by the use of drug and medicine that the hospitals got credit from the drug companies.

co-insurance payment has been canceled in 1990 by the MOPH. In 1991, the premium increased to 500 Baht for a family of five.

To get the medical benefit, each VHC patient had to start their treatment at a closet primary care unit or a health center.[9] If the health center was unable to treat the disease then patients would be referred to more equipped hospitals, either a community hospital, a general hospital or a regional hospital.

The premium collected for the VHC was shared between the health centers (15%), community hospitals (30%), and general or regional hospitals (30%). The rest was allocated to personnel costs (10%) and administration costs (15%).

A VHC evaluation conducted by the MOPH showed that the VHC faced many challenges. First and the biggest challenge was the adverse selection problem. The majority of card members tend to have chronic diseases or a need of high cost healthcare (MOPH, 1990: 141). As a result, hospitals suffered from operating loss. Many rules were changed to suit the situation, causing confusion to the users. Second challenge was poor rural villagers cannot afford the premium. Some of the VHC allowed the premium to be paid by installments. Without efficient premium collection, some villages did not have enough operating funds.

The VHC was financially unviable. The government subsidized the VHC through the user side. In 1994, the government subsidized THB 500 per family of 5 members. The subsidy was later increased to 1,000 Baht in 1999 (Gajeena *et al.*, 2000: 16). Each family paid the same amount for the premium to cover up to 5 household members. The MOPH strongly hoped that the VHC could be expanded to cover the majority of the population which would solve the adverse selection problem. On average, subsidy per head was THB 200, which was lower than the MWS.

Important lessons for the MOPH after implementing these two schemes are that collecting insurance premium and targeting health insurance program to the poor were proved to be difficult tasks. This

---

[9]Health center may only have rotating physicians and has no capacity of inpatient admission.

results in a later adaptation of healthcare system with no-premium and no-targeting the poor policies.

A major health insurance reform came after the general election in January 2001. The new government initiated many social policies[10] that aimed to reduce household expenditure as well as to improve household income. The policies focus on the low- and middle-income households in the rural areas. Two main targeting programs, MWS and village's revolving fund,[11] were redesigned and given new names. Figure 2 shows the summary of the public health insurance changes reported by Chandoevwit and Wibulpolprasert (2014). They have become the entitlement programs that provide benefits to a larger proportion of the population. Uninsured population dropped from 29% to 5.1%.

Three major components of the healthcare reform were: (1) the UHC which is an expansion of the coverage to everybody who is not covered by other public health insurance schemes; (2) health insurance system management; and (3) financing and funding mechanism to service providers. All uninsured and people under the MWS and VHC are covered under the new UHC. They are entitled to the comprehensive health benefit package including outpatient, inpatient, accident, emergency cares, high-cost care with minimal exclusion, and prevention and health promotion (HISRO, 2012). Beneficiaries are required to register at the district health systems and pay THB 30 for each hospital visit. This system covers the cost for every type of hospital.[12]

Before the reform, the MOPH took care of health insurance (MWS and VHC), healthcare services, disease prevention and health

---

[10]Including Debt Suspension for Farmers, Village and Urban Community Fund, One-Tambon-One-Product, People's Bank and UHC.

[11]The poor-targeting revolving fund was named Poverty Reduction Fund (*Gor-Khor-Khor-Jor*).

[12]Co-payment is not required for MWS beneficiaries. Co-payment was removed in November 2006 and came back again in late 2011. The successor (Pheu Thai Party) of the Thai-Rak-Thai Party who initiated the healthcare reform wants to remind people that this popular policy (widely called 30 Baht program) is their brand.

promotion. The reform introduced an autonomous organization, the NHSO, to look after the purchasing obligation of the new health insurance system. This new management system reduced the MOPH's budget and its budget allocation power to the healthcare service providers and hospitals.

Using the new financing mechanism, a capitation budget is allocated to the NHSO who purchases services from the district health system networks or contracting unit for the primary cares (CUPs) who provide primary care services and arrange the referral of patients to secondary or tertiary care services (HISRO, 2012: 53). The capitation budget in 2002 was THB 1,202. The total budget allocated for the health insurance of 45 million populations was about THB 51 billion (NHSO, 2013). However, only 40% of the budget was for healthcare services, the rest was for CUPs' health personnel cost. In 2012, the budget share for the healthcare services increased to 70%. Figure 3 shows that with the UHC system the budget allocation of MOPH and NHSO has increased from 7% of total budget in 1990s to 9% of total budget in 2013. Currently, the NHSO manages a higher budget than the MOPH who used to control all budget on public health.

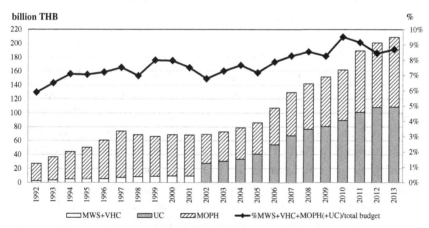

Figure 3. Budget allocation to MWS and VHC through MOPH and to UHC through NHSO.

*Source*: Bureau of the Budget (1991–2013).

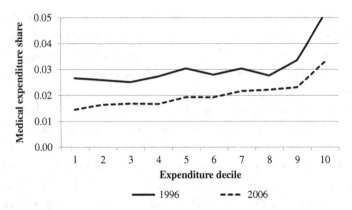

Figure 4. Medical expenditure as a fraction of total expenditure.
*Source*: Chandoevwit and Wibulpolprasert (2014).

A national survey shows that the share of medical expenditure by households declined after an implementation of the UHC (Figure 4). Conditioning on receiving healthcare, the beneficiary households spent a lesser fraction of their total expenditure in the out-of-pocket medical expenditure (OOP) in 2006 compared to 1996. The poorest household used to spend almost 30% of their total expenditure on healthcare in 1996, but this figure reduced to 15% in 2006. Limwattananon *et al.* (2015) shows that the UHC could reduce the OOP by THB 19 per capita or about 28%.

## 3.2. The issue of inequity

The development of health insurance in Thailand has ended up with three public health insurance schemes. Each of them is developed separately at different occasions as shown in Table 8. The CS was introduced in 1983, the SSS was introduced in 1990 and the UHC was introduced in 2001. The major problem with these three schemes is that they are not harmonized in many aspects. First, the contributions from public funds are unequal. Second, the benefit package and payment to the service providers are not the same. Lastly, these schemes are under different organizations that follow their own Laws and regulations. Healthcare providers have to understand each insurance scheme and charge differently for the same medical treatment.

Table 8. Summary of three public healthcare insurance programs.

| | CS | SSS | UHC |
|---|---|---|---|
| Type of insurance | Entitlement program for civil servant | Compulsory contributory insurance program from private employee | Entitlement program for people who are not eligible for CS or SSS. |
| Year started | 1980 | 1990 | 2001 |
| Beneficiary | Civil servants and their dependents (spouse, parents, and maximum 3 children), and government retirees | Private employee in non-agriculture sector | Thai population without public health insurance and migrant worker |
| Number of registered member | 5 million (12% of population) | 10.5 million (16% of population) | 48 million (72% of population) |
| Source of fund | General tax revenue | Equal contribution from employee, employer, and government (1.5% of insured wage from each party, maximum THB225 per month) | General tax revenue |
| Payment to service provider | Outpatient: Fee-for-service Inpatient: DRG | Outpatient and Inpatient: Capitation Chronic disease: DRG | Outpatient: capitation Inpatient: DRG |
| Average expenditure per registered member in 2013 | ~THB 12,589 | ~THB1,446 (capitation) | ~THB2,756 (capitation) |
| Administration | Comptroller's General Office, Ministry of Finance | Social Security Office, Ministry of labor | NHSO |
| Service provider | Any public hospital. | Registered public or private hospital. | Registered public hospital. |

(*Continued*)

Table 8. (*Continued*)

| | CS | SSS | UHC |
|---|---|---|---|
| | | Each member must register to only one hospital. | Each member must register to only one public hospital. Private hospitals are involved in a few provinces. |
| Benefit | Comprehensive medical benefit and child delivery | Comprehensive benefit or non-work related illness, child delivery and Cash compensation if not able to work. | Comprehensive benefit, child delivery and disease prevention and health promotion. |
| Annual check-up | Yes | No | No |
| Dental care | Extraction, filling, scaling, root canal treatment, orthodontic treatment caused by an accident. | Extraction, filling, scaling, and removal of embedded teeth; Maximum 2 visits each year with the ceiling of THB 300 per visit. Removable plastic denture once per 5 years period; maximum of THB 1,300 for 1–5 teeth, THB 1,500 for 6 and more teeth, THB 2,400 for Upper/lower plastic full denture and THB 4,400 for full plastic denture. | Extraction, filling, scaling, removable plastic partial denture and full denture, pulp treatment for primary teeth, and obturator for cleft child patients. |
| Special ward | Yes | No | No |
| Emergency | Yes Maximum THB 300 for private hospitals | Yes | Yes |

(*Continued*)

Table 8. (*Continued*)

| | CS | SSS | UHC |
|---|---|---|---|
| Pharma-ceuticals | Free if drugs are in the National Essential Drug List (NEDL). Drugs not in NEDL can be used under doctor discretion. Free only if three doctors agree that they are necessary. | Free if drugs are in the NEDL. | Free if drugs are in the NEDL. |

*Source*: Summarized by the authors.

Thailand's health insurance systems are alleged to cause inequity across the beneficiary groups. Since each scheme pays different amount to the healthcare providers for the same treatment, patients carrying different insurance schemes could potentially get a different treatment. Given that public hospitals have limited resources, patients who pay more would implicitly get a priority for the treatment.

TDRI (2014) studies the equity of medical care of Thai elderly in their last year of life. Majority of Thai elderly are under two health insurance schemes; either the UHC or the CS. The study selects only elderly with at least one of the following five chronic diseases: cancer, cerebrovascular disease, diabetes mellitus, hypertensive disease, and heart disease between 2007 and 2011. TDRI shows that access to medical treatment was unfair. Hospital admission of elderly in the UHC scheme concentrates at the younger ages compared to elderly in the CS scheme and the elderly in the UHC scheme have a shorter life span. Within the last year of life, 95% of elderly under the UHC scheme admitted to the hospital for the first time in their last quarter of life, while elderly in the CS scheme admitted to the hospital throughout the year. Figure 5 shows that elderly patients under the CS stay longer in the hospital, given that all elderly have the same diseases. This is because unequal rates of pay of the two healthcare

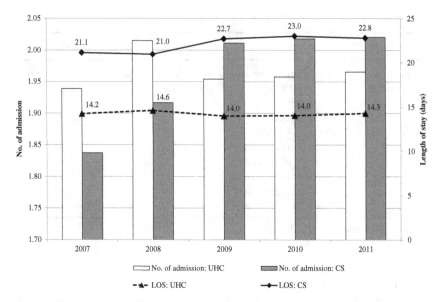

Figure 5. Length of stay of elderly patients in their last year of life.
*Source*: TDRI (2014).

schemes motivate hospitals to select their patients or to lower quality
of care to patients with lower payments.

## 4. Public pension for elderly

The development of the pension system in Thailand follows the policy formation patterns of the public health insurance schemes. Civil
servants are the first group to have access to the pension for elderly.
The history of civil servant pension is long before the revolution in
1932 that changed Thailand from an absolute monarchy to a constitutional monarchy. The current civil servants' pension is under the
Civil Servant Pension Act 1961 and the GPF Act 1996. According to
the Act, civil servants who have been working for at least 25 years
with the government or have turned at least 50 years old[13] are eligible

---

[13]Retirement age is 60. But, civil servants can retire at the age 50 ask for the
pension benefit.

to receive monthly pension. In addition, civil servants who are members of the GPF receive additional pension or lump sum payment when they retired (Chandoevwit, 2006).

The private employee in the non-agricultural sector is the second group to receive pension, either pension or lump sum payment depending on which type of payments an individual is eligible for. The system was started in 1998. With this system both the private employees and their employers have to contribute 6% of the wage to the SSF for at least 180 months to be eligible for the pension benefit.

Provided that Thailand has two pension systems covering only the civil servants and private employees in the non-agricultural sector, only 6% of elderly's main source of income in 2011 was from pension (Figure 6). In fact, all of these 6% were government retirees as the pension from the SSF was paid for the first time in 2014.

About 40% of elderly live on their children's income, reducing from 60% in 2007 (Chandoevwit, 2013). 35% of the elderly was still in the workforce due to the fact that they have no other source of income or saving. The Survey of Elderly in Thailand (NSO, 2011) shows that about 64% of the elderly had no saving. Social assistance

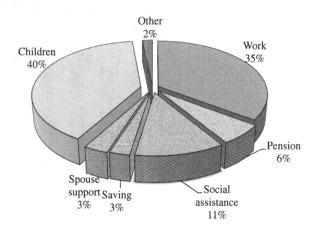

Figure 6. Main source of income of elderly (age 60 and above).
*Source*: NSO, Elderly Survey 2011.

program that provides cash benefit to elderly was the main source of income of 11% of elderly.

## 4.1. Social assistance program for the elderly

Social assistance program for the population aged 60 years or older was initiated in 1993. It was a targeting program aiming at helping the poor elderly who lived alone or abandoned by their children. The cash benefit of THB 200 was paid to the poor elderly who were selected by their village committee. The benefit was increased to THB 300 after Thailand was hit by the financial crisis in 1997. This program was targeted to the poor, but many of the beneficiaries were not poor. In 2009, the cash benefit increased to THB 500 and was paid to every elderly who registered with the government. The number of beneficiaries increased from 1.7 million to 5.5 million (Figure 7). In 2011, the amount beneficiaries received became 600, 700, 800, and 1,000 THB for elderly in age groups 60–69, 70–79, 80–89, and 90 and above, respectively. The Survey of Elderly in Thailand in 2011 shows that about 18% of elderly earned less than THB 10,000 per year and about 35% of this group thought that their

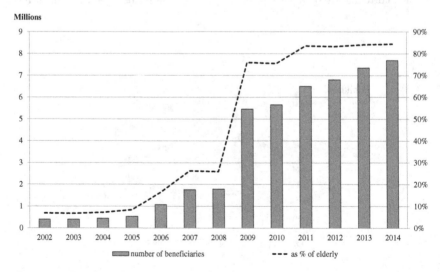

Figure 7. Elderly receiving monthly cash benefit.
*Source*: Department of local administration.

earning was not enough for a living. To increase public spending on the elderly cash benefit, however, would be difficult as the number of elderly is continuously increasing.

## 4.2. Saving for retirement of workers in the informal sector

As a small proportion of elderly is entitled to the pension and the level of cash assistance is not high enough for the living, therefore policy makers are proposing to promote saving for retirement. A further increase of the cash benefit system cannot be sustained as it may cause a fiscal constraint in the future when Thailand has a higher old-age dependency rate.

In 2011, the policy makers proposed the pension system for workers in the informal sector. The pension system was formulated and enacted in the National Savings Fund (NSF) Law. Any individual who is not an employee in the private enterprises, the government offices or private schools is allowed to save for retirement with the NSF. The government encourages private saving by contributing into the NSF. The contribution from the government varies between 50%, 80% and 100% of the individual savings depending on the age of account owner (Table 9). The minimum saving per month is THB 50.

Up until 2014, the government had not yet implemented the NSF law. It was the political battles between the two political parties that want to stop one another from gaining popularity from formulating good public policies. The delay of the NSF causes a delayed saving which in the future could lower the amount of benefits that an elderly should have received.

Table 9. Government contribution to the NSF.

| Age of saver | % of individual saving | Maximum contribution to each individual account (THB per year) |
|---|---|---|
| <30 years old | 50 | 3,000 |
| 30–50 years old | 80 | 4,800 |
| >50 years old | 100 | 6,000 |

*Source*: The National Saving Fund Act 2011.

## 5. Conclusions

The public health insurance and pension policies development in Thailand has developed in the shorter period compared to the other developing countries. The country's economic, employment environment and the bureaucracy have shaped Thailand's public health insurance and pension for elderly to the fragmented inefficient and unfair systems.

Three healthcare schemes provide unequal benefits, receive unequal subsidy per head from the government, and pay to service providers under different mechanisms. People were treated according to the type of health insurance they are entitled to which could lead to unfair health treatments and outcomes. To achieve fair the healthcare systems and health outcomes across population groups, the governance of the systems must be modified. At least the basic benefits package, government subsidy per head, and payment to hospitals must be harmonized.

The income security for elderly or pension for elderly has been developing very slowly. An implementation of policy does not answer the needs of the citizens. Thailand is reaching a complete ageing society. Large proportion of the population needs to prepare for retirement. Any delay of implementing the income security system for elderly could possibly put more burdens on the younger generations. Moreover, the recent development of the pension systems in Thailand results in a fragmented system where each pension system is administrated under different organizations. Each system does not allow their members to transfer their savings to another pension system if the members change their occupations. Basic need for elderly has never been determined by any government agency. The pension for each scheme has no connection with the elderly's need.

Other low- or middle-income countries could learn from this experience when structuring the public health insurance and pension policies. Harmonization of the public welfare schemes is crucial for the whole population to receive fair treatments and benefits from the central government.

# References

Bureau of the Budget, Office of Prime Minister (1991–2013). *Budget in Brief: Fiscal year*. Office of the Prime Minister, Bangkok.

Chandoevwit, W. (2006). *Social Security Systems in Thailand*. Thailand Development Research Institute, Bangkok.

Chandoevwit, W., and A. Chawla (2011). Economic impact and human capital. In *Impact of Demographic Change in Thailand*, Gavin Jones and Wassana Im-em (eds.), United Nations Population Fund, Bangkok, pp. 85–98.

Chandoevwit, W. (2013). Social and economic aspects of the elderly in Thailand. *Malaysian Journal of Economic Studies*, 50, pp. 193–206.

Chandoevwit, W., and W. Wibulpolprasert (2014). *Thailand's Universal Health Coverage Program and Household Expenditure*. TDRI research submitted to the Rockefeller Foundation.

Department of Employment, Ministry of Labor (2015). *The Statistic of the ASEAN Migrant Workers Allowing to Work in Thailand*. Office of Foreign Worker Administration. (In Thai)

Gajeena, A., S. Srithamrongsawat, and N. Gailard (2000). *Harmonizing the Execution of Voluntary Health Card and Medical Welfare Scheme*. Ministry of Public Health, Nonthaburi. (In Thai)

Health Insurance System Research Office (2001). *A Proposal to a Universal Health Coverage*. Health System Research Institute, Nonthaburi. (In Thai)

Health Insurance System Research Office (2012). *Thailand's Universal Coverage Scheme: Achievements and Challenge. An Independent Assessment of the First 10 Years (2001–2010)*. Health Insurance System Research office, Nonthaburi.

Khoman, S. (1997). Rural healthcare financing in Thailand. In *Innovations in Health Care Financing: Proceedings of a World Bank Conference*, G. J. Schieber (ed.), the World Bank, Washington, DC, pp. 183–193.

Limwattananon, S., S. Neelsen, O. O'Donnell, P. Prakongsai, V. Tangcharoensathien, E. Van Doorslaer, and V. Vongmongkol (2015). Universal coverage with supply-side reform: The impact on medical expenditure risk and utilization in Thailand. *Journal of Public Economics*, 121, pp. 79–94.

Ministry of Public Health (1990). *Evaluation of the Health Card Project*. Ministry of Public Health, Nonthaburi. (In Thai)

NHSO (2013). *Health Insurance Information Service Center*. Available at http://eis.nhso.go.th/FrontEnd/home.aspx (download on 3 April 2013). (Accessed on April 3rd, 2013).

Rojvanit, A. (1993). *Pricing Policy of Public Hospitals.* Faculty of Economics, Thammasat University.

Thailand Development Research Institute (2014). *Health Status and Health Equity.* Thailand Development Research Institute, Bangkok. (In Thai)

United Nations, Department of Economic and Social Affairs, Population Division (2013). *World Population Prospects: The 2012 Revision.* DVD Edition.

CHAPTER 9

# China: Economic Structure Change and Outward Direct Investment (ODI)[1]

Yongzhong Wang[*], Guoxue Li[†] and Bijun Wang[‡]

*International Investment Department*
*Institute of World Economics and Politics*
*Chinese Academy of Social Sciences*
*No. 5 Jianguomennei Street, Beijing, China 100732*
[*]*wangyzcass@163.com*
[†]*lgxlne@sina.com*
[‡]*wangbijun007@126.com*

## 1. Introduction

Over the past three decades, China's export-led growth mode has obtained tremendous success in economic growth and export promotion. Now, China's GDP ranks second just next to U.S. in the world, and it is the largest exporter and foreign reserve accumulator and the second largest foreign trader. In accordance with the fame of "World Factory," China is also the largest manufactured goods producer, fixed capital investor, energy and raw materials consumer and $CO_2$ emitter in the world, which has engendered prolonged worldwide impacts on manufactures supply, commodities demand and environmental conservation.

However, due to the rising costs of production factors, rapid aged tendency of population, lack of advanced technology and gloomy global economy, China's current growth mode featuring with overdependence on export and investment cannot be sustainable. To

---

[1]Sections 1, 2, 3, and 4 is contributed by Yongzhong WANG, Bijun WANG, and Guoxue LI respectively. Section 4 is part of research achievements in Basic Research Scholarship Project funded by Chinese Academy of Social Sciences.

escape the middle income trap and realize the target of the new normal state formulated by the Chinese new administration, the most emergent and challenging task for China is to restructure the economy, charactering with the transformations of the growth mode from export-led and investment-driven to consumption and innovation driven, and the replacement of resources intensive and heavy emission manufacturing industries by service and high technology industry.

Regarding the restructure and upgrade of industrial structure, a successful experience of China in the past decades is to open-up, and attract FDI inflow and foreign technology and management skills. Through the adoption of export promotion measures and the encouragement of FDI policies, China has successful shifted from an agriculture country to an industrial state in the past three decades. In the future economic restructure and upgrade, China certainly should continue the policy of FDI encouragement and welcome the FDI inflow with high quality or technology.

It is worthy of noting that Outward direct investment (ODI) can play an important role in attracting foreign technology and upgrading the economic structure, through acquiring oversea natural resources and advanced technology, establish market distributional channels and transferring domestic overcapacity industries. In the past, a mistake that China had made is to neglect the role of ODI, and China started to encourage ODI activities in 2001, and even so the stock of the ODI cannot compare to that of the FDI, Chinese huge foreign assets are collectively held by its monetary authority — the PBOC, and current Chinese firms have only a modest international presence. In recent years, the pace of Chinese enterprises' ODI has significantly accelerated due to domestic strong demand on strategic resources and technology, and reasonable asset prices in advanced countries attributed to the global financial crisis and European sovereign debt crisis. With the implementation of the initiative of "One Belt One Road" and the diversification of Chinese foreign reserve, it is expected that China's ODI will entered a stage of rapid growth, and there are more Chinese capital will be invested in infrastructure, high-end manufacturing industry, labor-and-resource intensive standardized technology industry and service sectors. Hence, China's ODI will play a more important role of stimulating the economic structure upgrade, through acquiring key technology and famous brands, transferring overcapacity sectors such as steels and cements, and making use of the idle labors of the host countries.

In this regard, this chapter will undertake a comprehensive and systematic investigation on China's economic structure change and ODI. The framework of the following sections is arranged as follows: the Section 2 will conduct a comprehensive analysis on the facts, challenges and prospect of Chinese economy; the Section 3 will discuss over the current circumstances and challenges of China's ODI, and put forward some policy suggestions; the final section will carry out an in-depth research in the issue of ODI, the extension of production chains and China's upgrade in the global value chains.

## 2. Chinese economy: Facts, challenges, and prospects

In this section, we undertake a comprehensive investigation on the current circumstances of Chinese economy in terms of economic growth, foreign trade, fixed capital investment, cross-border direct investment, foreign reserve accumulation, and outward investment return. The most comprehensive and complicate challenges of Chinese economy is middle income trap. The new normal state is a vitally important target for Chinese economic development in the coming decade.

### 2.1. China's economic growth, trade and investment

Since the reform and open-up in 1978, China has experienced continuous and dramatic high economic growth, and the GDP size rose substantially from 189 bn USD in 1980 to 10,330 bn USD in 2014 in current term. Featuring with high savings, heavy investment and export stimulation, China's export-led growth mode has achieved great success over the past thirty-five years, with average annual growth of 9.8%, the highest economic growth rate in the world. In 2010, China's GDP reached 5,930 bn USD in current price, overtook Japan's GDP scale of 5,474 bn USD and became the second largest economy in the world. If China's strong growth momentum maintains, it will overtake USA as the largest economy in the near future. According to a prediction of OECD, if calculated in constant

PPP international dollar, China economy size has surpassed that of eurozone and will become the largest economy in 2016.

In the past three decades, China's export-led strategy has achieved unbelievable success and became the world factory. China sequentially overtook Japan as the third largest foreign trader in 2004, Germany as second largest trader in 2010 and USA as the largest exporter in 2011. The amount of China's import and export of goods in 2014 reached 1,960 bn USD and 2,343 bn USD respectively. China's trade surplus has increased sharply and become an excessive exporter since 2005. The share of China's trade surplus of GDP firstly rose dramatically from 1.66% in 2004 to 7.57% in 2008, and then steadily fell to 2.02% in 2014.

A typical feature of China's economic growth mode is heavy investment. The scale of Chinese fixed capital investment has experienced persistent and substantial growth in the past decades, rising sharply from 55 bn USD in 1980 to 4,370 bn USD in 2013. China surpassed USA in 2009 and became the largest nation in fixed capital investment. Over the period of between 1990 and 2013, the average share of China's fixed capital investment in GDP attains 37.7%, and which is much higher than the world average level of 22.8%. This means that it is a tough task for China to adjust its economic structure by reducing overdependence on investment.

## 2.2. China's inward and outward foreign direct investment (FDI)

China's regulatory system discriminates among different kind of cross-border capital movements. Encouraging FDI is China's long-held policy. With features of relative stability and associated with benefits such as transfers of technological and managerial expertise, FDI has generally been the dominant form of China's capital inflows under the background of capital transactions restrictions.

With the establishment of China's status as "world factory" after entry into WTO and the revaluation pressure of the RMB gradually accumulated, China's FDI inflow has expanded steadily since 2001, with an average annual growth rate of 8.1%. The flow and stock of China's inflow FDI in 2014 was 119.6 bn USD and 2677.9 bn USD respectively. Recently, the growth speed of China's FDI inflow has substantially declined due to foreign investors' tight fiscal constraints originating from the global financial crisis, and China's enhancing requirements on the quality of foreign capitals, average annual growth rate falling from 13.1% over the period between 2001 and 2008 to 2.2% during the period from 2009 to 2014. However, China is still a main and popular destination for FDI capital.

With strong pressure of growing foreign exchange reserves, China has changed fundamentally the ODI policy and began to implement the policy of encouraging Chinese companies to "Go Globally" in 2001. This policy shift intends to increase capital outflows to reduce external surplus, acquire oversea natural resources and advanced technology, establish market distributional channels for Chinese products, and enhance investment revenues of China's huge foreign assets. China's outward investment has accelerated substantially since 2003. The flow and stock of China's ODI rose from 2.9 bn USD and 33.2 bn USD in 2003 to 116.0 bn USD and 744.3 bn USD in 2014 respectively.

## 2.3. China's FX (foreign exchange) reserve accumulation and outward investment return

Since joined in WTO in 2001, China has experienced large and persistent trade surplus, FDI and speculative capital inflow, and hence China has accumulated huge foreign exchange reserve. The size of China's foreign exchange reserve skyrocketed at 3.84 tn USD at the end of 2014. As a natural consequence of the accumulation of huge foreign exchange reserve, China has successfully shifted from a capital-scarce country to relatively capital-abundant one. As Table 1 shows, the size of China's foreign assets has experienced a rapid growth in the past decade, rising sharply from around 1.22 tn USD in 2005 to 6.41 tn USD in 2014. The value of China's net foreign asset has maintained positive since 2004, and this means that China has always been a net capital export or a debtor in the past decade.

China is an abnormal debtor. Although China has large amount of net foreign asset, its net outward investment reward has always recorded minus profits in the past decade. Over the period between

Table 1. The position and revenue of China's international investment (in billion USD).

|  | 2005 | 2010 | 2011 | 2012 | 2013 | 2014 |
|---|---|---|---|---|---|---|
| Foreign Asset | 1223.3 | 4118.9 | 4734.5 | 5213.2 | 5986.1 | 6408.7 |
| — ODI Asset | 64.5 | 317.2 | 424.8 | 531.9 | 660.5 | 744.3 |
| — FX Reserve | 818.9 | 2847.3 | 3181.1 | 3311.6 | 3821.3 | 3843.0 |
| Foreign Liability | 815.6 | 2430.8 | 3046.1 | 3346.7 | 3990.1 | 4632.3 |
| — FDI Liability | 471.5 | 1569.6 | 1906.9 | 2068.0 | 2331.2 | 2677.9 |
| Net Foreign Asset | 407.7 | 1688.0 | 1688.4 | 1866.5 | 1996.0 | 1776.4 |
| Net Investment Return | −17.6 | −38.1 | −85.3 | −35.2 | −94.5 | −59.9 |
| Net Investment Yield | −5.16% | −2.40% | −5.05% | −1.98% | −4.89% | −3.17% |

*Source*: SAFE and Author's calculation.
*Note*: The net investment yield equals to the net investment return divided by the average value of China's net foreign asset, which is the mathematical mean of the outstanding of China's net foreign asset at the end of previous year and current year.

2010 and 2014, China's average net outward investment return equals to −62.6 bn USD, and whose average net outbound investment yield is −3.50%. This phenomenon can be mainly attributed to China's insufficient capacity in outward investment. The predominant component of China's foreign asset is foreign exchange reserve, with a share of 60.0% in 2014, and which is mainly invested in high-credit-rated but low-yield public debt securities of advanced countries, particularly U.S. government bonds and agency bonds, while the share of risky but high-yield ODI asset is just 11.6% in 2014. As Figure 1 displays, the average annual investment yield of China's foreign asset is 3.27% during the period between 2005 and 2014.

It is obvious that ODI activities are much more complicate, risky and profitable than purchases of government debt securities, and need more business knowledge. Opposite to the side of foreign asset, the predominant component of China's external liability is FDI, with an average share of 61.0% during the period between 2010 and 2014. According to estimations of some scholars, the average annual investment yield of foreign investors in China was around 20% due to China's large economic and market potentials (Yu, 2008). The average annual investment yield of China's foreign liability is 6.65%

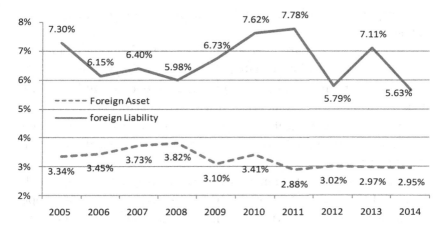

Figure 1. The investment yield of china's foreign asset and foreign liability.

*Source*: safe and author's calculation.

*Note*: The investment yield equals to the investment return divided by the average value of China's foreign asset or liability, which is the mathematical mean of the outstanding of China's foreign asset or liability at the end of previous year and current year.

over the period between 2005 and 2014, and which is 3.38% higher than that of China's foreign asset. This reflects that the international investment capabilities of foreign enterprises are much stronger than those of Chinese enterprises.

## 2.4. The challenges of Chinese economy

Due to limitations in politics, society, endowment and environment, it is impossible that the development process of Chinese economy will be gone smoothly without a setback. China will encounter some serious challenges in the coming years. These challenges are as follows:

First, the most comprehensive and complicated challenge that China has faced is middle income trap. Owing to the rising costs of production factors, rapid aged tendency of population, lack of advanced technology and slow growth of global demand, China's high speed growth mode featuring with overdependence on export and investment cannot be sustainable. The challenging task for China is to restructure its economy and replace the resources intensive and heavy emission manufacturing industries with service and high technology industry.

Second, China's current economic growth mode has faced increasingly serious constraints in labor, land, resources, energy and environment. China has faced the potential threats of social instability, such as, disparity in urban and rural areas, income gaps in different stratums, social emergent incidents, corruption, environment pollution, real estate bubble, and unjust in education, health care and endowment insurance.

Third, The global financial crisis and European sovereign debt crisis and the resultant gloomy world economy could dampen hopes for moderate world growth over the next several years, and which has caused the resurgence of trade and investment protectionism in the world so that some countries have set up many non-tariff barriers against Chinese firms, such as, anti-subsidy, anti-dumping and product standards. This has constituted a serious obstacle to the sustainability of China's export-led growth mode.

Fourth, Chinese enterprises have faced fierce competition and political obstacles in international market. This can be reflected in three aspects: (1) Due to low entrance barriers, standardized technology and low value-added ability, Chinese firms have undergone fierce competitions in the world and their temporary competitive advantages in international production chains can easily lose. (2) The reindustrialization plan of U.S. will constitute a serious threat to the competitive capability of Chinese firms. Comparing to Chinese firms, U.S. manufacturing enterprises have substantial advantages in capital financing cost, energy cost and technology. (3) The application of the principle of competitive neutrality will make Chinese firms particularly SOEs experience many obstacles in carrying out ODIs, such as, investment motives investigation, state security examine, market monopoly investigation, and industrial entrance barriers.

## 2.5. The new normal state of Chinese economy

Currently, the "new normal" is a popular term in China. The new normal state means that Chinese economy has entered a new phase that features more sustainable, mid-to-high-speed growth with higher efficiency and lower costs, and environmentally friendly. It has four key characteristics: the GDP growth will shift from high-speed growth of around 9 to 10% to now mid-to-high rate growth of about 7% (and even lower); the economic structure will undergo comprehensive and fundamental changes, the service industry will gradually play a dominant role in the Chinese economy; consumption will gradually replace investment as the dominant source of demand, the income disparity will be shrink, and people's income will account for a larger share of the economy; the engine of Chinese economy will gradually transform from the investment-driven model into an innovation-driven model.

To realize the target of the new normal, Chinese new government has adopted some concrete measures since it took office in late 2012 and early 2013, such as, reducing overdependence on investment, deepening the economic reform, substantially loosening regulation on economic activities, and accelerating open-up. These new attempts has produced some elementary achievements: (1) quarterly GDP growth rate significantly falls from 7.9% in the fourth quarter of 2012 to 7.0% in the first quarter of 2015; (2) the share of service industry in Chinese economy amazingly rises from 45.5% in the fourth quarter of 2012 to 51.6% in the first quarter of 2015, while that of manufacturing industry significantly declines from 45.0% to 42.9%; (3) the growth rate of high technology industry and equipment manufacturing industry is obviously higher than that of manufacturing industry, meaning that Chinese economy is gradually more driven by innovation; (4) the service sectors have provided more new jobs than the manufacturing industries; (5) the income gap between rural and urban areas is gradually narrowed, and if the trend maintains, consumption will play a more important demand source of Chinese economy; (6) the environment protection law and relevant regulations have been revised, features with strengthening supervision on enterprises' environment related activities.

However, in the transition to the new normal state, the Chinese economy has some uncertainties and challenges, such as, middle income trap, large fluctuation in economy, real estate bubbles, local government debt and financial uncertainties. The largest challenge for Chinese economy is middle income trap. Under the environment of the declining potential growth rate and increasing environmental pressure, if China cannot improve growth quality and efficiency, restructure the economy and boost the economy by innovation, the sharp slowdown of Chinese economy will weaken investors' confidence in investment, real estate market and local government debt, and trigger a chain reaction and even economic crisis.

In sum, under the background of gloomy global demand, rapidly rising labor cost and serious environment pollutions, China's current growth mode cannot be sustainable, with an overdependence on exports of low-and-middle-end manufacturing products and heavy investment. To realize the state of new normal, China should enhance its economic structure, encourage the development of the sectors of service, high-technology and middle-and-high-end manufacture, and restrict the expansion of industries of low value added, resource intensive and heavy $CO_2$ emission. As a large nation with huge oversea assets, China can make use of ODI activities to effectively upgrade its industrial structure and improve the status in the international specifications and global value chains, through acquiring advanced technology, well-known brands, marketing networks and resources, and transferring domestic overcapacity industries. The initiative of "One Belt One Road" will provide large potential for Chinese enterprises to go globally. However, as a late comer in international investment field, Chinese enterprises have faced more obstacles and prejudices than those of their western counterparts, such as fewer investment opportunities, insufficient international business experience, and political intention suspicions. The following two sections will investigate the current circumstances and challenges of China's ODI, and how ODI can enhance China's status in the global value chains and upgrade the industrial structure.

## 3. Chinese ODI's facts, challenges and policy suggestions

China has become an important player in the global international investment scene. In flow terms, Chinese ODI realized 11-year sustained growth with the average rate of 39.8% between 2003 and 2013. From an international comparison, China has been ranked for the first time the world's third largest ODI source nation after the United States and Japan in 2012. Thereafter, Chinese ODI has maintained a strong growth pattern and reached a new high record in 2013 with the total investment of $107.8 billion, up 22.8% over the previous year.

The rapid expansion of Chinese ODI is a result of policy support and economic development. Before 2000, a key strategy for China is to attract foreign capital while overseas investment is strictly controlled. Since the release of "going out" policy in 2000, making overseas investments get encouraged and supported by Chinese government. And the accumulated huge amount of foreign exchange could be used for Chinese ODI. In addition to government support, the economic reality also requires overseas expansion. With rising domestic costs and heightened competitiveness, investing overseas becomes entrepreneur's natural choice.

Along with the phenomenal growth, risks and barriers against Chinese ODI have also been strengthened. State owned enterprises (SOEs) as the dominant players of Chinese ODI are usually considered by host country the threat to fair market competition and even national security. Chinese investors are also often accused of bringing technology, resources, and jobs in host country back to China and thereby undermining sustainable development in local communities. Chinese enterprises' overseas journey is filled with twists and turns. Considering most Chinese enterprises being inexperienced in overseas operation, governmental guidance and service is vital for their subsistence and development.

## 3.1. Investor, industry and destination

By the end of 2013, the number of Chinese ODI investors had reached 15,300. Among these investors, a key feature is the significance of SOEs, especially those centrally-administered SOEs (CSOEs). In 2013, among the non-financial ODI investors, CSOEs accounted for only 3.5%, while local enterprises from provinces, autonomous regions and municipalities took a lion's share of 96.5%. Nevertheless, China's non-financial ODI flows reached $56.3 billion in the same year, accounting for as many as 60.7% of China's total non-financial ODI flows.

CSOEs are a special enterprise group in China. They are few in number with one hundred and twelve in total under the state-owned assets supervision and administration commission of the state council. But they are more powerful compared with private enterprises and local-administered SOEs in the sense that CSOEs enjoy more financial and administration resources. Besides, China's CSOEs face less competition since they are more likely to be in monopolized or highly-controlled industry, such as finance, power and utility, petrochemical and energy, and aircraft and telecommunications. China's CSOEs are keen in making overseas investment under the ambition to be larger, stronger, and globally influential and competitive. But they are often criticized to threaten fair competition because of their special status, as well as have strategic intention which might pose threats to host country's national economic security.

East China is the engine of local Chinese ODI. In 2013, China's local non-financial ODI reached $36.4 billion, with a year-on-year increase of 6.5%. Among these overseas investments, $29.2 billion, or 80.2%, was from East China, with a year-on-year increase of 14.8%; $3.5 billion and $3.7 billion was respectively from Central China and West China with the year-on-year growth rate of 9.6% and −33.9% for each. Guangdong, Shandong, Beijing, Jiangsu, Shanghai, Zhejiang, Liaoning, Tianjin, Fujian and Hebei were top 10 provinces (municipalities) in terms of local Chinese ODI (see Table 2). They accounted for 73.8% of China's total local ODI flows in 2013.

In the aspect of industrial distribution, Leasing and business service attracts the largest amount of Chinese ODI. There were $27.1 billion Chinese overseas investments to this sector in 2013, basically the same as last year, accounting for 25.1% in total (see Table 3). After Leasing and business service, mining, finance, wholesale and retail trade were another three industries that respectively attracted Chinese ODI of $24.8 billion, $15.1 billion and $14.7 billion in 2013. These four industries were over 75% of total Chinese ODI,

Table 2. Top 10 provinces (municipalities) in terms of local Chinese ODI, 2013.

| No. | Province (Municipality) | Flows ($ Billion) |
|---|---|---|
| 1 | Guangdong | 5.9 |
| 2 | Shandong | 4.3 |
| 3 | Beijing | 4.1 |
| 4 | Jiangsu | 3.0 |
| 5 | Shanghai | 2.7 |
| 6 | Zhejiang | 2.6 |
| 7 | Liaoning | 1.3 |
| 8 | Tianjin | 1.1 |
| 9 | Fujian | 1.0 |
| 10 | Hebei | 0.9 |

*Source*: 2013 Statistical Bulletin of China's Outward FDI.

Table 3. Industrial distribution of China's ODI flows.

| | 2013 $ Billions | 2012–2013 Change % | Share in 2013 % |
|---|---|---|---|
| Leasing and business service | 27.1 | 1.2 | 25.1 |
| Mining | 24.8 | 83.2 | 23.0 |
| Finance | 15.1 | 50.0 | 14.0 |
| Wholesale and retail trade | 14.7 | 12.3 | 13.6 |
| Manufacturing | 7.2 | −17.0 | 6.7 |
| Construction | 4.4 | 34.2 | 4.0 |
| Real estate | 4.0 | 95.5 | 3.7 |
| Transport, storage and post | 3.3 | 10.7 | 3.1 |
| Agriculture, forestry, husbandry fishing | 1.8 | 24.0 | 1.7 |
| Scientific research and technical service | 1.8 | 21.0 | 1.7 |
| Information transmission, computer services and software | 1.4 | 13.0 | 1.3 |
| Residents service, repair and other services | 1.1 | 27.0 | 1.1 |
| Production and supply of electricity gas and water | 0.7 | −65.0 | 0.6 |
| Culture, sports and entertainment | 0.3 | 55.0 | 0.3 |
| Hospitality and Catering | 0.1 | −42.9 | 0.1 |

*Source*: 2012 and 2013 Statistical Bulletin of China's Outward FDI.

which further increased by 3.6 percentage points compared with last year.

Although China is called "world factory," the scale of Chinese manufacturing ODI is relatively small, and Chinese manufacturing firms do not move their factories abroad on a large scale. This is likely due to the diversity and imbalance of the economic development among different areas of China. In face of rising domestic production cost, Chinese enterprises are able to relocate their factories inward to the country's less prosperous central and western regions from the more developed eastern coastal areas rather than setting up new facilities in foreign countries which could entail more uncertainties. However, the amount of Chinese manufacturing ODI is likely under-reported, and disguised as Leasing and business service.

It can be implied from the distribution of top 10 countries (regions) of Chinese ODI destinations that offshore financial center, developed economies and resource-rich countries are attractive places for Chinese enterprises (see Table 4). Among these, Hong Kong is the most important transit and destination of Chinese ODI. It received $62.8 billion in 2013, accounting for 58.3% of the total. A large share of Chinese overseas merger and acquisition is conducted through re-investments from Hong Kong, such as the acquisition of

Table 4. Top 10 countries (regions) as destinations for China's ODI flows.

| No. | Countries (Regions) | 2013 $ Billions | 2012–2013 Change % | Share in 2013 % |
|-----|---------------------|-----------------|--------------------|-----------------|
| 1 | Hong Kong (China) | 62.8 | 22.6 | 58.3 |
| 2 | Cayman Islands | 9.3 | 1018.9 | 8.6 |
| 3 | United States | 3.9 | −4.3 | 3.6 |
| 4 | Australia | 3.5 | 59.1 | 3.2 |
| 5 | British Virgin Islands | 3.2 | 43.9 | 3 |
| 6 | Singapore | 2.0 | 33.8 | 1.9 |
| 7 | Indonesia | 1.6 | 14.8 | 1.5 |
| 8 | United Kingdom | 1.4 | −48.8 | 1.3 |
| 9 | Luxembourg | 1.3 | 12.5 | 1.2 |
| 10 | Russia | 1.0 | 30.2 | 0.9 |

*Source*: 2012 and 2013 Statistical Bulletin of China's Outward FDI.

the Canadian oil company Nexen by China National Offshore Oil Corporation (CNOOC) and etc.

## 3.2. Challenges and risks

Along with the increasingly significant presence of Chinese enterprises in overseas investments, their journey is filled with twists and turns. Several major investments have run into obstacles, blocked or subject to long delays. Even for those finally completed projects, in many cases, they go through hardship and some come to a bad end.

The first challenge is investment barriers and resistance. A typical case is a series of difficulties that Chinese telecoms giant Huawei has experienced in some developed countries, especially in the United States and Australia. National security is one pretext that host country's regulatory body use to justify their concerns over Chinese ODI. A key reason is that China adopts the non-alignment policy, the independent diplomatic policy that does not form an alliance with any superpowers, and does not form any military ally of countries like the United States. Another reason is that the major players of Chinese ODI are SOEs. They are considered to be agents of the Chinese government, and their ODI is usually seen as having some hidden agenda.

But things are more complicated underneath the national security fears. Some Chinese ODI are being adversely affected by the tensions of international relations. The failure of Huawei's proposed acquisition in 2010 of a U.S. internet software provider 2 Wire came at a time in the U.S. mid-term elections when members of Congress were especially sensitive because they were concerned about their prospect of reelection and scandals over cyber-attacks and data theft sparked fears over internet security. It seems that Chinese ODI tend to fall victim to the domestic politics of host countries. Opposition parties favor to utilize Chinese investments as an easy target to attack the ruling party. The investment by Chinese private enterprise Zhongkun Group in an undeveloped land in Iceland for tourism in 2011 is a case in point. In addition to political considerations, sometimes commercial interests hide behind claimed national security concerns. The series of frustrations that Huawei has met in the United States at least partly bears on opposition from existing U.S. telecommunications firms.

The second challenge is investment risks in politically vulnerable countries and regions. China has large amounts of investments in Afghanistan, Sudan, Iran, Iraq, Libya, Venezuela, North Korea and other unstable regions. Chinese ODI in these regions accounted for 11.4% in total stock in 2011. The political changes in Middle East, North Africa, and South America have triggered turbulence and instability in these regions. Besides, the fact that commodities bull market has run its course brings huge pressure to those emerging markets that rely heavily on strong prices of major commodities. Chinese investment is easy to become a target and suffer heavy losses wherever there is political turmoil, terrorist attacks, civil wars or sudden regime changes. In fact, Chinese companies have suffered huge losses in the Libyan and Iraq unrest.

Although other foreign investors share the same concern and need to guard against such investment risk, Chinese enterprises are more likely to suffer losses. A key reason is that most Chinese companies, big or small, SOEs or private, are newcomers in the international investment arena. A survey in 2010 shows that more than 80% of Chinese ODI firms began investing abroad after 2000, while only 4% of them had outward investments before 1990.[2] It is easy for them to ignore the potential risks in overseas markets. Moreover, some Chinese investors are accustomed to building close connections with juntas, local strongmen, and powerbrokers, but do not know how to communicate with the local community and its people. Is there any political turmoil or sudden regime changes, they have trouble winning support from local community and its people.

The third challenge is the international recognition of its unique identity. China has overtaken Japan to become the world's second

---

[2]China Goes Global 2011: Survey of ODI Intentions of Chinese Companies, prepared by China Council for the Promotion of International Trade, the United Nations Conferences on Trade and Development and the Asia Pacific Foundation of Canada.

largest economy. But it is still a developing country and a middle income country. So it needs some space to maneuver when negotiating with developed countries. What's more, China is a socialism country with its own characteristics and does not follow the orthodox 'Washington Consensus', a set of policy proposals made by the International Monetary Fund (IMF) and the World Bank to reduce government interventions, and promote trade and financial liberalization. To the Western eye, China's growth and rising influence remains a mystery. In fact, China itself does not have a clear idea of what the 'China Model' is, and has been 'crossing the river by feeling the stones'.[3] But what is certain is that Chinese government has played an important role in the country's economy. And the state ownership is the pillars of Chinese economy.

Such domestic situation has exercised an inevitable influence upon its overseas investment. The former U.S. Secretary of State Hilary Clinton during her visit to Zambia in 2011 criticized China's "reckless misuse" of the continent's resources as a "new colonialism." Hilary's criticism as well as other label of Chinese ODI as pursuing 'state capitalism' is not fair. The issue of state ownership has been overestimated.

## 3.3. Policy suggestions

The large scale of Chinese ODI is still a recent phenomenon. Most Chinese enterprises are inexperienced in overseas operation, and their investment risk awareness is very weak. Therefore, governmental guidance and service is vital for their subsistence and development. As the third largest ODI nation in the world, China should based on its own characteristics to systematize and institutionalize its policies for promoting, supporting and reducing risks of overseas investments.

Chinese ODI policy system should be on the one hand in line with global conventions, and on the other in the service of the nation's overall economic development. The first principle is to guide

---

[3] "Crossing the river by toughing the stones" means there is no fixed mode to follow, but groping in the forward step by step.

but not control, service but not intervene. Making overseas investments is the spontaneous behavior and commercial activity for the micro-enterprises. The governmental ODI policy system should guide but not control the enterprises' overseas investment. It's a service-oriented system, and should refrain from involvement in microeconomic decisions.

We think there are several key policies that should be high on agenda.

The first is to develop and strengthen the function of overseas chamber of commerce in risk elimination, disputes settlement and promotion of the communications between Chinese investors and host country's each side. Overseas chamber of commerce is familiar with local laws and regulations, market structures and conditions as well as social customs. It could maximize the synergy between domestic and foreign cultural differences, bring together solitary enterprises, and therefore greatly enhance viability and the ability to resist risks. Besides, it is needed to establish information consulting service system and support the development of local intermediaries to provide high-quality investing, financial, legal, accounting and other ODI services.

The second is to alleviate the financing problem at various levels. The problem of financing is one impediment of Chinese ODI. This is largely blamed on the underdevelopment of Chinese domestic financial market as well as low degree of internationalization of Chinese domestic financial institutions. To alleviate this problem, it requires to make better use of both domestic and international financial markets and resources.

This includes: (1) built up a promotion platform for enterprises to be listed in China and overseas. (2) Increase the share direct financing, in particular, encourage large enterprises to issue corporate bonds and small and middle-sized enterprises (SMEs) to issue set bond. (3) Increase the government support to SMEs finance. For instance, establish a SMEs ODI fund with the focus on supporting those overseas investments that facilitate the restructure of Chinese economy or move abroad domestic excess capacity. (4) Sign strategic cooperation agreement with foreign banks so as to encourage them providing financial support for Chinese ODI in host countries. (4) Enrich and expand overseas business by Chinese local commercial banks to support overseas investments by Chinese enterprises. (5) Integrate "bring in" and "going global." For example, when Chinese enterprises make overseas merger and acquisition, the target foreign enterprises are also allowed to have the stake of investing Chinese enterprises in the form of stock-for-stock deal. This strategy is likely to reduce financial burden of Chinese enterprises as well as lower investment resistance in the host country.

The third is to accelerate negotiation of Bilateral Investment Treaties (BITs) with the United States and Europe. Although China has concluded BITs with 131 countries, these BITs have not played an enough role in protecting Chinese ODI. A key reason is that most of existing BITs were concluded in the 1980s and 1990s, and thus do not reflect Chinese interests as the major source of foreign capital. China should push ahead with bilateral BIT negotiations with the U.S. as well as Europe. China–U.S. BITs negotiations started in 2008 while China–Europe BITs negotiations began last year.

There are several points of disagreement in both negotiations, include the degree of market access and investor protection; fair competition issue that what standards should be set as a treatment of SOEs, labor practices and the environment; and dispute settlement issue that to which extent arbitration is governed by the Convention on Settlement of Investment Disputes between States and Nationals of Other States. Through exceptional arrangements and other legislative techniques, coming to an agreement does not mean the resolution of all these differences. But each side should make its part of concessions. China has taken the lead in making a major concession. During the fifth Sino-U.S. strategic and economic dialogue in July 2013 in Washington, China for the first time promised pre-establishment national treatment for investments. The next breakthrough depends on whether China could give a satisfactory negative list in 2015 that balance a greater openness and domestic economic interests.

## 4. Outward FDI, the extension of production chains and upgrading of China's GVCs

In the global production networks, the international division of labor is beyond industry and into intra-product. Even in the labor intensive industry, there are capital and technology intensive segments, and in capital and technology intensive industry, there are still labor intensive segments. So, upgrading of industrial structure is mainly embodied by upgrading of GVCs.

### 4.1. The connotation of upgrading of GVCs

In global production networks, production is no longer limited to traditional manufacturing and processing, and consists of a series of value-added activities. The global production chains can be broadly divided into three elementary phases: the first is about technical aspects including research and development, creative design, technical improvement, technical training and so on; the second is concerned with traditional production aspects such as logistics and procurement, module production, production systems, terminal processing, quality control, packaging and inventory management; the third is related to marketing aspects covering wholesale and retail, advertising and after-sales service.

The distribution of revenue along GVCs is represented visually using a U-shaped graphic which is so-called "smile curve." In general, R&D is often the core of the whole GVCs in producer-driven global production networks, while marketing and brands are usually crucial to the whole GVCs in buyer-driven global production networks. So value captured by the technical phase and the marketing phase are relatively high, and that for traditional production phase is correspondingly low in global production networks.

Depending on the capability to control and manipulate the GVCs, firms involved in global production networks can be classified as global flagships, "higher-tier" suppliers, and "lower-tier" suppliers. Global flagships usually possess strategic assets such as core technologies, marketing channels or famous brands, "higher-tier" suppliers also possess other valuable proprietary assets except for hard-core R&D and strategic marketing, "lower-tier" suppliers normally lack proprietary assets. In global production networks, global flagships dominate the whole value chains, "higher-tier" suppliers are inferior to global flagships but superior to "lower-tier" suppliers, and "lower-tier" suppliers are typically used as "price breakers" and "capacity buffers" which are highly vulnerable to abrupt changes in market and technology (Ernst, 2003).

Based on the above attributes of global production networks, the connotation of upgrading of GVCs can be defined in terms of promotion of a firms' position and improvement of capability to create and capture value in global production networks. In existing literature, the upgrading of GVCs covers process upgrading, product upgrading, functional upgrading and inter-sector upgrading in terms of production, or inter-industry upgrading, inter-factorial upgrading, upgrading of demand, upgrading along functional activities and upgrading of forward and backward linkages from the perspectives of industrial system. Although upgrading of GVCs is characterized by its variety, the final destination is to create and capture more value than ever. In global production networks, the upgrading of GVCs is broadly embodied by the shift from manufacturing and processing stages to R&D and marketing stages, and the transition from "lower-tier" suppliers to "higher-tier" suppliers and further to global flagships, the gradient industrial transfer around the world is correspondingly characterized by the gradient transition of all the phases along GVCs in turn.

## 4.2. China's "world factory" position in a dilemma

In global production networks, most Chinese firms are locked in "low end" due to lack of key technology and well-known brands. With the "demographic dividend" is gradually disappearing, China's is faced with serious challenges.

### 4.2.1. *Low-End Locking in Global Production Networks*

China has been integrated into global production networks as the "Manufacturing Factory of the Globe." From the 1990s to the early

2000s, especially after Deng Xiaoping's southern tour speech, China tried to promote technological progress and upgrading of the value chains by technology spillover of FDI. Under the guidance of thoughts behind FDI policies, local governments competed to attract FDI by a series of preferential policies such as tax exemption, land and resource price concessions, and even provide "super-national treatment" for foreign firms in some areas. Driven by such preferential policies, labor-intensive industries, and labor-intensive processing stages in technology-intensive and capital-intensive industries are transferred from Japan and "four tigers" in Asia to China, and therefore China has been integrated into global production networks.

China is becoming more innovative, but it is not yet an innovation powerhouse. Although China has developed a more conducive ecosystem for entrepreneurship and innovation than ever, there is still much room to improve. According to the Global Competitiveness Report 2015–2016, access to finance, policy instability, inflation, inefficient government bureaucracy, insufficient capacity to innovate and so on impede further improvement of productivity and global competitiveness.[4] What's more, China's domestic market is large but domestic demand is relatively inadequate, especially human capital and technological readiness cannot fully meet the demand of high value-added stages. Compared with the percentage of more than 50% in many developed countries, about one quarter of China's economic growth is attributed to productivity improvement in terms of TFP, and the rest is broadly ascribed to input of factors of production.

Under the circumstances, apart from a few global contract manufacturers such as Huawei and Lenovo, the majority of Chinese firms pursue projects which are small, low-budget and effective quickly in short term, and therefore they play the role of "lower-tier" suppliers, and are locked in "low end" in global production networks. Jason Dedrick *et al.* (2011) analyze the distribution of value along the global supply chains of iPad and iPhone, and find that China's

---

[4]World Economic Forum (2015).

economy captures a tiny fraction of total value. The main financial benefit to China takes the form of wages paid for the assembly of the product or for manufacturing of some of the inputs, while the price for an iPhone is about $200 or so, only $10 or less in direct labor wages is paid to China workers (Kraemer *et al.*, 2011).

### 4.2.2. *Severe Challenge Faced with "World Factory"*

The reserve of coal, oil, natural gas, and mineral resources cannot meet the tremendous demand of a world factory. As is well known, China acts as the Manufacturing Factory of the Globe in global production networks and therefore consumes a large amount of energy and mineral resources while supplying large numbers of inexpensive products to the world. Although China is a large developing country, but the reserve of coal, oil, natural gas, and mineral resources and so on is inadequate, and natural resource per head is much lower relative to most countries in the world, and China's natural resources cannot meet the tremendous demand of a world factory at all, which means China's current economic development mode is unsustainable. In order to drive China's sustainable development, China has to transfer from a manufacturing-driven economy to an innovation-driven economy.

Rising labor costs and aging undermine China's competitiveness of manufacturing and processing sectors. On the one hand, Chinese government has driven up minimum wages, aggressively enforced labor and environmental regulations. According to China's Employment Promotion Plan, the minimum wage in each jurisdiction must be increased at least once every two years, and the Twelfth Five-Year Plan stipulates an average increase of 13% per year. On the other hand, different from developed countries, China has already entered an aging society with lower GDP per capita. In 2014, the number of seniors over 65 has reached about 138.55 million, and the share in the population is 10.1%. However, the China's GDP per capita is just $7589, ranks 80th in the world. In order to drive China's sustainable development, China has to transfer from a manufacturing-driven economy to an innovation-driven economy.

### 4.3. The extension of production chains: A solution to the dilemma

In order to enhance China's capacity to create and capture value-added, China should develop a Multinational Diamond Model with China as the core by the extension of production chains driven by outward FDI.

#### 4.3.1. *The Diamond Model of National Competitive Advantage (NCA)*

Michael Porter, a Harvard University professor, has developed NCA which is represented visually using a diamond-shaped graphic. The Diamond Model of NCA outlines the framework of four interrelated attributes which determine a firm's innovative capability (Porter, 2011). The four interrelated determinants are factor conditions, demand conditions, related and supporting industries, and firm strategy, structure, and rivalry. In addition, the government and chance are just viewed as two exogenous parameters which influence the four determinants of the diamond model. Factors can be further divided into basic factors such as raw-material resources and advance factors such as specialized human capital, and the latter are more important than the former. Demand conditions involve customer needs and wants, a company's capacity and growth rate and so on, especially sophisticated buyers prod companies to innovate faster. Internationally competitive related and supporting industries not only deliver the most cost-effective inputs in an efficient, rapid, and sometimes preferential way, but also provide new ideas and technical interchange which speed up the rate of innovation and upgrading. In addition, the modes choice of establishment, organization and management are usually influenced by national circumstances and context, and especially domestic rivalry often spurs innovation of products and processes as well as improvement of quality and service (see Figure 2).

#### 4.3.2. *The Expanded Diamond Model of NCA*

However, multinational activities have not been taken into account in Porter's Diamond Model. With trade and investment liberalization

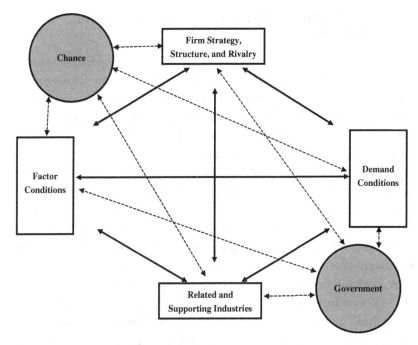

Figure 2. Diamond model of NCA.
*Source*: Porter (2011).

and facilitation, the barriers to cross-border movement of factors
and goods have been reduced or canceled, the process of regional
economic integration has greatly accelerated. Therefore, one country's NCA are also influenced by the four determinants of other
countries. Based on the facts, the expanded diamond models have
been developed whereby international flows of factors and goods are
formally incorporated into the model. For example, Dunning (1993)
views multinational activities as a third exogenous variable except
for the government and chance; Rugman and D'Cruz (1993) propose
the Double Diamond Model and North American Diamond based on
the Canada-U.S. Free Trade Agreement; Moon, Rugman and Verbeke
(1998) develop the Generalized Double Diamond with both domestic
and global factors taken into account to assess the global competitiveness of Korea and Singapore.

### 4.3.3. *Multinational Diamond Model with China at Its Core*

Expanded Diamonds give China clues on how to gain competitive advantage at high value-added stages. As we all know, Porter's Diamond Model is based on the patterns of competitive success in ten leading nations such as the U.S., Japan, and Germany which possess abundant advance factors and relatively sound national innovation systems. However, China is a developing country, and the four determinants of NCA at value-added stages are far from those of ten leading nations. What's more, China's economic environments cannot change overnight due to path dependence. In view of above facts, China can enhance its own competitive advantage at high value-added stages by means of economic environments of other countries. An alternative way is to pool together complementary factor conditions, demand conditions, related and supporting industries of China and other countries, and to develop a Multinational Diamond Model with China at its core. In the Multinational Diamond Model, China can enhance competitive advantage at high value-added stages based on innovative capability gained in developed countries and resources obtained in developing countries (see Figure 3).

The extension of production chains driven by OFDI contributes to development of the Multinational Diamond Model with China at its core. In global production networks, countries are different in economic environments which result in distinct stage-specific competitive advantages. In order to gain competitive advantage at high value-added stages, enterprises from China can make cross-border matching between various production stages and respective corresponding economic environments via outward FDI on a global scale (Li 2015). On the one hand, through OFDI in developed countries such as the U.S. and Germany, Chinese companies are embedded in production networks of host countries, thereby getting access to globally competitive related and supporting industries, obtaining specialized factors such as talented personnel, patents and well-known brands, and making full use of local innovation systems to meet sophisticated demands; on the other hand, through OFDI in

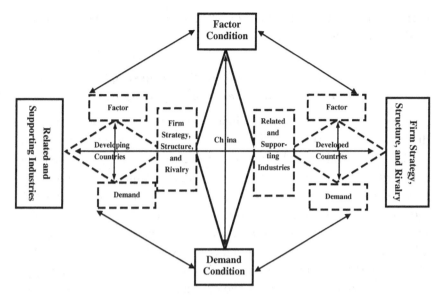

Figure 3. Multinational diamond model with China at its core.
*Source*: The figure is originated by author.

developing countries which are abundant in natural resources and
labor, Chinese companies can not only lower the costs of manufacturing and processing stage, but also make room for the development of
R&D and marketing stages. In the end, the Multinational Diamond
Model with China at its core comes into being through which China
is moving upward along the "smile curve."

## 4.4. The ways to develop multinational
## diamond model

The development of Multinational Diamond Model with China as
the core is essentially the extension of China's production chains
with the intention to gain competitive advantage at high value-added
stages. To this end, Chinese firms should transfer marginal industry
or marginal segments of production chains to other developing countries, meanwhile, make asset-specific investment on marketing and
R&D in developed countries. At the government level, China together

with other countries should promote facilitation of investment and trade along "one belt, one road."

### 4.4.1. Expand Manufacturing and Processing
### Segments in Other Developing Countries

The expansion of marginal industry or marginal segments of production chains optimizes allocation of resources and improves social welfare. Generally speaking, there are gaps in factor cost, managerial skill, and technical knowledge between China and countries at lower stages of economic development, and therefore a particular industry which is losing competitiveness as a result of rapid changes in factor endowments in China may be a potentially comparatively-advantaged industry in the countries at lower stage. In global production networks, the international division of labor is beyond industry and into intra-product. Under the circumstances, even in the sunrise industry, there are still segments which are losing competitiveness, and therefore expansion driven by OFDI not only involves traditional marginal industries, but also includes marginal segments of production chains. The successful expansion of marginal industry or marginal segments of production chains through OFDI will exploit cheap natural resources and labor of host countries, transfer China's overcapacity, make room for the development of sunrise industry or higher value-added stages transferred from developed countries.

In fact, many developed countries and newly industrialized countries promote upgrading of industrial structure or GVCs by this way. In the 1950s, the United States transferred iron and steel, textile and other industries which were losing comparative advantages to Westdeutschl and Japan which were inferior to the U.S. in economy, and focused on emerging industries such as semiconductors, communications equipment and computer. From the 1960s to 1980s, Westdeutschl and Japan expanded such labor and natural resources intensive industries to Newly Industrial Economics, and specialized in technology intensive industries such as integrated circuit, precision machinery, automobile, household appliances, and fine chemicals. Since the 1990s, the United States, Germany, Japan and other developed countries as well as Newly Industrial Economics have transferred labor intensive industry or low-value added production stages of capital and technology intensive industries to China, India and other developing countries, and they are mainly engaged in R&D, marketing, brands and so on.

### 4.4.2. *Make Asset-Specific Investment on R&D and Marketing in Developed Countries*

It is vital for Chinese firms to get tacit knowledge from "higher-tier" suppliers or global flagships in order to upgrade CVCs. According to difference in knowledge needed, tasks along global production chains can be further classified into those that require explicit knowledge and those that require tacit knowledge (Polanyi, 2012). Explicit knowledge can be expressed in a linguistic, mathematical, or visual symbol, and is often embodied in a standardized — or even outdated — technology or usual routine; while tacit knowledge is deeply rooted in the human body and only can be expressed through action, commitment, and involvement in a specific context and locality, and often provides the fertile intellectual ground for all knowledge management and for the effective performance of an economy (Ernst, 2002) by which Chinese firms can create and capture more value added.

It is necessary for Chinese firms to be integrated into global production networks of developed countries in order to acquire tacit knowledge. The process of knowledge diffusion and capability formation in the GPNs involves four steps such as socialization (tacit-to-tacit conversion), externalization (tacit-to-explicit conversion), combination (explicit-to-explicit conversion), and internalization (explicit-to-tacit conversion). Chinese firms can achieve combination and internalization of explicit knowledge by the transactions of intellectual property and procurement of equipment, but often suffer export restrictions to high technology. Only by integration into production networks of developed countries, can Chinese firms achieve the socialization and externalization of tacit knowledge.

It is a prerequisite of integration into global production networks of developed countries that Chinese firms have made asset-specific investments. Asset-specific investments on R&D and marketing not only improve the capability of Chinese firms to assimilate tacit and explicit knowledge, but also make Chinese firms functionally and territorially embedded into aspects of the social and spatial arrangements of "higher-tier" suppliers and global flagships. Based on asset-specific investments on R&D and marketing, there is a symbiosis among Chinese firms, "higher-tier" suppliers and global flagships by which relation contracts come into being. In line with the changing requirements of markets, "higher-tier" suppliers and global flagships will actively provide technical literature and technical assistance and share related marketing experience to help Chinese firms meet their requirements.

### 4.4.3. *Promote Facilitation of Investment among Countries along "One Belt, One Road"*

"One belt, one road" is the longest economic corridor with the greatest potential in the world. It involves 65 countries and more than 4 billion people. The development and construction of "one belt, one road" creates a large market. Many countries along "one belt, one road" are abundant in natural resources, but insufficient in capital, human resources and infrastructure. There is great potential for countries along it to cooperate in transportation, finance, energy, telecommunications, agriculture and tourism. Especially, it is reported that many countries in Asia and Europe have indicated their support for China's construction of "one belt, one road."

China's pivotal role helps develop the Multinational Diamond Model with China at the Core. "One belt, one road" runs through the whole Eurasia, borders on the Asia-Pacific Economic Circle on the East, and enters the developed European Economic Circle on the West. The Belt and Road initiative covers five areas-policy communication, road connectivity, unimpeded trade, money circulation and understanding between peoples. In order to fully utilize factor conditions, demand conditions, related and supporting industries of Eurasia, China together with other countries along it should further refine the Belt and Road initiative, and formulate specific measures on trade and investment facilitation, infrastructure development, industrial and sub-regional economic cooperation, and financial cooperation.

## References

Dunning, J. H. (1993). Internationalizing porter's diamond. *MIR: Management International Review*, 33(2), 7–15.

Ernst, D. and L. Kim (2002). Global production networks, knowledge diffusion, and local capability formation. *Research Policy*, 31(8), 1417–1429.

Ernst, D. (2003). *Digital Information Systems And Global Flagship Networks: How Mobile Is Knowledge In The Global Network Economy*. Edward Elgar, Cheltenham.

Kraemer, K. L., G. Linden, and J. Dedrick (2011). *Capturing Value in Global Networks: Apple's iPad and iPhone*. University of California, Irvine, University of California, Berkeley, Syracuse University, NY. Available at http://pcic.Merage.Uci.Edu/papers/2011/value_iPad_iPhone.Pdf.

Li, G. (2015). Cross-border institutional matching and upgrading of industrial structureF An explanation on outward FDI from developing countries. *Journal of Central University of Finance & Economics*, 6, 82–90, forthcoming.

Moon, H. C., A. M. Rugman, and A. Verbeke (1998). A generalized double diamond approach to the global competitiveness of Korea and Singapore. *International Business Review*, 7(2), 135–150.

Porter, M. E. (2011). *Competitive Advantage of Nations: Creating and Sustaining Superior Performance*. Simon and Schuster, New York.

Rugman, A. M., and J. R. D'Cruz (1993). The double diamond model of international competitiveness: The Canadian experience. *Management International Review*, 33(2–1), 17–39.

Polanyi, M. (2012). *Personal Knowledge: Towards A Post-Critical Philosophy*. University of Chicago Press.

World Economic Forum (2015). The Global Competitiveness Report 2015–2016. Available at http://www.weforum.org/reports/global-competitiveness-report-2015-2016. (Accessed on October 17, 2015).

Yu, Y. (2008). Managing Capital Flows: The Case of China. Research Center for International Finance, Institute of World Economics and Politics. CASS, Working Paper No. 0816.

CHAPTER 10

# The Role of Judiciary in India's Economic Development

Sukanya Natarajan

*Center for Policy Research*
*New Delhi, India*
*sukanyanatarajan@gmail.com*

## 1. Introduction

Historically, several scholars have committed themselves to calibrating the various factors including judiciary that determines economic growth and development and have sought to understand the nexus between law and growth (Dam, 2006a and 2006b; Sen, 2000; Posner, 1998; Messick, 1999, 2004; Voigt, 2005). Present different theories on the probable sources of cross country income differences suggest that the rate of economic growth is dependent upon the performance of a country's institutions — social, political, economic, and legal (North, 2003, 1993, 1989). Variables such as capital accumulation, political structure, legal systems, productivity, technological developments and selection of policy framework have been evaluated both theoretically as well as empirically. In this context, it is undeniably tricky to identify which institutions matter and precisely how do they count. Countries are open to restructure institutions in order to improve their economic performance.

Post financial crisis, there has been an incredible increase in the amount of interest that has been attributed to the role that structural reforms plays in promoting economic development. In this context, the present chapter traces the role of judiciary in India's economic development. The intention is to understand the underlying mechanisms of the legal apparatus, the prospects and challenges judicial reforms pose and the manner in which it influences the Indian economy.

## 2. Current state of the Indian economy: Developmental challenges and economic reform in India

Indian economy has recovered to 7.4% between April to December of 2014–2015 as compared with 7% during the same period of the previous year (Jaitley, 2015). India's growth is likely to surpass China by the year 2030 and will overtake China as the most populous country in the world (Lagarde, 2015). The global economy is slated to grow by 3.5% this year in 2015 and 3.7% in the subsequent year.[1] Analysis and growth forecasting of India's growth story has been perplexed by the emergence of a new GDP series (2011 base) that has made some fundamental changes in methodology and data sources (Virmani, 2015). According to certain analysts, this series provides less than three years of growth data and it is impossible to estimate the underlying trend growth rate using the same series. The Central statistical organization (CSO) has projected a growth rate of 7.4 for 2014–2015 and acceleration of growth to 8% in 2015–2016.[2] The recent IMF assessment in March 2015 on Indian economy claims that lower global oil prices as well as constructive policy actions have improved confidence in investment. Although the IMF report stresses that India needs to focus on revitalizing the investment cycle and accelerate structural reforms, the Indian economy presently maintains a positive outlook on the global development scale and is set to become one of the fastest emerging market economies in the world.[3] By 2030, India will have the largest labor force in the world and yet the youngest populations in the world which will be larger than

---

[1] *Ibid.*
[2] *Ibid.*
[3] *Ibid.*

the combined labor force in Indonesia, European Union and United States (Lagarde, 2015).

India has a hard task of having to create jobs for the roughly 100 million young Indians who will enter the job market in the forthcoming decade. In order to increase India's growth rate and to ensure it starts to generate sufficient jobs require implementation of deeper structural reforms. Various sectors that require reform include agriculture, mining, power sector, labor markets which can bolster economic growth. The present government's efforts to improve the climate of investment has gathered momentum in the past year through schemes such as 'Make in India' to attract foreign investment.

In this context, economic diplomacy has brought a lot of goodwill for India's presence as well as an invitation for foreign investors to come and invest in India (Rajamohan 2014). The prospect of how far Japan is involved in South Asia has been clearly established. With the recent visit of the Chinese Premier Xi Ziping and the Japanese PM Abe one tends to understand the gravity of the change in posture from strict reciprocity to unilateral cooperation. The economic diplomacy facilitated visits to countries in the West and East to target foreign investors to come and invest in India. Since 1991, the opening up of the Indian economy has enabled a drastic change in environment for private sector growth and development projecting India as one of the fastest growing economies in the world. The economic growth in India has been made possible due to the dynamic growth in the services sector (Eichengreen and Gupta, 2011).

## 3. Investment climate in India and make in India policy

To improve the investment scenario and India's image as a hub for economic activity, the present government has devised a new policy for export promotion. There are several challenges and advantages that exist for foreign investors and foreign firms that are operating in India that are not fully utilized at this moment and don't directly lead to economic development (Bajpai and Sach, 2000). Some of these challenges include inadequate physical infrastructure for the smooth operation of the firms, complicated regulatory environment to muddle through and insufficient availability of skilled population which continue to constrain the manufacturing sector within the country (GOI Report, 2002).

India's strength so far lies in the services sector as opposed to the manufacturing sector. The present government is projecting its focus on the manufacturing sector to improve and facilitate growth within the manufacturing sector. In cognition of the multiplier effect that manufacturing sector would induce, the government is garnering to focus on the creation of 100 million jobs and therefore has announced a policy of manufacturing with the aim of enhancing the share of the manufacturing sector to about 25% in GDP within a time span of 10 years.[4]

In this context, the Make in India program will be an important indicator of India's rising challenge in the present economic situation. The 'Make in India' programme has been specifically modeled to improve investment and innovation, target skill development, enable protection of intellectual property rights and in the process provide physical infrastructure for the firms and investors.[5] The sectors have been slotted for the programme are as follows: automobiles, biotechnology, chemicals, construction, electrical machinery and systems, automobile components, mining, oil, gas, pharmaceuticals, food processing, media and entertainment, roads, highways, space, garments, thermal power, tourism, hospitality, aviation, renewable energy, textiles, and garments. The positive aspects of the manufacturing sector are being focused upon through policy instruments, simplifying the processes of setting up business in India as well as focused on raising the competitiveness of the Indian manufacturing sector which is imperative for the long term economic growth of India.

The policy intends to grapple with problems of regulation, technology, financing as well as exit mechanisms, infrastructure, skill set

---

[4]National Manufacturing Policy, Ministry of Commerce and Industry, Department of Industrial Policy and Promotion.

[5]Make in India Policy, Government of India, and Accessed at http://www.makeinindia.com/policy/foreign-direct-investment/.

improvement and other factors important for growth generation. The policy has been met with caution as well as praise from various quarters. RBI governor Raghuram Rajan (2015) has very particularly caustic in his approach towards the manufacturing policy announced by the present government. His main focus was to question why the focus on manufacturing sector was being showcased in a manner similar to that of China.[6] He underlined that Asia already has a manufacturing powerhouse in China, in this context; it would be wise to focus on the advantage of the services sector which drives India's growth story.[7]

## 4. Legal institutions and economic growth in India

In the past, policymakers and academics keenly sought to understand the relationship between legal institutions and economic performance whereas development community pursued research on legal and judicial reform projects. This pursuit has been revived in large part by a keen interest in understanding the role that legal apparatus in the country plays in promoting improvements in aiding poverty reduction especially in low and middle income countries in Asia.

Enormous literature exists in understanding the correlation between sound legal machinery, judicial reforms, and economic development especially in developing economies in Asia (Santos, 2012; Perry, 2000). Some of these studies reveal the following results: predictability as well as transparency in a system, less judicial corruption, speedy legal proceedings, and enhancement in investment environment for foreign investors may lead to economic development (Pistor and Wellons, 1999; Brown and Gutterman, 1998; Jayasuriya, 1999). Western literature on developed economies exclaims that for sustained economic growth, efficient legal machinery and enforcement are mandatory. In the case of developing economies, there have been success stories of countries escaping the middle income trap irrespective of the performance of legal

---

[6] *Ibid.*
[7] *Ibid.*

institutions depending upon whether they were democracies or not (Dam, 2006).

In the context of India, there is a definite need to understand the connection between performance of legal apparatus and economic growth. The intention of the chapter is to comprehend relevant knowledge as well as reconfigure our intellectual understanding of the relation between legal institutions and economic growth as well as the capacity of judicial reforms to resolve problems of governance. India is one of the few developing countries where the legal machinery in action, adjudicated by judges and enforced by the Indian state plays a crucial role despite well-known shortcomings which can be altered by implementing judicial reforms.

The general notion that exists is that there is a strong correlation between legality and economic development denotes that only developed countries mostly democracies can afford better institutions (Dam, 2006). Further, in his work on judiciary and economic development, Dam (2006) claims that 'No degree of substantive law improvement nor world best practice substantive law will bring the rule of law to a country without effective enforcement'. In the case of India, this section seeks to analyze how legal apparatus poses challenges and opportunities to remaking the developmental Indian state. Although there are adequate laws in India to cope with the investors grievances, the problem lies in the implementation of these laws due to delayed judgments in Indian courts. Justice delayed is justice denied is a common phrase one contends with when one tries to grapple with the Indian legal machinery.[8] This is hardly shocking as legal scholars have tacit understanding in quality of law on paper does not guarantee the enforcement of laws.

In order to analyze how law mattered for economic development, interdisciplinary research undertaken by legal and economic experts from Asia and the west, commissioned by ADB, TCA Anant and ML Mitra (1995) examined the Indian story on the role of law in economic development. The authors posed the following query: Did law matter

---

[8]The famous phrase justice delayed is justice denied is attributed to William E. Gladstone although some claim that it is attributed to 1215 Magna Carta.

for economic development in India between 1960 and 1995? In their work, they separated the time period from 1960–1965 as high growth in a closed economy, from 67–80 as a stagnant socialist economy and from 1980 to 1995 as a period of reform and liberalization. The authors analyzed the impact of law separately for each period.

Despite having a well-established legal system, India's economic development storyboard fails to grapple with the origin, structure, pathologies of judicial delays. The Indian judicial system is a three tiered system which includes 18,000 courts under the helm of the supreme court of India. The Supreme Court is headed by the Chief Justice of India and has 31 judges. The Supreme Court takes up appeals against the judgments of high courts and petitions of serious violations on its own or based on petitions filed by Supreme Court lawyers. There is an argument that confirms that India's courts in the process of protecting civil rights as well as political rights might not contribute to growth Peerenboom, Randall (2008: 08).

Investors who throng to India are bothered by judicial corruption, lack of resources, long delays, and pendency of cases and largely view the system as inefficient (Law Commission Report, 2003). In a globalized economy, especially when the present government is keen to win over investors from all over the world, specialized commercial courts are required to deal with investors issues and problems.[9] One of the Law Commission (2014) reports noted that the U.S. and UK courts are increasingly admitting cases which ought to have been filed before Indian courts on the ground that in India almost all cases take 25 years for disposal. To catapult India to act as a significant player in the globalized market, it is not just important to bring in stricter enforcement of laws.

Judicial reforms need to be systemically implemented not in a haphazard piecemeal manner with due emphasis given to prioritizing and sequencing judicial delays as soon as possible. The report on doing business based on factors such as cost, time, complexity of procedures resolving commercial disputes published by the World Bank in 2014 compares business regulations for domestic companies

---

[9] *Ibid.*

in about 189 countries wherein India ranks on the 158th position with respect to starting a business, similarly, with respect to enforcement of contracts, India ranks at about 186th position.[10] If India is projecting itself as a manufacturing hub and invites foreign investors to come and invest in the country, it is vital that it channelizes its energies on constructing an effective judicial system as an integral part of the economic reform agenda.

## 4.1. Judicial reforms in India

Before we look at the special case of India, scholars such as Mathew Stephenson (2007) claim that 'there are three problems that bedevil efforts to design and implement effective legal and judicial reform projects'. He summarizes the three problems as follows: improving the efficiency of a judicial system requires financial and human resources that are in short supply in developing economies, the potential of judiciary to perform a positive role in promoting development depends on the willingness of affected parties to employ the courts to dispute settlement; when the judiciary is in suboptimal stage improving the courts along one dimension might not improve overall institutional performance. Permanent Member of the NITI Aayog,[11] Bibek Debroy (2006) claims that there are three layers to judicial reform in the case of India. First, there is an element of statutory law reform weeding out old and dysfunctional elements in legislation, unification and harmonization. Second, legal reform has to have an administrative law reform component, meaning the subordinate legislation in the form of rules, orders, regulations and instructions from ministries and government departments. He claims that constraints to efficient decision making comes about through administrative law rather than through statutory law and bribery and rent seeking are fallouts. Third, the element of legal reform is

---

[10]World Bank Report on Doing Business, Accessed at http://www.doingbusiness. org/data/exploreeconomies/india.
[11]NITI Aayog is the new institution that has replaced the Planning Commission which was under the helm of Montek Singh Ahluwalia during the congress rule. Presently, Bibek Debroy is a permanent member to Niti Aayog.

what may be called judicial reforms, though faster dispute resolution and contract enforcement are not exclusively judicial issues.

Debroy and Hazra's (2007) work on Judicial Reforms in India examines how economic understanding of judicial reforms is not necessarily the correct approach as they measure efficiency of the system largely pertaining to property rights, enforcement of contracts and maintenance of order. Their contribution revolves around property and contract in addressing legal and judicial problems such as judicial strength, judicial infrastructure, judicial productivity and management of judicial administration. Practicing lawyers such as Arun Mohan (2009) have argued that delayed justice slows down economic development and growth. He claims:

> "A proper set of laws that are fine-tuned and an efficient judicial system that acts as an accelerant while an improper set of law, tardy justice, poor governance and inefficient administration act as a retardant. An inefficient law and justice system could become a dead weight to development efforts. An agreement or a business transaction must be enforceable at law and so in a reasonable time. The ability of the law to settle matters quickly and make itself more agile is imperative. The greater the justice system's support the faster is the growth of the economy and therefore development." [12]

Researchers such as Nick Robinson (2012) have analyzed the Indian Supreme Court docket in great detail from the year 1993 to 2011. He states that court data is imperfect in a certain way and analyses court data and pendency to show that 'the Supreme court is disproportionately accessed by those close to Delhi and then the rest of the supreme court's multiplicity of benches and cases which may be undercutting the following of precedent in the Indian judicial system'.[13] Robinson (2014) argues that 'the Indian judiciary is unusually top-heavy, with more cases, more judges, and more administrative power located in the upper judiciary, and especially the Supreme Court, than in most other systems.' In his work on pendency of cases in India, Robinson (2009) claims that the backlog is caused by

---

[12] *Ibid.*
[13] *Ibid.*

the number and the type of cases the court accepts than having far
few judges who handle the cases. He argues that owing to the low
barriers to petitioning to the Supreme Court, combined with the high
percentage of cases the court ultimately accepts, lie at the root of
the high backlog. He presents the international system of admission
policy in other countries to give a broader context to his argument
as follows:

> "The importance of the court's admission policy becomes clearer when
> placed within an international context. In the United States, for instance,
> an appeal to the Supreme Court is fairly easy, but its court only accepts
> about 1% of these appeals and so generally hears less than a hundred
> cases each year. Several European constitutional courts have very high
> acceptance rates but appeals can often only be generated upon request
> by the legislature or a lower court judge. Because of this, the Italian
> constitutional court decides about 500 cases a year, while the French
> constitutional council which has even stricter grounds for appeal may
> decide only 50 cases in a year." [14]

He argues that the 'Supreme Court by and large remains popular. Yet, if one digs a bit, beneath the surface is an institution
that has strayed from its mission and may even be undermining the
rest of the judicial system'.[15] Robinson (2013) further claims that
the Supreme Court centralizes and creates uncertainty deliberately.
Robinson claims:

> "Such an extremely active Supreme Court demoralizes High Court and
> lower court judges, who now have difficulty determining what the law
> actually is, and exasperates litigants, who can now expect that any given
> case will be appealed to the Supreme Court, which means squandering
> years and money in the process." [16]

He further notes[17]:

> "The Supreme Court has centralized judicial authority in Delhi, micro-
> managing the decisions of the rest of the judicial system, with seemingly
> counterproductive results. By taking on so many cases, the Supreme

---

[14] *Ibid.*
[15] *Ibid.*
[16] *Ibid.*
[17] *Ibid.*

Court instead of clarifying precedent has confused it. Instead of making the system more accessible, it has normalized an expensive layer of appeal that the wealthy and those closer to Delhi are best positioned to navigate. The current arrangement has enriched Supreme Court lawyers but arguably weakened the health of the rest of the judicial system."

He argues that public interest litigation and important constitutional cases have a high entry barrier as opposed to the other cases. He claims that increasing the number of judges alone will not solve the backlog problem. The traditional understanding of the literature available on the supreme court portrayed how the main advantage lay in understanding how the importance of judiciary lay in checking abuses of state power, enforcing property rights, enabling exchanges between private entities as well as ensuring public order.

The logic and rationale behind understanding nuances was to underline how economic policies require strong and accountable institutions to support and implement them. The literature on Judicial Reforms amongst other things stressed that the key aspect without which economic reforms alone will not help is judicial reforms to ensure timely as well as effective delivery of justice in commercial cases. According to the Department of Justice, the Indian judiciary has employed 18,000 judges at the subordinate level amounting to 13 judges per million.[18] The tally is against 50 judges per million in developed countries and 35–40 in developing countries. India Spend has prepared a report that states that over 30 million cases are pending in several courts spread across the country; lower level courts roughly have about 27 million pending cases; higher level courts have about 4 million pending cases.[19]

Study undertaken by Barry Walsh (2008) on judicial productivity in India shows a vivid comparison that the disposal ratio in Delhi in 2005 was estimated at 701 disposals per year when juxtaposed with Australian courts where the figure stands double at 1,511 disposals.

---

[18]Committee on Empowerment of Women, Parliament House, New Delhi, Lok Sabha Secretariat, Press Release, Para 2.8.
[19]India Spend Report, Pendency of Cases in Indian Judiciary.

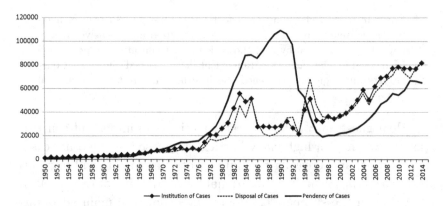

Figure 1. Historical perspective: Supreme Court case status: admission, disposal and pendency.

*Source*: Annual Report 2014–2015, Supreme Court of India.[20]

For a historical perspective of case disposal, institution and pendency of India's Supreme Court — please see Figure 1. In April 2015, as per the statement made by Law Minister Sadananda Gowda in the Indian Parliament, there are about 1.89 crore cases pending in subordinate courts as of 2014 whereas in higher courts the cases stand at 89,164 cases.

## 4.2. Judicial accountability

In this context, it is impossible to attain judicial productivity by deciding on the ratio of judges to cases disposed every year. Law Commission headed by Justice A. P. Shah submitted its recommendations for judicial reforms to support economic growth from a legal perspective in January 2015. Some of the troubling information with regard to the report includes please see Figure 3: there are 32,656 civil suits pending in 5 high courts, increase of 6.27% in pendency every year as noted, overload of cases on few judges, for e.g., Madras HC contains only 4 judges who were disproportionately allocated 41,702 cases pending on the original jurisdiction. To understand the volume of commercial disputes in high courts with original jurisdiction,

[20] Annual Report 2014–2015, Supreme Court of India. Available at http://supremecourtofindia.nic.in/annualreports.htm, http://supremecourtofindia.nic.in/annualreport/annualreport2014-15.pdf.

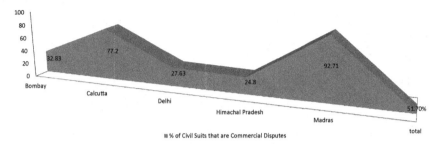

Figure 2. Percentage of commercial disputes in high courts with original jurisdiction.

*Source*: The Law Commission of India Report No. 253, 2015, Ministry of Law and Justice, India.

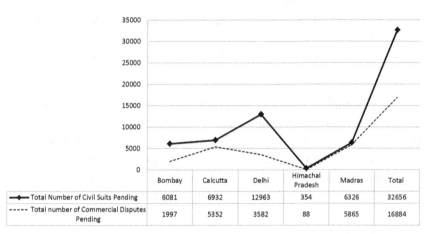

Figure 3. Pendency of commercial disputes in high courts with original jurisdiction.

*Source*: The Law Commission of India Report No. 253, 2015, Ministry of Law and Justice, India.

please see Figure 2. Also see Figure 4 depicting the present scenario of delays in civil suits in high courts. The recommendations of the report include the following:

(i) Commercial disputes of high complexity and value to be disposed in a speedy manner;

(ii) To tackle with the commercial cases pending in all the three courts, the commercial division and commercial appellate

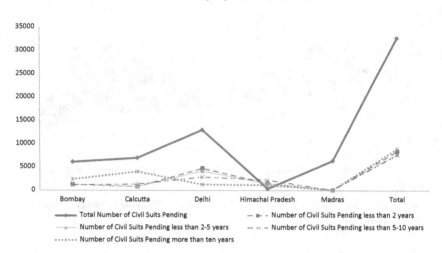

Figure 4. Breakdown of delays in disposal of civil suits in each high court with original civil jurisdiction.

*Source*: The Law Commission of India Report No. 253, 2015, Ministry of Law and Justice, India.

division of high courts and commercial courts bill 2015 will soon be tabled in the parliament.[21]

(iii) The bill stresses the need for an efficient dispute resolution mechanism to the growth and development of trade and commerce underlining the requirement of quick enforcement of contracts, mechanism to recover monetary claims and compensation of damages are critical to encourage foreign investors to come to India.

(iv) This bill aims to improve the investment climate perception pertaining to India as a difficult country to carry out business due to a slow and inefficient judicial system.

(v) Some of the other reforms suggested within the bill include: promised increase in the judicial strength of high courts.

If the bill is passed, the commercial courts will be setup, which will ensure that disposal of cases are speedy thereby encouraging

---

[21]The Law commission of India Report No. 253 in-depth analyses the Commercial and Commercial Appellate Division of High Courts and Commercial Courts Bill, 2015.

foreign investors to come to India to invest especially in the light of make in India campaign. The report also underlines in-depth study of commercial courts abroad indicating that courts will revamp the inefficient judicial system. As per the bill, the power to constitute commercial vision within high courts or commercial courts will now lie with the central government.[22] To establish these commercial courts, new norms of practice will be setup for commercial litigation which can be expanded to civil litigation in India.

Some measures to be introduced include e-courts, online operations to maintain voluminous accounting and efficacy of functioning.[23] In addition, judges of commercial courts will be made to undergo training at the National judicial academy that will improve the level of exposure. In terms of court infrastructure, better maintenance of court records, digitization of proceedings of commercial courts and e-filing as well as facilities for audio visual recording will be instituted.[24] From the increase in commercial dispute definition to speedy disposal of cases and effective training of the judiciary, the law commission has suggested the enhancement of professionalism of Indian legal system.

In the context of broader judicial reforms being discussed about, the judicial accountability bill has been long dormant due to some of the clauses proposed to lay down standards of conduct for judges of the Supreme Court and the High courts. The bill was passed in the Lok Sabha in 2012 but it is still pending to be passed in the Rajya Sabha. The judicial standards and accountability bill at large tries to lay down enforceable standards of conduct for judges in addition requiring judges to declare details of their assets as well as liabilities which were passed by the former UPA government in the Lok Sabha in 2012. This bill later lapsed after the dissolution of the 15th Lok Sabha. The bill was later amended in Rajya Sabha following protests by several members of judiciary. In May 2015, the present government

---

[22] *Ibid.*
[23] *Ibid.*
[24] *Ibid.*

has put off the introduction of the Judicial Standards and Accountability Bill till the notification of the National Judicial Appointments Commission.

The National Judicial Appointments Commission Bill was passed in both the houses of the parliament in 2014.[25] The passage of this bill replaced the collegium system of appointing judges to the Supreme Court and the higher courts to usher in transparency in the judiciary. The Bill was passed by both the houses of the parliament in August 2014. Subsequently, 16 Indian states have ratified the same and the bill was assented by the President of India in December 2014. The NJAC Act came into being in April 2015. The composition of the commission includes the Chief Justice of India, two senior judges of the Supreme Court, the union minister for law and justice and two eminent persons to be nominated by CJI, Prime Minister, and Leader of Opposition for a period of three years and shall not be eligible for re-nomination. Political Scientists such as Pratap Bhanu Mehta (2015) claims that the argument over NJAC will likely weaken the institutional credibility of the judiciary, he discusses the previous method of appointing judges through a system of collegiums of judges wherein the method of appointment of judges had excluded the other branches of government.

The main responsibility of the commission is to recommend and oversee the appointment of Chief Justice of India, Judges of the Supreme Court, Chief Justices of High Courts, and Judges of High Courts. The functions of the commission would be to ensure that the persons recommended are of ability, merit and other criteria to be fulfilled by the office of the High Court/Supreme Court Judge.[26] Additional Solicitor General Indira Jaising argues that an assessment of the new law introduced to appoint judges will convert the independent judiciary subservient to the executive and that it poses a fundamental challenge to the Constitution and Indian democracy. The long pending demands for transparency and accountability of

---

[25]http://rajyasabha.nic.in/rsnew/bill/bill_main.asp.
[26]For further details, please see PRS Legislative Research http://www.prsindia. org/billtrack/the-national-judicial-appointments-commission-bill-2014-3359/.

judges and for making the judiciary more inclusive have been long forgotten in these above mentioned new bills (Jaising, 2014).

Supreme Court Judgement released on the 16th of October 2015 on the NJAC:

*The Supreme Court in October 2015 quashed the NJAC and declared the constitutional amendment as unconstitutional. It maintained that the previous collegium system will continue and that it is open to bring changes in the collegium system. The NJAC was proposed by former Law Minister Kapil Sibal which was adopted by the present government (BJP) and passed by the parliament but presently has been struck down by the Supreme Court. Due to this lockjam, for the past 16 months, no judicial appointments were made. According to the majority opinion of the judgement, the judicial primary is lost due to veto accorded to 2 eminent persons of which One member would be a woman/minorties/other backward class/scheduled caste/scheduled tribe. Scholars such as Pratap Bhanu Mehta claim that judging is too important to be left to the judges and that NJAC is not a violation of the basic structure of the constitution. worldover including UK and US, judges are appointed in consultation with the Executive. In India, presently, the SCAORA vs Union of India (NJAC) case, Supreme Court of India has been favourable to the judiciary.*

In addition to the adoption of the NJAC and the introduction of commercial courts, the present government is reviewing the National Litigation Policy of the former UPA government which was launched in the year 2010.[27] The previous government had formulated a National Litigation Policy to reduce the cases pending in various courts in India under the National Legal Mission to reduce average pendency time from 15 years to 3 years. This policy intends to regulate the manner in which the state should behave as an efficient litigant in handling disputes.[28] The states and the center together amount for 70% of the 3 crore cases left pending thereby

---

[27]National Litigation Policy, Ministry of Law and Justice http://pib.nic.in/newsite/erelease.aspx?relid=62745.
[28] *Ibid.*

making government the largest litigant in India.[29] The aim of NLP is to reduce this percentage to roughly about 50%. Even this percentage is not enough. The 2014 report on the National Litigation Policy with further amendments states[30]:

"The National Litigation Policy is based on the recognition that Government and its various agencies are the pre-dominant litigants in courts and Tribunals in the country. Its aim is to transform Government into an Efficient and Responsible litigant. This policy is also based on the recognition that it is the responsibility of the Government to protect the rights of citizens, to respect fundamental rights and those in charge of the conduct of Government litigation should never forget this basic principle."

## 5. Alternate path of east Asia

There is tension present between the centrality of legal institutions in the context of economic development and existing evidence from Asia. The experience of East Asia presents a rich source of material for consideration of the relationship of law and economy especially by widespread use of informal alternatives to law and role of state in facilitating economic growth. The growth trajectory of China to escape middle income blues was by postponing democratization until a higher level of economic growth was achieved and institutions had sufficient time to develop. At this juncture, only reform story will tell whether China and India will join the ranks of upper income countries where rule of law, good governance, human development and higher standards of living and in the case of China, democracy. The Chinese model followed the trajectory of several East Asian countries that were able to process the transition from middle to upper income countries, from authoritarianism to democracy and rule of law to strong institutions (Peerenboom, 2008: 13). Indian case is diametrically opposite to the China story. Only time will tell

---

[29] *Ibid.*

[30] Ministry of Law and Justice http://www.electroniccourts.in/blog/wp-content/uploads/2014/10/National-Litigation-Policy-Of-India-NLPI-2010.pdf.

if India can manage to analyze judicial assessment in a manner that promotes economic development.

Dam (2006) in his work suggested that it is too soon to acknowledge the idea that the Chinese growth story is a counterexample to the existing notion that legal institutions matter for the developing world. He claims with considerable confidence that 'there is little thus far in the Chinese experience to lead to the conclusion that rule of law issues are not important in economic development.[31] Scholars such as Donald Clarke, Susan Whiting *et al.* (2008) argue that the relationship between legal and economic development was bidirectional. They claim that it is impossible to make the case that formal legal institutions have contributed in an important manner to China's exemplary economic success. Infact, the authors claim that economic success has fostered the development rather than the reverse.

Cumings, Meredith Woo (2006) in her work for UNI-WIDER argues in a compelling manner that legal traditions and institutions do not ascertain the nature of the state, its impact on the economy or the course of economic development. She argues her case by presenting the 'real and informal' mechanisms of state intervention in the economy in East Asia. In her paper, she presents the argument posed by La Porta *et al.* on the 'superiority of the anglo American common law system' as opposed to the civil law tradition of Europe as well as East Asia in propagating financial development. She examines the mechanisms of state intervention by presenting the example of the Gyosei Shido in Japan as well as the Haengjong Chido in Korea and the Xuanxi in China which acted as informal mechanisms which had a tangential relationship to formal law or law traditions.[32] Cummings claims:

"The concern with the origins of the legal system also has the effect of putting the cart before the horse. Investor protection tended to develop in most countries only after the period of transplanting major legal system and much of that transplantation involved civil

---

[31] *Ibid.*
[32] *Ibid.*

law countries adopting Anglo-American Law. This was particularly true for Japan, Republic of Korea and Taiwan."[33]

Dam (2006) in his work on 'Legal Institutions, Legal Origins, Rule of Law and Governance' argues that 'the two legal families central to the scholarship on understanding the nexus between rule of law and economic development are English Common Law and Continental Civil Law-in particular, French civil law'. He poses three questions to the readers: What is it about law that makes its origin important? Why should law play an important role in economic development, and therefore what differences in legal systems make a difference in rates of economic development? Why should common law or civil law system be superior to the other? He answers the above by employing the reasoning provided by Cross:

"The reasoning, much of which suggests analogies of the case law system to Darwinian natural selection with good precedents replacing bad precedents, largely ignores two crucial points: first, most law today, especially that involving the economy, is statutory in both common law and civil law countries. And second, civil law countries have extensive bodies of case law."[34]

Further Dam points out that 'lack of enforcement of property rights in the developing world are more to do with public law than with private law'. He claims:

"The biggest threats to property rights are the state itself and favoritism towards friends of the government. Difficulties in enforcing contracts do not normally arise from weaknesses in substantive law."[35]

The issue of whether civil law tradition or common law tradition will ascertain how efficient a country's legal system falls outside the limits of this project as this study is more of a governance model which has been employed by the World Bank officials to monitor the development of the judicial reform projects in the developing world. The extensive work carried out by Douglas North on Institutions and

---

[33] *Ibid.*
[34] *Ibid.*
[35] *Ibid.*

Economic Performance can be used here to explain this alternative pathway.

Faundez (2014) discusses North's work in the context of Legal Institutions:

"Law figures prominently in North's theory: It is the main source of the formal rules of the game and plays a crucial role in supporting market exchange. In particular, it provides enforcement mechanisms that help to strengthen the efficacy and credibility of commitments made by economic and political entrepreneurs. Law is also the standard used to identify political regimes and — in its guise as the rule of law provides the institutional mechanism that facilitates the transition of natural states to open access orders. Thus, law in North's theory is ubiquitous, which is unsurprising since his definition of institutions as rules of the game has strong normative overtones, and it is difficult to distinguish his general concept of formal institutions from legal rules. Yet, despite the seemingly strong affinity between his theory of institutions and the notion of law, it is difficult to assess law's role in his theory. Does he regard law as an independent component or as a mere adjunct to political and economic processes? In order to address this question it is necessary to revisit his distinction between institutions and organizations."

Douglas North's contribution to develop a conceptual framework to study institutions and economic development has not been fruitful despite the wealth of reasoning and analysis that enrich research on institutions.

"The law and development movement in the 1960's were abruptly abandoned when its main proponents realized that understanding the role of law in developing countries was not straightforward as expected. Their retreat opened the way for economists who encouraged by the wave of economic globalization and political change brought about by the collapse of the Soviet Union, began to generate facile policy advice on how to improve legal systems and institutions in developing countries. North does not agree with their simplistic policy recommendations. Instead, he constructed a theory of institutions grounded in history. Although he encountered many conceptual problems while building his theory he did not give up. Rather than abandon his project, he turned to other disciplines and sought the assistance of colleagues. Today he continues to refine his conceptual framework, which he still regards as tentative. Law and development scholars should follow his example, for his resilience and determination are worthy of our respect."[36]

In this context, scholars attempting to continue research in understanding the role of law in economic development do so by analyzing how the present day concerns differs from the prior efforts undertaken to employ law as a policy tool to achieve economic progress and escape the middle income blues.

## 6. Conclusion

Most scholars trying to link and establish a relationship between judiciary and economic development in India have done so by judging the quality of the legal systems by the various parameters. Wolfgang Koehling (2002) stressed on the importance of speedy legal proceedings as opposed to pendency, backlog of cases and predictability of the outcome of the cases. In his work, Matthieu Chemin (2007) developed a game theoretical model to understand the manner in which efficiency of the Indian legal system would affect the contracting behavior of firms. Chemin's claims that negative implications of having an inefficient judiciary are enormous. Robinson's (2012) work throws light on the manner in which the supreme court micromanages and undermine the judicial system rather than focusing on the pendency and backlog of the cases.

The present chapter depicts the broad contours of the challenges that present itself before India's judiciary which matters for the economic development of the country. The judicial reforms which have been promised and assessed so far need to be implemented in a non-piecemeal manner so as to be able to leave a credible impact on the growth and development story. Key implication emerging from this research is that the efficiency of the judicial system has effects on economic growth but not at the cost of democracy if compared with

---

[36] *Ibid.*

China. Although India opened up its economy in 1991 as opposed to China in 1979, India holds better prospects for the long haul. For India to make the leap forward and embrace the judicial reforms including accountability to ensure timely and effective delivery of justice in commercial cases. At the present moment, the focus is narrowly limited and focused on economic reforms alone cannot reap long term dividends.

## References

Anant, T. C. A. and N. L. Mitra (1995). India. In *The Role of Law and Legal Institutions in Asian Economic Development 1960–1995*, K. Pistor and P. Wellons (eds.), Asian Development Bank.

Bajpai, N. and J. Sachs (2000). Foreign Direct Investment in India: Issues and Problems. Development Discussion Paper No. 759, Harvard Institute for International Development, Harvard University.

Brown, R. and A. S. Gutterman (1998). *Asian Economic and Legal Development: Uncertainty, Risk and Legal Efficiency.* Luwer Law International, Boston, p. 477.

Chemin M. (2007). Does the Quality of the Judiciary Shape Economic Activity? Evidence from India. CIRPEE Working Paper.

Clarke, D. C., P. Murrell, and Whiting, S. H. (2008). The role of law in Chinas economic development. In Chinas Great Economic Transformation, T. Rawski and L. Brandt (eds.), Cambridge University Press, 34 375428.

Clarke, D. C., P. Murrell, and Whiting, S. H. (2008). The role of law in China's economic development. In *China's Great Economic Transformation*, T. Rawski and L. Brandt (eds.), Cambridge University Press, 375–428.

Committee on Empowerment of Women. Parliament House, New Delhi, Lok Sabha Secretariat, Press Release, Para 2.8.

Comments made by RBI Governor Raghuram Rajan at Bharat Ram Memorial Lecture on Make in India, Largely for India. Available at http://www.dnaindia.com/money/report-rbi-governor-raghuram-rajan-s-word-of-caution-on-make-in-india-campaign-2043407.

Cumings, Meredith Woo (2006), "The Rule of Law, Legal Traditions, and Economic Growth in East Asia", Research Paper No. 2006/53, UNU Wider, World Institute for Development Economics Research, United Nations University, pp.1–15.

Dam, K. W. (2006a). *The Law-Growth Nexus: Rule of Law and Economic Development.* Brookings Institution.

Dam, K. W. (2006b). *Judiciary and Economic Development.* Brookings Institution.

Debroy, B. (2006). Judicial reforms — law and contract enforcement. In *Documenting Reforms: Case Studies from India,* Narayan, S. and Observer Research Foundation (eds.), Macmillan in association with Observer Research Foundation, New Delhi.

Eichengreen, B. and P. Gupta (2011). The Services Sector as India's Road to Economic Growth. NBER Working Paper Series No. 16757.

Faundez, J. (2014). Douglass North's Theory of Institutions: Lessons for Law and Development. Warwick School of Law Research Paper No. 2014/13. Available at SSRN: http://ssrn.com/abstract=2493052 or http://dx.doi.org/10.2139/ssrn.2493052.

Hazra, A. K. and B. Debroy (2007).*Judicial Reforms in India: Issues and Aspects.* Academic Foundation in Association with Rajiv Gandhi Institute for Contemporary Studies, New Delhi.

IMF Annual Assessment of Forecast (March 11, 2015).

IMFC Statement made by Arun Jaitley, Finance Minister, India to the IMF committee held on the 18th April 2015, Washington DC.

India Spend Report, Pendency of Cases in Indian Judiciary.

Jaising I. (2014). National Judicial Appointment Commission, A Critical Commentary, Vol XLIX, No. 35.

Jayasuriya K. (Ed.) (1999). *Law, Capitalism and Power in Asia: The Rule of Law and Legal Institutions.* Routledge, New York, p. 345.

Lagarde, C. (2015). Seizing India's Moment. Managing Director, IMF speaking at LSR, New Delhi.

Law Commission Reports Law Commission of India, Report No. 245 (2014). Arrears and Backlog, Government of India. Available at http://lawcommissionofindia.nic.in/reports/Report245.pdf.

Koehling, W. (2002). The Economic Consequences of a Weak Judiciary: Insights from India. EconWPA, Law and Economics 0212001.

Make in India Policy, Government of India. Available at http://www.makeinindia.com/policies/.

Mehta, P. B. (2015). Whom do you trust? Accessed at http://indianexpress.com/article/opinion/columns/whom-do-you-trust/.

Messick, R. E. (1999). Judicial reform and economic development: A survey of the issues. *World Bank Research Observer,* 14(1), pp. 117–136.

Messick, R. E. (2004). Judicial Reform and Economic Growth: What a Decade of Experience Teaches. A Liberal Agenda for the New Century: A Global Perspective. Russian Federation, Moscow.

Mohan, A. (2009). *Justice, Courts and Delays Volume I and II.* Universal Law Publishing, New Delhi.

National Judicial Appointments Commission Bill, PRS Legislative Research. Accessed at http://www.prsindia.org/billtrack/the-national-judicial-appointments-commission-bill-2014-3359/.

National Manufacturing Policy, Ministry of Commerce and Industry, Department of Industrial Policy and Promotion.

North, D. (2003). The Role of Institutions in Economic Development. ECE Discussion Papers Series 2003_2, UNECE.

North, D. C. (1989). Institutions and economic growth: An historical introduction. *World Development*, Elsevier, 17(9), pp. 1319–1332.

North, D. C. (1993). The New Institutional Economics and Development. Economic History 9309002, EconWPA.

Peerenboom, R. (2008). Law and Development in China and India: The Advantages and Disadvantages of Front-Loading the Costs of Political Reform, La Trobe Law School Legal Studies Research Paper No. 2008/15.

Perry, A. (2000). An ideal legal system for attracting foreign direct investment? Some theory and reality. *American University International Law Review*, 15(6), 1627–1657.

Pistor K. and P. A. Wellons (1999). *The Role of Law and Legal Institutions in Asian Economic Development, 1960–1995.* Oxford University Press, New York, p. 294.

Posner, R. A. (1998). Creating a legal framework for economic development. *The World Bank Research Observer*, 13(1), pp. 1–11.

Proposal for constitution of Hi-tech Fast Track Commercial Divisions in High Courts (2003). 188th Law Commission Report.

Rajamohan, C. (2014). *States and the SAARC.* Indian Express.

Rajya Sabha News. Available at http://rajyasabha.nic.in/rsnew/bill/bill_main.asp.

Report of the Steering Group on Foreign Direct Investment (2002). Planning Commission, Government of India.

Robinson, N. (2014). India's Judicial Architecture. Available at SSRN: http://dx.doi.org/10.2139/ssrn.2505523.

Robinson, N. (Forthcoming). A quantitative analysis of the Indian supreme court's workload. *Journal of Empirical Legal Studies.* Available at SSRN: http://ssrn.com/abstract=2189181 or http://dx.doi.org/10.2139/ssrn.2189181.

Robinson, N. (2009). Too many cases. *Frontline*, 26(1), 03–16. Available at http://www.frontline.in/static/html/fl2601/stories/20090116260108100.htm.

Robinson, N. (2013). Court Adrift. *Frontline.* Available at http://www.frontline.in/cover-story/a-court-adrift/article4613892.ece.

Santos, A. (2012). The World Bank's Uses of the 'Rule of Law' Promise in Economic Development. The New Law and Economic Development: A Critical Appraisal, pp. 253–300. Available at SSRN: http://ssrn.com/abstract=2034333.

Sen, A. (2000). *What is the Role of Legal and Judicial Reform in the Development Process?* World Bank Legal Conference, Washington, DC.

Stephenson, M. (2007). Judicial reform in developing countries: Constraints and opportunities. In *Beyond Transition*, Francois Bourguignon & Boris Pleskovic (eds.), Oxford University Press, Oxford.

Supreme Court of India, Court News, New Delhi. Available at http://www.supremecourtofindia.nic.in/courtnews.htm.

The Law commission of India Report No. 253 (2015). Commercial and Commercial Appellate Division of High Courts and Commercial Courts Bill.

Virmani, A. (2015). *India and China, Tracking the Two Growth Stories.* The Hindu.

Voigt, S. (2005). The Economic Effects of Judicial Accountability — Some Preliminary Insights. Discussion Papers in Economics 72/05, University of Kassel, Institute of Economics.

Walsh, B. (2008). Judicial productivity in India. *International Journal for Court Administration*, 1(1), pp. 23–30.

World Bank Report on Doing Business. Available at http://www.doing business.org/data/exploreeconomies/india.

# Index

242

*Index*